Henry Gannett

The Building of a Nation

The growth, present condition and resources of the United States with a forecast of

the future

Henry Gannett

The Building of a Nation

The growth, present condition and resources of the United States with a forecast of the future

ISBN/EAN: 9783744730204

Printed in Europe, USA, Canada, Australia, Japan

Cover: Foto ©ninafisch / pixelio.de

More available books at **www.hansebooks.com**

THE BUILDING OF A NATION

THE BUILDING OF A NATION

THE GROWTH, PRESENT CONDITION
AND RESOURCES OF THE UNITED STATES
WITH A FORECAST OF THE FUTURE

BY

HENRY GANNETT

CHIEF GEOGRAPHER OF THE GEOLOGICAL SURVEY AND OF
THE TENTH AND ELEVENTH CENSUSES

ILLUSTRATED WITH MAPS, CHARTS AND DIAGRAMS

NEW YORK
THE HENRY T. THOMAS COMPANY
1895

Press of J. J. Little & Co.
Astor Place New York

CONTENTS

	PAGE
AN INDUSTRIAL REPUBLIC	1
THE NATIONAL DOMAIN	4
Our Coasts	5
The Relief of the Country	5
The Appalachian Mountain System	6
The Appalachian Valley	6
The Atlantic Plain	7
The Mississippi Valley	7
The Ozark Hills	7
The Great Plains and the Cordilleran Plateau	8
The Cordilleras of North America	8
The Plateau Region	9
The Great Basin	10
Salt Lake Basin	11
Sierra Nevada	11
Cascade Range	11
Temperature	12
Rainfall	13
Forests	15
GOVERNMENT	16
GENERAL GOVERNMENT	17
Cabinet	18
Senate	18
House of Representatives	18
Judiciary	19
DISTRIBUTION OF POWERS	20
Executive Divisions	20
Department of State	21
Treasury Department	21
War Department	22

	PAGE
Department of Justice	22
Post Office Department	22
Navy Department	22
Department of the Interior	23
Department of Agriculture	23
Other Departments and Bureaus	23
Smithsonian Institution	24
ORGANIZATION OF STATES AND TERRITORIES	24
District of Columbia	25
Alabama	25
Alaska	25
Arizona	25
Arkansas	25
California	26
Colorado	26
Connecticut	26
Delaware	26
Florida	26
Georgia	26
Idaho	26
Illinois	26
Indiana	26
Indian Territory	26
Iowa	26
Kansas	27
Kentucky	27
Louisiana	27
Maine	27
Maryland	27
Massachusetts	27
Michigan	27
Minnesota	27
Mississippi	27
Missouri	28
Montana	28
Nebraska	28
Nevada	28
New Hampshire	28
New Jersey	28

CONTENTS

	PAGE
New Mexico	28
New York	28
North Carolina	28
North Dakota	28
Ohio	29
Oklahoma	29
Oregon	29
Pennsylvania	29
Rhode Island	29
South Carolina	29
South Dakota	29
Tennessee	29
Texas	29
Utah	29
Vermont	29
Virginia	30
Washington	30
West Virginia	30
Wisconsin	30
Wyoming	30
SUB-DIVISIONS OF STATES AND COUNTIES	31
GOVERNMENT DEBTS	32
National Debt	33
State Debts	36
Debts of Counties and Municipalities	37
BUDGET	40
MILITARY FORCES	41
The Regular Army	41
Organized Militia	41
Potential Militia	42
THE NAVY	44
PENSIONS	45
PUBLIC LANDS	45
State Cessions	46
Annexation of Territory	46
Method of Survey	47

	PAGE
Methods of Disposal.............................	48
Amount Alienated...............................	49

POPULATION................................. 51

Early Settlements.............................	51
Increase of Population.........................	52
Population of States...........................	56
Rate of Increase of Population of States........	56
Considerations Affecting Increase...............	58
Recent Changes................................	60
Relative Standing of States....................	62

DENSITY OF POPULATION............................ 62
Extent of Settlement...........................	63
Settlement in 1890.............................	65
The Settled Area...............................	66
Density of Population by Groups................	67
Density of Population of States................	68

CENTER OF POPULATION............................. 71
Movements of the Center........................	71

URBAN POPULATION................................. 74
Distribution of the Urban Element..............	77
Great Cities...................................	80
The Greater New York...........................	81

GEOGRAPHIC DISTRIBUTION.......................... 82
Distribution According to Temperature..........	82
Distribution Under Rainfall Conditions.........	83
Distribution in Altitude.......................	84
Size of Families...............................	86

SEX... 88
Distribution of the Sexes in European Countries.	88
Distribution of the Sexes by States............	89

RACES.. 90
History of the Races...........................	91
Relative Diminution of the Colored Element.....	92
Distribution of the Races by States............	94

THE CHINESE...................................... 98

CONTENTS   ix

	PAGE
THE INDIANS	99
Treatment of the Indians	100
NATIVITY	102
IMMIGRATION	103
Distribution of the Foreign Born	105
Constituents of the Foreign-born Element	108
History of the Several Elements	109
The Foreign Element in Cities	113
Occupations of the Foreign Born	114
Illiteracy of the Foreign Born	115
Effect of Immigration upon Natural Increase	115
Foreign Parentage	118
Summary	123
POTENTIAL VOTERS	124
ALIENS	126
ILLITERACY	127
EDUCATION	130
Public Schools	130
Enrollment	130
Expenditure	131
OCCUPATIONS	133
Occupations of Immigrants	140
Changes in Occupations	141
Wages	142
TRADES UNIONS	143
INVENTION	144
RELIGION	146
Catholics	147
Methodists	147
Baptists	148
Presbyterians	148
Lutherans	148
Christians	148
Episcopalians	149

	PAGE
Congregationalists	149
Other Denominations	149
Distribution of Communicants	149
MORTALITY	151
Census Statistics	151
Causes of Death	153
Mortality in Registration Cities	154
Death Rates of Countries	155
CRIME	156
PAUPERISM	158
CONJUGAL CONDITION	159
Divorce	161
AGRICULTURE	163
Relative Importance of Agriculture	163
General Statistics	164
Improved Land	166
Tobacco	166
Wheat	167
Corn	168
Oats	169
Cotton	169
Hay	171
Potatoes	171
Live Stock on Farms and Ranches	171
Distribution of Live Stock	172
Irrigation	173
MANUFACTURES	176
General Statistics	176
Iron and Steel Manufactures	180
Cotton Industry	182
Wool Industry	182
Silk Industry	183
Books, Periodicals and Newspapers	183
Spirits, Wines, and Malt Liquors	184

CONTENTS

	PAGE
MINERAL RESOURCES	186
Coal	187
Iron	189
Steel	190
Gold	190
Silver	191
Copper	191
Lead	192
Zinc	193
Quicksilver	193
Petroleum	193
Natural Gas	194
Salt	194
TRANSPORTATION	195
Wagon Roads	195
RAILWAYS	196
Extent	196
GENERAL STATISTICS	200
Traffic Statistics	200
Organization	201
Consolidation	201
Cost of Transportation	202
Rolling Stock	203
Accidents	203
Objects of Construction	203
ENGINEERING WORK	204
WATER TRANSPORTATION	206
Vessels Engaged in Foreign Trade	207
Coast and Internal Traffic	208
COMMERCE	209
Foreign Commerce	210
Shipbuilding	214
TELEGRAPH LINES	215
TELEPHONES	215
STREET RAILWAYS	216
MAIL SERVICE	217

	PAGE
FINANCE AND WEALTH	219
NATIONAL BANKS	220
SAVINGS BANKS	221
WEALTH	221
Methods of Estimating	221
Wealth in 1890	223
Historical Résumé	224
Assessed Valuation in 1890	227
Sources of Wealth	227
DISTRIBUTION OF WEALTH	228
A FORECAST OF THE FUTURE	231
The Government	231
The People	233
Woman	235
Language	235
Cities	236
Corporations	236
Agriculture	236
Manufactures	238
Coal	238
Electricity	239
FINIS	240
INDEX	241

LIST OF ILLUSTRATIONS

COLORTYPE

THE CAPITOL AT WASHINGTON.................. ...*Frontispiece*
(From a Sketch by F. HOPKINSON SMITH.)

COLORED PLATES.

PLATE		FACING PAGE
1.	Net Public Debt, by Classes of Organizations in 1890 ...	32
	Net National Debt, by Rates of Interest in 1890........	32
2.	State Debt per Capita, in Dollars, 1890................	36
3.	Accessions of Territory (except Alaska)	46
4.	The Settled Area in 1790........................	64
	The Settled Area in 1890........................	64
5.	Number of Inhabitants to a Square Mile in 1890........	70
6.	Proportion of Urban to Total Population in 1890.......	78
7.	Proportion of Sex to Total Population in 1890..........	88
8.	Number of Colored Persons to a Square Mile in 1890....	96
	Proportion of Colored to Total Population in 1890......	96
9.	Number of Foreign Born to a Square Mile in 1890.......	106
	Proportion of Foreign Born to Total Population in 1890.	106
10.	Elements of the Population at Each Census............	110
	Nationalities of the Foreign Born, 1850 to 1890.........	110
11.	Proportion of British to Total Population in 1890......	112
	Proportion of Germans and Austrians to Total Population in 1890	112
12.	Proportion of Canadians to Total Population in 1890....	112
	Proportion of Irish to Total Population in 1890.........	112
13.	Proportion of Scandinavians to Total Population in 1890	112
	Proportion of Native Whites of Native Parentage to All Whites in 1890	112
14.	Constituents of the Population of the States in 1890. ...	120
15.	Constituents of the Population of the Great Cities in 1890	122
16.	Population at Each Census Classified by Race and Nativity	124
17.	Proportion of Persons who Cannot Write, to Population, Ten Years of Age or Over, in 1880	128
	Proportion of Native Whites who Cannot Write, to All Native Whites of Ten Years of Age or Over, in 1880.	128

PLATE		FACING PAGE
18.	Proportion of Colored Persons who Cannot Write, to All Colored Ten Years of Age or Over, in 1880	128
	Proportion of Foreign Born who Cannot Write, to All Foreign Born Ten Years of Age or Over, in 1880	128
19.	Proportion of Enrollment in All Schools, to Children of School Age in 1890	132
	Expenditure in Dollars, per Capita, of Children Enrolled in Public Schools in 1890	132
20.	Proportion of Persons Engaged in Agriculture to All Wage-Earners in 1880	134
	Proportion of Persons Engaged in Manufacturing and Mining to All Wage-Earners in 1880	134
21.	Proportion of Catholics to Total Population in 1890	148
	Proportion of Methodists to Total Population in 1890	148
22.	Proportion of Baptists to Total Population in 1890	148
	Proportion of Presbyterians to Total Population in 1890	148
23.	Proportion of Lutherans to Total Population in 1890	148
	Proportion of Christians to Total Population in 1890	148
24.	Proportion of Episcopalians to Total Population in 1890	148
	Proportion of Congregationalists to Total Population in 1890	148
25.	Proportion of Church Members to Total Population in 1890	150
26.	Proportion which the Number of Deaths from Certain Diseases Bore to All Deaths in the United States in 1890	152
27.	The Prisoners of the United States in 1890	156
28.	Relative Value of the Industries of the United States in 1890	164
29.	Proportion of Cultivated Land to Total Area of the Country	164
30.	Proportion of Cultivated Land to Total Area in 1890	166
31.	Production of Wheat, in Bushels, per Square Mile of Total Area in 1889	168
	Yield of Wheat per Acre, in Bushels, in 1889	168
32.	Production, in Bushels, of Indian Corn per Square Mile of Total Area in 1889	168
	Yield, in Bushels, of Corn per Acre in 1889	168
33.	Production, in Bushels, of Oats per Square Mile of Total Area in 1889	168
	Yield, in Bushels, of Oats per Acre in 1889	168

LIST OF ILLUSTRATIONS xv

PLATE / FACING PAGE
34. Yield of Cotton, in Bales, per Square Mile of Total Area in 1889.. 168
Yield of Cotton per Acre, in Tenths of Bales, in 1889.... 168
35. Number of Tons of Hay Raised per Square Mile of Total Area in 1888..................................... 168
Number of Bushels of Potatoes Raised per Square Mile of Total Area in 1888................................ 168
36. Proportional Value of the Principal Products of Agriculture in 1889.................................. 170
37. Number of Horses and Mules per Square Mile in 1892.... 172
Number of Cattle per Square Mile in 1892............. 172
38. Number of Sheep per Square Mile in 1892............. 172
Number of Hogs per Square Mile in 1892.............. 172
39. The Circulating Media in 1893....................... 220
40. Assessed Valuation per Capita, in Hundreds of Dollars, 1890... 238

TEXT ILLUSTRATIONS.

MAPS AND DIAGRAMS.

PAGE
National Debt of the World, 1848 to 1890................... 32
The National Debt, 1856 to 1891.......................... 34
  The National Debt Less Cash in the Treasury.
  The National Debt per Capita, Less Cash in the Treasury.
The National Debt, 1856 to 1891.......................... 35
  Annual Interest Charge.
  Annual Interest Charge per Capita.
Indebtedness of States in 1890............................ 38
State Debt per Capita in 1890............................ 39
Population of Countries of the Globe in 1890.............. 54
Population of Each State and Territory in 1890............ 56
Density of Total Population at each Census................ 63
Number of Inhabitants per Square Mile in Various Countries in 1890.. 64
Number of Inhabitants per Square Mile in 1890............ 70
Position of the Center of Population at the Close of Each Decade from 1790 to 1890............................... 73
The Total Urban and Rural Population at Each Census..... 76

	PAGE
Aggregate Population and Urban Element in Cities of 8,000 or More Inhabitants, by States, in 1890	79
Average Number of Persons to a Family in 1890	87
Rate of Increase—White and Colored	93
Constituents of the Total Immigration and of the Immigration Between 1880 and 1890	106
Principal Constituents of the Foreign Born in 1890	109
Rates of Increase of All Whites and of the Native Element of the North and of All Whites of the South	116
Proportion of Aliens to Total Population in 1890	126
Proportion of Church Members to Aggregate Population in 1890	150
Death Rate of the Great Cities in 1890	155
Death Rates of Various Countries in 1890	156
Value of Farms, Implements and Machinery	165
Number of Farms	165
Average Size of Farms, 1850 to 1890	165
Yield of Tobacco, in Pounds, per Square Mile of Total Area in 1889	167
Products of Manufactures in Leading Cities in 1890	180
Annual Production of Iron and Steel	181
Value of Principal Mineral Products in 1889	187
Railway Mileage of the United States, 1830 to 1890	197
Railway Mileage of the World for 1890, by Countries	198
Miles of Railway per 10,000 Inhabitants, by Countries, in 1890	199
Principal Articles of Foreign Commerce	212
Imports and Exports, 1843 to 1892	213
Total Wealth of the United States	225
Wealth per Capita	225

LIST OF TABLES

GOVERNMENT.

	PAGE
Areas of the States and Territories in Square Miles	30
Civil Divisions of the United States in 1890	32
Government Debts in 1880 and 1890	33
Principal Items of Expenditure	40
Receipts and Expenditures per Capita, 1872 to 1891	40
Classification of the Regular Army	41
Distribution of Organized State Militia	42
Classification of the Militia	42
Proportions of Potential Militia and Population	43
Cost and Area of Acquired Territory	46
Disposition Made of Public Lands	49

POPULATION.

Estimated Population prior to 1790	52
Population and Rate of Increase by Decades	53
Total Population by States in 1890	55
Percentage of Increase of Population by Decades	57
Area and Density of Population at Each Census	62
Settled and Unsettled Area at Each Census	66
Rates of Increase of Settled Area and of Population	67
Classification of Settled Area	67
Area in Square Miles of the Different Classes of Settlement	68
Population per Square Mile, by States, in 1890	69
Position of the Center of Population	71
Urban and Rural Elements of Population	75
Urban and Rural Increase by Decades	77
Urban Population by Geographic Divisions	78
Cities of Over 100,000 Population in 1890	80
Number of Cities, Classified According to Population	81
Distribution of Population as to Mean Annual Temperature	82
Distribution of Population as to Mean Annual Rainfall	84

	PAGE
Distribution of Population as to Altitude	85
Size of Families at Each Census	86
Proportion of the Sexes, 1850 to 1890	88
Proportions of the Sexes in Foreign Countries	88
Percentage of the Sexes to Total Population in 1890	89
White and Colored Population at Each Census	91
Proportion of White and Colored by Decades	91
Increase of White and Colored by Decades	92
White and Colored Population in 1890	95
Percentage of Colored to Total Population	96
Proportion of the Colored Element at Each Census	98
The Chinese Population by Decades	98
Nativity of the Population, 1850 to 1890	102
Ratio of Native and Foreign Population, 1850 to 1890	102
Immigration, 1821 to 1890, by Decades	103
Principal Constituents of the Immigration	104
Native and Foreign Born Population in 1890	105
Percentage of Native and Foreign Born to Total Population, 1890	106
Percentage of the Foreign Element, 1850 to 1890	107
Foreign Born by Principal Nationalities, 1890	108
Percentages of Total Population	110
Proportion of Different Nationalities to the Total Foreign Population in 1890	112
Proportion of White Population of Native and Foreign Parentage	120
Constituents of the Population of the Great Cities	121
Proportion of the Principal Elements of Foreign Birth to the Total Foreign Born, in Cities	122
Composition of the Population, 1890	124
Proportion of Potential Voters and of Total Population	125
Colleges and Professional Schools, and Attendance	132
Distribution of Breadwinners by Classes	134
Proportion of the Number of Persons in the United States Engaged in Each Class of Occupations	134, 135
Proportion of Breadwinners of Each Nationality	138
Distribution of Breadwinners by Occupations	138
Ratio of Native and Foreign Born Wage Earners to Total Population, by Classes	139
Occupations of Immigrants, Classified	140

Ratio of Immigrants Engaged in Certain Classes of Labor to
    Total Immigrants.. 141
Elements of the American Federation of Labor................ 143
Membership of Principal Religious Denominations............ 146
Ratio of Deaths from Certain Diseases to Total Mortality.... 153
Mortality in Registration Cities.................................... 154
Death Rates per Thousand in Various Countries................ 155
Race and Nativity of Prisoners and of Population............. 157
Number of Prisoners of Each Class in 10,000 Inhabitants.... 157
Distribution of Paupers by Race and Nativity.................. 159

AGRICULTURE.

Value, Number, and Size of Farms, and Value of Products
    by Decades.. 165
Yield of Cotton in 1889, by States................................ 170
Number and Value of Farm Animals in 1892..................... 172
Irrigated Area and Total Area Compared......................... 174

MANUFACTURES.

Statistics of Manufactures from 1850 to 1890 by Decades..... 177
Average Capital Invested in Each Establishment............... 178
Average Wages per Hand Employed................................ 178
Proportions of Net Product Shared by Employes and by
    Capital.. 179
Ratio of Net Product to Capital................................... 179
Number and Circulation of Periodicals by Classes.............. 184
Spirituous and Malt Liquors Produced in 1891.................. 184

MINERAL RESOURCES.

Quantity and Value of Non-Metallic Products in 1891......... 186
Quantity and Value of Metallic Products in 1891............... 187
Coal Product of the Several States in 1891..................... 188
Production of Pig Iron in the United States and Great Britain
    by Decades.. 190
Sources of the Production of Zinc in 1890...................... 193

TRANSPORTATION.

	PAGE
Railway Capital, Operating Expenses, Earnings, etc.	200
Railway Traffic for the Year Ending June 30, 1890.	201
Classification of the American Fleet	207
Freight Moved by Water in 1890	209
Value of Principal Imports in 1891, Classified.	211
Value of Principal Exports in 1891, Classified.	211
Number and Tonnage of Vessels Built in 1892	214

FINANCE AND WEALTH.

Money in Circulation in 1891	219
Coinage in 1890, Classified.	220
Total and Per Capita Wealth by Decades.	224
Rate of Increase of Wealth by Decades.	225
Holdings of the Different Classes of Wage Earners.	229
Holdings of All Wage Earners	229
Distribution of Wealth in Percentages of the Total	230

THE BUILDING OF A NATION

AN INDUSTRIAL REPUBLIC

LITTLE more than a century ago, a new nation came into being on the western shores of the Atlantic. When the contest with the mother country was at last ended, the rising smoke of battle disclosed a group of feeble colonies, held together only by the necessity for defense against a common enemy, and drawn asunder by difference of interests, difference of origin, class distinctions, and mutual jealousies. They were poor before the burden of war was laid upon them; they were bankrupt when the struggle closed. Their commerce, their petty manufactures, had been destroyed; their fields had been laid waste.

To unite and harmonize these colonies was the first step toward the building of the nation.

With vast labor and great wisdom, the fathers of the Republic devised a plan of confederation which on the one hand would weld the colonies into a stable nation, and on the other would antagonize as little as possible their varying interests and prejudices. This plan was embodied in the Constitution of the United States, a masterpiece of human creation. Prepared to serve the needs of thirteen small states, numbering only three millions of people, it now governs equally well sixty-five millions, distributed over fifty states and territories—a people more numerous and diverse, and having vastly more diverse interests, than the framers of that great work could have imagined.

They builded better than they knew. The freedom guaranteed by that great state paper to individuals, to communities, and to states, has contributed, more than any other single agency, to the career of magnificent prosperity which this country has pursued, almost without interruption.

As soon as the young nation had shaken off its load of debt, it gathered itself together and commenced the work of development—a work which, with trifling interruptions, it has continued at a constantly accelerating pace. Nation after nation has been overtaken in the industrial race. Nation after nation has struggled to maintain its lead; but the young giant of the West has set them too hot a pace, and, one after another, all have fallen behind. The last competitor was the mother country, and long and hard was the struggle she made against her offspring; but at last, in industry as in war, she has been forced to give way, and see her child not only pass, but distance her in the race.

As in the regatta for the Queen's cup at which an American yacht first entered, America is in the lead, and "there is no second."

In numbers, wealth, industry, enterprise, ease, and dignity of living—in short, in all that goes to make civilization, the American Republic, at the end of its first century, stands the acknowledged leader of the nations of the earth.

What has conspired to induce this remarkable career of prosperity? It is not due to any single cause, as may be easily shown by comparison with countries in which the same conditions operate, but to a combination of causes. First among these are the freedom and liberality of its institutions, which, by favoring none and giving an equal chance to all, have stimulated ambition and enabled every man to make the most of his career. That this has had a tremendous effect upon the people of the country, may be seen by comparing its history with that of other countries under much the same physical conditions, but under very different institutions. Compare, for instance, the history of the United States with that of Canada, with the Australian colonies, with Russia; or, to bring the comparison nearer home, compare the United States of the past century with the colonies during the century preceding. Although occupying the same territory, although substantially the same people, they made comparatively little progress either materially or socially while under the dominion of a monarchy.

Secondly, its domain of three and a half millions of square miles afforded ample room for expansion, with every variety of climate, and with surpassing resources of soil and mineral deposits. Its climate and soil are so varied as to make it agriculturally almost independent of the rest of the world. Its mineral resources are so vast and so varied that there is scarcely a metal or a mineral that need be purchased abroad.

The United States is an industrial nation. Its young men, instead of being trained to the profession of arms, are devoted to the arts and industries. Instead of maintaining great standing armies into which are drafted the strength of the nation, for the purpose of threatening the peace of the world, it has a vast industrial army, which is occupied in producing instead of destroying.

While enumerating the reasons for its prosperity, the character of the stock with which the country was peopled must not be forgotten. Energy and enterprise are qualities that specially distinguish the Anglo-Saxon. His power of adaptation to new conditions, and his inventive genius, render him preëminently a colonizer, and in this broad and virgin field he has displayed these qualities as they have been shown nowhere else in the world.

Add to all this, wise and liberal legislation, not forgetting the provision for free education, and the summary of the leading reasons for America's marvelous development is complete.

It is now in order to examine the present status of our population, our social life, and our industries, and to follow the course of their growth throughout the century.

THE NATIONAL DOMAIN

At certain intervals the prudent merchant balances his books, goes over his stock in trade, estimates its value, and strikes a balance with the world, to find out whether during the interval he has made or lost money, and how much. Most civilized nations do a similar thing, some more, some less thoroughly, the United States the most thoroughly of all, for its decennial census is a taking account of stock. Although the census does not deal with all the items of national progress, those which it omits are omitted because they are the subject of special examination by other parts of the governmental organization. This volume undertakes to bring together all the physical and material items concerned in the nation's progress.

First of all to be described in such a schedule of assets, is the home of the American people, the country in which we were so fortunate as to have been planted, and in which we have so wondrously developed. This involves a description of the country with its variations of surface, of its streams with their adaptability to navigation and to irrigation, of its coast line as it lends itself to the promotion of commerce, of its climate as it affects the distribution of the people, of its influence upon health, and of its latent resources hidden in the soil and rocks. All these collectively have had a tremendous influence upon the development of the American people.

Our territory consists of two distinct parts, the smaller of which, the territory of Alaska, comprising five hundred and seventy thousand square miles, occupies the extreme northwestern portion of the continent. The great body of the country, including five-sixths of its area, and containing nine hundred and ninety-nine out of every thousand of its inhabitants, occupies the middle portion of the continent, stretching from latitude twenty-five to forty-nine, and from the Atlantic ocean to the Pacific. Its area is 3,025,600 square miles, not greatly different from that of Canada or Australia, and not much less than that of all Europe.

Our Coasts.—The eastern or Atlantic coast is a very broken one, abounding in harbors, several of them deep and large enough to float the navies of the world. The coast of Maine, New Hampshire, and Massachusetts is, for the most part, an intricate one, with many long, narrow, rugged points sheltering deep, fiord-like bays, and studded with thousands of rugged islands. In southern New England the character of the coast is very different, being low and sandy, with lines of reefs against which the waves of the Atlantic beat, enclosing on the shoreward side bays, lagoons, and swamps, out of which gently rises the mainland. This character of coast extends southward to Florida and around the Gulf of Mexico.

The Pacific coast is of still another type. From Lower California northward to Puget sound it is simple, containing only two or three indentations which can be called harbors. From the coast the land rises steeply into mountains and descends abruptly to great depths. The Strait of Fuca, on the northern extremity of our western coast, is a gap in the mountains which lets the water of the sea into a depression in the great valley between the Coast and Cascade ranges, forming an immense harbor, Puget sound, in which the merchant marine of all nations could be easily anchored.

The Relief of the Country.—A correct idea of the relief of the country can be best obtained by considering first its broader outlines. It has two systems of uplift. The easternmost and smallest, known as the Appalachian system, runs from the northeast toward the southwest at a little distance back from the Atlantic coast, extending from Canada down into Alabama. The second and vastly greater system occupies most of the western half of the continent, extending from Colorado, New Mexico, Wyoming, and Montana, westward to the Pacific coast. Between the two mountain systems is a great valley, or depression, the southern and larger part of which is occupied by the Mississippi river and its tributaries, while the northern portion is drained by the system of the Great Lakes and the St. Lawrence. These are the broader features of the country. Let us now consider them somewhat more in detail.

The Appalachian Mountain System.—In the northeastern States the Appalachian mountain system is very irregular, consisting of detached groups and short ridges. Among these are the broken hills of northwestern Maine, and the White mountains of New Hampshire, which, with the exception of a few summits in North Carolina, are the highest of the whole system. Among them is Mount Washington, which reaches an elevation of 6,294 feet. The Green mountains of Vermont, and the Adirondacks of northern New York, form part of this system.

Passing into Pennsylvania, the system acquires a regularity which is unknown to the northward. It consists of two distinct parts, or members, the westernmost of which, known in this state as the Alleghany plateau, is a deeply eroded plateau with a well-defined escarpment, or cliff, on the southeast, and a gentle slope to the northwest. This plateau extends southwestward to Alabama, being known through the Virginias, Kentucky, Tennessee, and Alabama, as the Cumberland plateau. It presents everywhere the same uniform front to the southeast, consisting of a cliff from one to two thousand feet in height, and a similarly uniform slope to the west and north.

The Appalachian Valley.—The other member of this system lies southeast of the Cumberland plateau, and is known as the Appalachian valley. It is, in fact, a continuous valley, stretching from the Hudson river far into Alabama, with the general southwesterly trend of the mountain system. It is a region of extensive and complicated folding of strata, this folding being coupled with enormous erosion, which has produced a succession of mountain ranges and ridges, long, narrow, and sinuous, trending parallel to the direction of the valley.

Some of these ranges are of vast extent, stretching for hundreds of miles with scarcely a break; others form complicated loops, twists, and turns. The valley is terminated on the southeast by one of these ridges, known in Pennsylvania as South Mountain and farther south as the Blue Ridge. It reaches an elevation of twelve hundred feet at Harper's Ferry, and four thousand feet at the peaks of Otter in Virginia; while in North Carolina it widens out, and, in place of a single ridge, develops into a maze of high ranges, trending in various directions, and standing upon a base a thousand feet or more above sea level.

In this region are the Black mountains, the highest peak of which, Mount Mitchell, has an altitude of six thousand seven hundred feet above the sea; also the Big Smoky mountains on the boundary line between Tennessee and North Carolina, many peaks of which range between five and six thousand feet.

The Alleghany-Cumberland plateau forms an important water divide. Through most of its course its escarpment separates streams flowing directly to the Atlantic, from those flowing westward into the Mississippi. Certain streams, however, and those the most powerful ones, have broken through this escarpment, some in one direction, some in another. For instance, the Susquehanna, of Pennsylvania, heads far back in the plateau and cuts through this escarpment in its course to the Atlantic. The Potomac likewise heads back in the highest part of the plateau. On the other hand, the Kanawha river, with its main branch, New river, heads in the Blue Ridge, and flowing westward cuts through the plateau, making a gorge from its summit nearly to sea level. The Tennessee drains the southern part of the great Appalachian valley, and, collecting its waters, flows across the southern end of the plateau into the Ohio.

The Atlantic Plain.—East of the Appalachian system, the country slopes directly to the low ground bordering the Atlantic. From New Jersey southward, this Atlantic plain is comparatively level and unbroken, excepting for the beds of the streams. In New England, however, the country is much more broken, deeply scored by streams, and built up by glacial deposits.

The Mississippi Valley.—The great valley of the United States, speaking broadly, is a level expanse. In southern Ohio, however, the streams flowing into the Ohio river have eroded deep valleys.

The Ozark Hills.—The northwestern part of Arkansas and southern Missouri are occupied by what are known collectively as the Ozark hills, a region which until recent years was almost a *terra incognita*. This region presents many points of similarity to the Appalachian. South of the Arkansas river in Arkansas, the Ozark hills consist of east and west ridges rudely parallel to one another, but crooked and winding in detail, with many spurs and offshoots. That part of the hills north of the Arkansas river in Arkansas and Missouri is, on the other hand, an eroded plateau, where the streams occupy deep gorges which they have excavated in its originally level surface.

The Great Plains and the Cordilleran Plateau.— West of the Mississippi river the country gradually rises more and more rapidly, forming the eastward slope of a great elevated plateau, crowned by an interminable succession of mountain ranges extending from the middle of Colorado, New Mexico, and Wyoming, westward to the Pacific coast. This long slope of the plains, stretching for a thousand miles westward, and from the Rio Grande to the northern boundary of the country, with scarcely a break in its rolling expanse, is one of the grandest features of the continent.

The mountain system, also, is on a commensurate scale, extending from longitude one hundred and five degrees to the Pacific ocean, and from the Mexican boundary to that of Canada. It has a length from north to south of twelve hundred miles, and a breadth of a thousand miles. With its mountains, valleys, deserts, and plains, it comprises fully one-third of the area of the United States. This plateau reaches the greatest elevation near its eastern border in Colorado, where it is not far from ten thousand feet above sea level. From this summit it descends in all directions, to about four thousand feet in southern New Mexico and the same elevation in Montana on the British boundary. Descending toward the west, the plateau is four thousand feet in the valley of Great Salt lake, from whence it rises again to six thousand feet in central Nevada, and then sinks to the level of the Pacific.

The Cordilleras of North America.—This plateau is crowned by a vast number of mountain ranges of various elevations, the highest of them reaching nearly fifteen thousand feet. The system on our northern boundary is comparatively narrow, extending from longitude one hundred and twelve to one hundred and twenty-four, thus having a breadth of only about five hundred miles. Southward, its eastern boundary extends rapidly to the eastward, giving the system its maximum breadth in Colorado.

The easternmost ranges of this system are commonly classified as the Rocky mountains, and these again may be further subdivided into two parts, the northern and southern, which are separated from one another by a broad stretch of plateau. The southern Rocky mountain region comprises the ranges in southern Wyoming, Colorado, and New Mexico, and includes a series of ranges trending nearly north and south, and enclosing high mountain valleys which are called parks, the best known among them being the North, South, Middle, and San Luis parks, of Colorado.

With the exception of the Sierra Nevada, the mountains in Colorado are the highest in the country, exclusive of Alaska. These ranges contain scores of peaks whose altitude exceeds fourteen thousand feet, with great areas of country lying above the limit of timber, which in this state has the extreme altitude of eleven to twelve thousand feet. The easternmost of these ranges, the Front, Park, Sawatch, and Sangre de Cristo ranges, are broad and massive, while the Elk and San Juan mountains in the western portion of the group, are extremely rugged.

The northern group of the Rocky mountains extends from the Wind River and Bighorn ranges in northern Wyoming, across western Montana and Idaho. They are by no means as high as those of the southern group, varying from thirteen thousand seven or eight hundred feet in the Wind River range, down to nine or ten thousand feet in the more northerly ranges.

The Plateau Region.—The heart of this mountain region is drained by the Colorado river and its tributaries. Its drainage area is very peculiar. Around its borders are high mountains, the Rocky mountains on the east, the Wind River range on the north, and the Wasatch on the west. From these ranges flow the little streams which make up the Colorado. Leaving the mountains, these streams enter a region of plateaus, great level expanses stretching farther than the eye can reach, without hill or valley, and with scarcely an undulation in the level surface. Where a plateau ends there is a line of abrupt cliffs descending hundreds or even thousands of feet, to the level of another and lower plateau. And so, passing away from the mountains, one descends by a series of gigantic steps, a veritable giant's staircase, from an elevation of twelve thousand feet to the sea level.

These plateaus contain no valleys. Instead of valleys there are canyons and gorges, with rocky, precipitous sides and narrow beds. In many places these canyons are so numerous as to reduce the plateau to a mere skeleton of narrow, winding, flat-topped ridges. Most of the canyons are dry nearly all the year, and in but few do the streams flow continuously. When the rain comes it is usually in the form of spasmodic showers. It falls in sheets, and flowing rapidly off the upper land, fills these canyons to a great depth. For a few hours, perhaps, they are rushing torrents, and then the beds of the canyons are left as dry and hot as before. This region is, on the whole, an arid one. The high plateaus are, however, green and fertile, covered with pines, spruces, and waving grasses, and bedecked with gayly painted flowers. But as one descends the aspect of nature changes. The spruces, aspens, and waving grasses disappear, and are replaced by the pinon pine and cedar; then by artemisia, which is succeeded by the cactus, yucca, and mesquite; while finally, upon the lower plateaus, little if any vegetation exists. The lower plateaus of the Colorado are as completely a desert as any part of the Sahara.

The Great Basin.—West of the basin of the Colorado is another peculiar region, in which, owing to deficient rainfall, no system of drainage has yet been developed. It is an inland basin, without drainage to either ocean. Though known as the Great Basin, it is in reality a group of many basins. At ordinary seasons each of these basins is independent of every other. The streams flowing into them either sink into the soil or evaporate to the thirsty atmosphere. On those rare occasions when the rain falls heavily, several of the basins may be connected one with another by temporary streams. The surface of the Great Basin is an alternation of broad valleys, deeply filled with sand and soil washed from their sides, and with sharp, narrow, abrupt mountain ranges trending nearly north and south. Upon the east this basin is separated from the Colorado valley by the Wasatch range, and upon the west the Sierra Nevada separates it from the valley of California. The northern and southern boundaries are ill-defined, consisting in the main of gentle elevations in the midst of valleys.

Salt Lake Basin.—The largest of the basins of which the Great Basin is composed, is that of Great Salt lake, which collects most of the streams flowing down the west wall of the Wasatch range, into this Dead Sea of America, where the water is evaporated and restored to the atmosphere. Another of these basins, which lies at the eastern foot of the Sierra Nevada, collects the waters flowing from that range and from the interior of the basin, in a series of lakes and swamps, whence it is evaporated. These are known as the Carson and Humboldt sinks.

Sierra Nevada.—The Sierra Nevada forms the west wall of the Great Basin. It is a broad, massive range, rising steeply on the east, and descending by long spurs to the valley of California on the west. Near the southern end it has its greatest altitude, nearly fifteen thousand feet, thus exceeding all other elevations in the country, with the exception of certain mountains in Alaska. Toward the north it diminishes in height, and disappears as a range near the gorge of Pitt river.

Cascade Range.—Northward through Washington and Oregon, the line of elevation is continued by a volcanic plateau, upon which stand numerous extinct volcanoes, forming what is known as the Cascade range. Among these there are several peaks exceeding fourteen thousand feet in height, such as Shasta and Rainier.

West of these ranges lies a great valley, stretching from Puget Sound to southern California. Though broken in northern California by mountain spurs, it is practically a continuous valley. It lies for the most part not far above sea level; it is well watered in the northern portion, but in the southern part it becomes arid. Between this valley and the Pacific lie a series of ranges, the Coast ranges, consisting mostly of long, parallel ridges, which, with the narrow valleys included between them, extend to the Pacific coast.

This mountain region abounds in strange scenes. The forces of nature have here been exerted upon a tremendous scale, building up mountains and eroding canyons and gorges. In some places great floods of lava have been poured out, and have flowed over the land, producing immense basalt plains and lava beds. At other points volcanic eruptions have built up mountain peaks. Nowhere have the forces of erosion been displayed upon such a magnificent scale, and nowhere are their results so easily and clearly read. The great canyons, cliffs, mesas, and buttes of the Colorado basin, are their work. Their crowning labor is the grand series of canyons of the Colorado, which, stretching for a thousand miles, culminates in the Grand Canyon, six thousand feet in depth and scores of miles in length.

In some parts of this region the volcanic forces are still smouldering. A hot spring upon the summit of Mount Shasta, and smoke from other peaks in the Cascade range, bear witness that the internal fires are not extinct. But it is in Yellowstone Park, the region where in times past the god of fire has held high carnival, that the most striking evidences of his reign are still seen. Over this region has been poured a flood of molten rock. In it was buried the vegetation of the past, and in the midst of volcanic masses are now to be found trunks of trees changed to amethyst, opal, chalcedony, and quartz crystals.

In this region there are hot springs and geysers, in such abundance and magnitude as to throw all others, the world over, completely in the shade. Those of Iceland and New Zealand are petty affairs in comparison. Over an area of nearly four thousand square miles hot springs are omnipresent. They are found literally by the thousand, and are of all sizes, from a few inches across to areas of many acres. Where Iceland has two or three active geysers, the Yellowstone Park has hundreds. The amount of boiling water poured out from the bowels of the earth is simply fabulous. The water of the Firehole river flows hot from the Geyser Basins.

Temperature.—The United States lies entirely within the temperate zone, and the mean annual temperature ranges from seventy-five degrees Fahrenheit down to forty degrees; the temperature, of course, diminishing northward, and as the altitude above the sea increases. The mean temperature of the hottest month, July, ranges from eighty-five down to sixty-five degrees, and that of the coldest month, January, from sixty-five degrees down to near the zero point.

The maximum temperature rarely exceeds one hundred degrees, while the minimum is sometimes fifty degrees below zero. In the eastern, well-watered part of the country, where the atmosphere is moist, and upon the northwestern coast where similar conditions prevail, the range of temperature between summer and winter and between day and night is not excessive.

In the mountain region of the west, however, where the atmosphere is dry, the range is often very great. It is in this region that excessively high and excessively low temperatures are occasionally experienced. At Yuma, near the mouth of the Colorado river, the temperature in summer often exceeds one hundred and fifteen degrees, and when it falls to one hundred degrees people put on their flannels. On the other hand, in Montana, minimum temperatures of minus fifty-two degrees have been repeatedly recorded; although, on the whole, the climate of Montana is exceptionally mild, considering its latitude and altitude above sea level.

Rainfall.—The rainfall of the United States differs widely in different parts of the country. Over the eastern half it is abundant. It diminishes upon the plains, and in the mountain regions of the west it is scanty. Over the northwest coast, again, it is more than abundant. The rainfall of the east is derived in the main from the Gulf of Mexico and the Caribbean sea. The south winds come to the Gulf coast laden with moisture, and, encountering a cool land, deposit it as rain. Moving northward, they become dryer, and the rainfall is consequently reduced.

A similar action takes place upon the Atlantic coast, but the breadth of its area of operations is less. Thus we find along the Atlantic and Gulf coasts, the heaviest rainfall of the eastern part of the United States. On the Gulf coast it reaches, and sometimes exceeds, sixty inches per annum. Proceeding northward, the rainfall diminishes, and about the Great Lakes it is as low as thirty inches; but here the diminution in rainfall is partly made up by the diminished evaporation, due to the colder climate.

Passing westward up the slope of the Great Plains, the rainfall diminishes, and in the neighborhood of the one-hundredth meridian it commonly amounts to less than twenty inches. The rainfall within the mountain region as a rule ranges from ten inches upward, being greatest on the high mountains, whose altitude induces precipitation from the air currents, and lowest in the valleys and on the plateaus. The most arid part of the country is the Great Basin, whose rainfall rarely exceeds ten inches, and in many localities falls to four or five.

On the Pacific coast a different condition of things prevails. Here are found well-defined wet and dry seasons. Their wetness and dryness depend upon the latitude, the rainfall being much greater in the north than in the south. The annual rainfall at the Strait of Fuca has been as great as one hundred and twenty-five inches, while at San Diego it is often as low as five inches. This change in rainfall with the change of season and of latitude, is due to the relative temperatures of the sea and the land. Warm westerly winds from the Pacific reach the coast saturated with moisture. The temperature of these air currents does not vary much from summer to winter; but the temperature of the land varies greatly, so that in winter the currents, upon reaching the coast, encounter a relatively cold land, which chills them and induces precipitation.

The contrast between the temperatures of air currents and the land, increases as the latitude increases; consequently the precipitation increases northward and diminishes southward. After passing the Coast range and the great Pacific valley, these air currents encounter the peaks of the Cascade range and the Sierra Nevada. They are forced to great altitudes, are chilled, and shed upon these ranges all the moisture that is left in them, and in that desiccated condition they blow over the desert to the eastward as dry winds. Hence it is that the winter winds are dry in the western mountain regions.

In the summer all this is changed. Then the land, with the exception of the highest mountains, is relatively warmer than the sea, and the moist air currents coming from the sea blow over the Coast ranges with little loss of moisture, and climb the Sierra and Cascades, upon which they deposit a greater amount; but they still contain enough in their eastward progress to water with frequent showers the mountains and valleys of Colorado, New Mexico, and Texas. Hence it is that the summer season is the rainy season of these States.

From the above brief outline it is easy to understand the impropriety of speaking of the *climate* of the United States, for the country contains within itself the widest possible variations of climate. It is one of the wettest and one of the dryest countries on the globe, it is one of the hottest and one of the coldest; and the folly of the assumption of European writers, that the so-called American climate is developing an American species of mankind, is made apparent when the facts are stated.

Forests.—The eastern part of the United States, from the Mississippi to the Atlantic, including southern Missouri, Arkansas, and eastern Texas, is, on the whole, a forested region. Throughout this part of the country timber grows freely. It is true that portions of Illinois and adjacent States were prairies when settlement began; but, except where cultivated, they are fast growing up to woodland under the protective influences of man.

It is said, too, that the Appalachian valley was also a prairie; but it is now covered with forests, except where cultivated. The western part of Washington and Oregon, and the western part of California, are also forested regions, and most of the mountain ranges of the west are wooded; but the valleys, plains, and plateaus of this region and the Great Plains, are devoid of tree growth. In all this region the rainfall is not sufficient to support trees, if we except two or three scrubby species which are peculiar to an arid climate.

It is estimated that more than one-third of the area of the United States is at present covered with timber. This estimate takes account not only of the area naturally devoid of trees, but also of the areas which have been denuded for purposes of cultivation and other requirements of civilization.

GOVERNMENT

THE government of the United States is a pure democracy. It is in the most complete sense a government by the people, from the smallest political subdivision, the township, up to the national government. The machinery of government is absolutely controlled by the people governed. It is therefore home rule pure and simple. Matters concerning the township, and the township only, are controlled by the township government; those concerning a group of townships are controlled by the county government.

Matters which have a wider bearing and influence than the county are controlled by the state government, and in turn those of national importance and bearing are in the hands of the general government. Thus, speaking broadly, the powers and functions of the greater governments are restricted to matters of general importance and concern, and as far as is consistent with the general welfare, the powers of government are given to the minor units. Naturally enough, this distribution of power among the different units of government differs in different States, depending upon the stage of settlement, upon the character of the occupations of the people, and, to some extent, upon their traditions and social customs. Of the distribution of powers, more will be said later.

To the foregoing it is scarcely necessary to add that, under this system of government, the individual enjoys the greatest freedom consistent with the due protection of the rights of others. To this large measure of individual freedom is due, in great part, the development of the strong, and at the same time adaptable, American type of mankind, which has already made this country *facile princeps* in all the elements of national greatness.

In each unit of government three elements are to be plainly recognized—the legislative, executive, and judicial. In the national and state governments, these are clearly distinguished by different sets of officers and related organizations. In county and township governments, the legislative and executive functions are often exercised by the same officers. The judicial function is everywhere distinctly differentiated from the others.

GENERAL GOVERNMENT

In the general government the President is the chief executive officer. Under the Constitution he must be a native of the United States, and must be at least thirty-five years of age at the time of his election. His term of service is four years, and he may be reëlected; but precedent has decreed that he shall be reëlected only once. His election is effected by what the fathers designed to be a very judicious piece of machinery, but this has degenerated into a mere formality. The Constitution requires that the qualified voters shall choose electors, such electors being in the proportion of one for every senator and representative in Congress: that the electors of each state thus chosen shall meet on a certain day within that state and vote for President and Vice-President, transmitting the result to Congress, which publicly declares it.

It was intended that the electors should be men chosen for the purpose of sitting as a deliberative body, and selecting according to their judgment the men best fitted for these high offices. As a matter of fact, while this routine is carried out to the letter, the selection of candidates for the Presidency and Vice-Presidency is made beforehand by conventions of the great parties, and the party electors are pledged in the strongest possible way to vote for the candidates of their respective parties and thus simply carry out the dictates of the party which elected them. Wooden men would answer the purpose equally well.

A majority, not a plurality, of the electors decides the election, and when, as has happened on rare occasions, there is no choice by the electors, it goes to the House of Representatives, the members of which vote, not individually, but by states; so that in this event each state, whatever the number of its delegation, has the same weight in electing the President as every other.

Cabinet.—The President, upon assuming office, selects a number of advisers, known collectively as his Cabinet. These are as follows: Secretary of State, Secretary of the Treasury, Secretary of War, Attorney-General, Postmaster-General, Secretary of the Navy, Secretary of the Interior, and Secretary of Agriculture. These selections are subject to confirmation by the Senate. In case of the removal, death, or inability of both the President and Vice-President, these officials succeed to the Presidency in the order here given: first, the Secretary of State; or, in case of his death, the Secretary of the Treasury, and so on.

The members of the Cabinet, besides being the President's advisers, are executive heads of departments of government, the scope of their departments being indicated to a certain extent by their designations. Within these departments the work of government is further subdivided into bureaus, the heads of which are subordinate to the Cabinet officers; and these bureaus, in turn, are separated into divisions and sections. The salary of the President is fifty thousand dollars a year; that of the Vice-President and of members of the Cabinet, eight thousand dollars.

Senate.—The legislative branch consists of two houses of Congress, known as the Senate and House of Representatives. The former consists of two members elected from each state for a term of six years, so arranged that one-third of the body goes out of office every two years. A senator must be a resident of the state from which he is elected, and must be at least thirty years of age. The Vice-President is the presiding officer of the Senate.

As there are now forty-four states in the Union, the number of senators is eighty-eight, and, being elected for terms of considerable length, they are not as closely in touch with their constituents as members of the House of Representatives. They are more deliberative and less likely to be swayed by the impulse of the moment. The Senate is therefore regarded as the more conservative of the two legislative bodies. The compensation of a senator is five thousand dollars a year.

House of Representatives.—The House of Representatives at present comprises three hundred and thirty-six members, including the delegates from the territories who are permitted to participate in debates but have no vote. The representation from each state is proportioned to the number of inhabitants. Representatives are elected for two years only. Each representative must be a resident of the district from which he is elected, and must be at least twenty-five years of age. This body chooses its own presiding officer, who is known as the Speaker, and in cases of contested elections decides upon its membership. Being the popular branch of the government—that is, the branch in closest touch with the people—it claims and as a rule maintains the right to originate business, and especially to propose the appropriation of funds from the Treasury. The salary of a representative is five thousand dollars a year.

The work of Congress is carried on mainly by means of committees. In the House of Representatives there are in all fifty-seven standing committees for specific purposes, the members of which are chosen by the Speaker. To these committees are referred bills and measures presented to the House which fall within their respective provinces. In committee measures receive careful consideration, and, as a rule, the House accepts the committee's report. Under this method careful legislation is possible, while otherwise it would be impossible. A similar committee system prevails in the Senate; but there the committee is a less powerful organization, and justly so, since the Senate is a smaller and more deliberative body, and moreover originates fewer measures.

Judiciary.—The judiciary of the general government consists of three classes of courts: First, the Supreme Court of the United States, which sits in Washington, and is composed of a chief justice and eight associate justices, who are appointed by the President and confirmed by the Senate; their tenure of office is for life, unless impeached. Second, the United States circuit courts, which are held at various places throughout the country, and are presided over by individual members of the Supreme Court. Third, the United States district courts, over which preside district judges, who are also appointed by the President and confirmed by the Senate.

DISTRIBUTION OF POWERS

There has been a constant struggle ever since the organization of the government, as to the powers vested in the general government and those retained by the states. All the difficulties encountered by the fathers in attempting to form the federal government arose from this jealousy of centralization. With the exception of the war of the Rebellion, this has been a peaceful struggle, but none the less it has been constant and intense. However, the general government has steadily maintained and extended its control over questions of common interest to all or several of the states.

All matters connected with foreign relations, the coinage or printing of money, the postal system, the collection of revenue whether by customs or excise taxes, the taking of the decennial census, the administration of the public lands, the issuance of patents and copyrights, the lighting and protection of the coasts, and the public defense whether by land or sea, are in the hands of the general government. There are many other matters in which it shares the control jointly with the States. Through its Department of Agriculture and through its Surveys, it aids in the development of agricultural and mineral resources. It collects and furnishes information concerning the progress of education. It aids in the maintenance of the supply of food fishes, and of numerous agencies which assist in the collection and dissemination of scientific information.

Executive Divisions.—The executive departments of the government are eight in number: The Department of State, which has jurisdiction over foreign affairs; the Treasury Department, which has charge of all matters relating to the collection and disbursement of the revenues of the government; the War Department, which controls the army; the Department of Justice, which prosecutes all government cases in the United States courts, and acts as the legal adviser of the Executive; the Post Office Department, which manages the transportation and distribution of the mails; the Navy Department; the

Department of the Interior, which has general control over internal matters of administration, and which embraces a great variety of bureaus; and, finally, the Department of Agriculture, which is primarily concerned in fostering that great branch of industry. Besides these, there are several bureaus or institutions which are not attached to any of the regular departments.

Department of State.—This department, which is regarded as first in rank, has jurisdiction over all matters connected with our foreign relations, including treaties in extradition of fugitives from justice and the granting of passports. It has control of the ministers to foreign countries and consuls in foreign ports, and is the custodian of the Great Seal of the United States. It also publishes the laws and resolutions of Congress, amendments to the Constitution, executive orders and proclamations. The bureaus of this department are six in number; namely, the Bureau of Indexes and Archives, the Diplomatic Bureau, Consular Bureau, Bureau of Accounts, Bureau of Rolls and Library, and Bureau of Statistics. The duties of these several bureaus are indicated by their names.

Treasury Department.—This is a large department, comprising many bureaus and employing an army of clerks. The collection of the revenues is done under two bureaus, those of the Commissioners of Customs and of Internal Revenue. The disbursement of public funds is supervised by two comptrollers, who pass upon legal points connected therewith, and by six auditors, who examine the correctness and validity of accounts. The Treasurer has charge of the funds or deposits in the Treasury. The Register of the Treasury is the book-keeper of the United States. The Comptroller of the Currency has control over the national banks. The Mint Bureau supplies the coinage, and the Bureau of Engraving and Printing supplies the issues of paper money. Besides all these, which may be classified as executive bureaus, there are others, attached to the Treasury Department, of a scientific or semi-scientific nature. The construction of public buildings throughout the United States is also controlled by one of its bureaus, presided over by the supervising architect.

The Treasury Department maintains a Bureau of Statistics, for the collection and publication of statistics of foreign trade and immigration. It also maintains a Life-Saving Service, the best in the world; by this service much of our coast, including the most important portions, is patrolled day and night by parties fully equipped with the most modern appliances for saving life and property from shipwreck. It includes the Light House establishment, by which the entire coast and most of the navigable rivers are lighted. It also controls the Coast and Geodetic Survey, to which is intrusted the survey of the coast and the geodetic triangulation of the interior of the country.

War Department.—A partial enumeration of the bureaus of which the departments are composed, with a slight account of the work carried on by each, will illustrate the scope and great variety of the functions of the general government. The War Department is divided into twelve bureaus, or sub-departments, whose names in most cases describe their functions. They are: Army Headquarters, Adjutant General's office, Inspector-General's office, Judge-Advocate-General's office, Bureau of Subsistence, Quartermasters', Ordnance, Medical, and Pay Departments, Engineers' Department, Department of Public Buildings and Grounds, and Office of Publication of War Records.

Department of Justice. This is a small department, whose functions, as stated above, are to advise the President and the heads of other departments upon legal points, and through assistant attorneys-general and United States district attorneys, to prosecute cases in the United States courts on behalf of the general government.

Post Office Department.—The work of the Post Office Department is entirely of an executive character, and a statement of its operations is presented in a later portion of this work.

Navy Department. The Navy Department embraces a large number of bureaus and offices, among which are the following: Bureau of Ordnance, of Equipment, of Navigation, of Yards and Docks, of Provisions and Clothing, of Steam Engineering, of Medicine and Surgery, of Construction, of Inspection and Survey, and of Naval Intelligence. It contains a Hydrographic office, whose function is to supply charts to the navy, and for that purpose it not only engraves and prints charts of the coasts of foreign lands, but makes surveys with the same end in view. It contains also the Naval Observatory, one of the best equipped in the world, and the Nautical Almanac office, which prepares the American Nautical Almanac, for the use of the merchant marine as well as the navy.

Department of the Interior.—The Department of the Interior was not created, but has grown. To it have been attached bureaus which did not fit elsewhere, and consequently it contains a great variety of them. It has control of the survey and disposition of the public lands, of the issuance of patents, of the granting of pensions, and of the relations of the government with the Indians, a bureau being assigned to each of these matters. The Bureau of Education collects and publishes statistics of education throughout the country. The Geological Survey studies and reports upon the geology and mineral wealth of the national domain, and, incidentally, is preparing a topographic map thereof; indeed, this great work, although an incidental, has for ten years been the principal work of the Geological Survey office. Finally, the Interior Department contains the Census office, a temporary bureau, constituted every ten years for the purpose of taking account of stock.

Department of Agriculture.—It is the function of the Department of Agriculture to aid and foster the agricultural industry. To this end it collects and disseminates statistics of crops. It searches for the means of protecting crops from disease and insect enemies. It tests the fitness of soils and climates for new products, it studies the forest resources, and thus in many ways it advances the interests of the farmer. To this Department is attached the Weather Bureau, whose principal function is to predict the weather.

Other Departments and Bureaus.—The Fish Commission, an independent bureau, exists for the purpose, primarily, of increasing the supply of food fishes. Incidentally it has contributed greatly to our knowledge of the life and habits of the denizens of the briny deep and of our lakes and rivers.

The Interstate Commerce Commission is likewise unattached. It has jurisdiction over the railways of the country, under the laws regulating interstate commerce.

The Department or Bureau of Labor is an office for the collection and dissemination of statistics relating to labor, its compensation, hours, relation to capital, etc.

Most of the civil employés of the United States are under the protection of a civil service law, whose chief provision is that appointments to the service can be made only as a result of competitive examination, free to all, with some slight restrictions as to residence, etc. There is a commission, known as the Civil Service Commission, for conducting such examinations.

Smithsonian Institution.—There is under the control of the government one institution of a peculiar character. Many years ago, Mr. James Smithson bequeathed a large sum of money to the United States for the increase and diffusion of knowledge. Partly with the income from this bequest, and partly by appropriation from the United States Treasury, the Smithsonian Institution has been founded and maintained, and to it have been added the National Museum, the Bureau of Ethnology, and the National Zoölogical Park.

The work of this institution has been mainly in pure science. Its uniform policy has been to aid original investigation, and, whenever practicable, to assist it to aid itself. Thus it supported the first tottering steps of the science of meteorology, and at last saw it recognized by the government in the form of the Weather Bureau. Similarly with fish culture, now supported in the Fish Commission. It deserves no small share of the credit of establishing the Geological Survey, the National Museum, and the Bureau of Ethnology.

ORGANIZATION OF STATES

The Union, which originally consisted of thirteen states, is now composed of forty-four states, five territories, and the federal District of Columbia. The political organization of each state is very similar to that of the general government, the chief executive officer being the governor. The legislative functions are carried on by a legislature, which consists in each case of two houses. Each state has a judiciary of its own, for the purpose of interpreting and enforcing state laws. The government of the territories rests in part with the people of the territories, and in part with the general government. The President appoints the territorial governors, while the people elect their legislatures.

District of Columbia.—The District of Columbia, the seat of the national government, is the only portion of this great domain which is not in any respect under home rule. Strange to say, this, the capital of the greatest and freest Republic, is in its form of government an absolute monarchy. Its executive consists of three commissioners, who are appointed by the President of the United States. Its laws are enacted by Congress, and its judiciary is appointed by the President. Therefore the people of the District have no voice in the management of their public affairs, beyond the privilege of protest and petition. As originally constituted, the District of Columbia comprised an area ten miles square. The Virginia portion was ceded to the United States, July 16, 1790, and the Maryland portion, March 30, 1791. Subsequently, July 9, 1846, the Virginia portion was re-ceded to that state.

The following is a list of the states and territories, with a brief account of their organization:

Alabama.—Alabama territory was created from a part of Mississippi territory, March 3, 1817. Its limits were those of the present state, excepting that the thirty-first parallel was its southern boundary. It was admitted as a state, December 14, 1819.

Alaska.—Alaska was obtained by purchase from the Russian government in 1867, for the sum of $7,200,000 in gold. It was given a territorial government, July 27, 1868.

Arizona.—This territory was formed in part from the first Mexican purchase, and in part from the Gadsden purchase, by act of Congress, February 24, 1863.

Arkansas.—Arkansas territory was created by act of March 2, 1819, from a part of the Louisiana purchase, then known as Missouri territory. It was admitted as a state with its present boundaries, June 15, 1836.

California.—This state was admitted September 9, 1850, its area being taken from the territory acquired from Mexico by the treaty of Guadalupe Hidalgo.

Colorado.—Colorado territory was created February 28, 1861, its area being taken partly from the Louisiana purchase, partly from the territory acquired from Mexico, and partly from the area purchased from Texas. It was admitted as a state, August 1, 1876.

Connecticut.—One of the Thirteen Original States. It ratified the Constitution, January 9, 1788.

Delaware.—One of the Thirteen Original States. It was the first to ratify the Constitution, having taken this step January 7, 1787.

Florida.—Florida territory was created March 30, 1822, from the area purchased from Spain three years previously. It was admitted as a state, March 3, 1845.

Georgia.—One of the Thirteen Original States. It adopted the Constitution, January 2, 1788.

Idaho.—Idaho territory was formed March 3, 1863, from Oregon, which was acquired by prior settlement. It was admitted as a state, July 3, 1890.

Illinois.—The territory of Illinois was formed by act of February 3, 1809, from a part of the territory northwest of the Ohio river. It was admitted as a state, with its boundaries greatly reduced, December 3, 1818.

Indiana.—Indiana territory was created May 7, 1800, from a part of Northwest territory. Its boundaries then enclosed a much greater area than those of the present state. December 11, 1816, it was admitted as a state, with its present boundaries.

Indian Territory.—This is not in the proper sense a territory of the United States, but rather a group of Indian reservations, established from time to time as occasion has arisen. The area included in the present territory is a part of the original Louisiana purchase.

Iowa.—Iowa territory was created July 3, 1838, when it included a much greater area than at present. Its area was embraced in the Louisiana purchase. March 3, 1845, it was admitted as a state, and December 28, 1846, its northern and western boundaries were changed, giving to the state its present limits.

Kansas.—The territory of Kansas was created May 30, 1854, its area being taken from that of the Louisiana purchase. January 29, 1861, it was admitted as a state, with its present limits.

Kentucky.—Kentucky was admitted June 1, 1792, with its present limits, having been taken from the western portion of Virginia.

Louisiana.—The territory of Orleans was created March 3, 1805, and comprised nearly the same area as the present state of Louisiana. April 30, 1812, this territory was admitted as a state, under the name of Louisiana, and in the same year its limits were extended to include the present area.

Maine.—The area of the state of Maine was originally a part of Massachusetts, and was known as the District of Maine. It was detached from Massachusetts and admitted as a state, March 15, 1820.

Maryland.—One of the Thirteen Original States. It adopted the Constitution, April 28, 1788.

Massachusetts.—One of the Thirteen Original States. It adopted the Constitution, February 6, 1788.

Michigan.—The territory of Michigan was formed June 30, 1805, its area being taken from what was originally the Northwest territory. It was admitted as a state, January 26, 1837, with its boundaries considerably changed from those of the territory.

Minnesota.—The territory of Minnesota was created March 3, 1849. Its area was derived in part from the old Northwest territory, and in part from the Louisiana purchase. It was admitted as a state, May 11, 1858, with its limits greatly reduced.

Mississippi.—The original territory of Mississippi, organized April 7, 1798, was very different from the present state, and comprised an area in the southern part of the present states of Alabama and Mississippi. In 1804 this territory was enlarged to include almost the entire area of these two states.

It was subsequently diminished by the formation of the territory of Alabama, and December 10, 1817, it was admitted as a state with its present boundaries.

Missouri.—The original Missouri territory, as constituted by act of April 30, 1812, included all the Louisiana purchase with the exception of the present state of Louisiana. One after another, states were carved from it, and August 10, 1821, the state of Missouri was admitted, with its boundaries the same as at present, excepting the western boundary, which was extended westward in 1836.

Montana.—Montana territory was created May 26, 1864, its area being originally part of the Louisiana purchase. It was admitted as a state, November 8, 1889.

Nebraska.—The territory of Nebraska was organized under the act of May 30, 1854, and originally comprised a large proportion of what was the Louisiana purchase. It was reduced by the formation of several states and territories, and March 1, 1867, was admitted as a state.

Nevada.—Nevada territory was created by act of March 2, 1861, from a part of the territory first acquired from Mexico. Its original area was much less than at present. It was admitted as a state, October 31, 1864, with its eastern limits enlarged, and subsequently, in 1866, it was still further enlarged so as to include the present area.

New Hampshire.—One of the Thirteen Original States. It ratified the Constitution, June 21, 1788.

New Jersey.—One of the Thirteen Original States. It ratified the Constitution, December 18, 1787.

New Mexico.—The territory of New Mexico was created by act of December 13, 1850. Originally it included its present area, with the exception of that part of the Gadsden purchase which it now embraces. This was added by Congress, December 30, 1853.

New York.—One of the Thirteen Original States. It adopted the Constitution, July 26, 1788.

North Carolina.—One of the Thirteen Original States. It adopted the Constitution, November 21, 1789.

North Dakota.—The territory of Dakota was created by

act of March 2, 1861, from a part of the original Louisiana purchase. From it several states have been formed, and the remainder was cut in two parts and these parts admitted as states, November 2, 1889, under the names North and South Dakota.

Ohio.—Ohio was formed and admitted as a state, November 29, 1802, its area being taken from Northwest territory. In 1836 the northern boundary was slightly changed, a narrow strip of land being added.

Oklahoma.—The territory of Oklahoma, originally a part of the Louisiana purchase, was formed May 2, 1890.

Oregon.—The territory of Oregon was created by act of August 14, 1848, and originally included the present areas of Oregon, Washington, and Idaho, which were acquired by prior settlement, immediately after the purchase of Louisiana. It was admitted as a state, with its present boundaries, February 14, 1859.

Pennsylvania.—One of the Thirteen Original States. It adopted the Constitution, December 12, 1787.

Rhode Island.—One of the Thirteen Original States. It was the last to adopt the Constitution, the act bearing date May 29, 1790.

South Carolina.—One of the Thirteen Original States. It adopted the Constitution, May 23, 1788.

South Dakota.—(See North Dakota.)

Tennessee.—Tennessee was admitted as a state, with its present boundaries, June 1, 1796. Its area was taken from the territory south of the Ohio river.

Texas.—This state, which in 1836 achieved its independence of Mexico, was admitted December 29, 1845. It then included a large territory subsequently sold to the United States, which now forms portions of New Mexico, Colorado, and Kansas.

Utah.—Utah territory was created by act of September 9, 1850, and originally embraced, besides its own area, that of Nevada.

Vermont.—This was the first state admitted to the Union after the adoption of the Constitution. The act of Congress bears date March 4, 1791. Its area was in dispute between New York, New Hampshire, and Massachusetts.

Virginia.—One of the Thirteen Original States. It adopted the Constitution, June 25, 1788.

Washington.—The territory of Washington was created by act of March 2, 1853, from a part of Oregon territory. It originally included, besides its own area, that of Idaho. It was admitted as a state, with its present boundaries, November 11, 1889.

West Virginia.—The state of West Virginia was set off from Virginia and admitted, June 19, 1863.

Wisconsin.—The territory of Wisconsin was formed by act of June 3, 1836, from a part of the Northwest territory. It was admitted as a state, May 29, 1848, with its present boundaries.

Wyoming.—Wyoming territory was created, July 25, 1868, with its present area. It was admitted as a state, July 10, 1890.

The following table presents the

AREAS OF THE STATES AND TERRITORIES IN SQUARE MILES

States and Territories	Gross area	Water surface	Land surface	States and Territories	Gross area	Water surface	Land surface

*Including Cherokee Outlet and No Man's Land

SUBDIVISIONS OF STATES AND COUNTIES

Each state and territory is divided for governmental purposes into counties, and these counties are further subdivided. The distribution of political power between the counties and their subdivisions, differs widely in different states; indeed, three distinct systems are apparent in various parts of the country. In the New England states the county government has very few functions, indeed scarcely any beyond judicial ones, while its subdivision, the town or city, has jurisdiction of all local concerns, and is by far the most powerful political unit.

In the southern states, and in the sparsely settled states and territories of the west, the county has jurisdiction over practically all local matters, and the subdivisions of the county, which are known variously in different states as civil districts, magisterial districts, beats, hundreds, militia districts, wards, etc., have merely minor judicial powers, and serve as election districts and for other minor uses.

In the northern states outside of New England, beginning with New York, New Jersey, and Pennsylvania and extending westward to the frontier of settlement, a compromise system prevails, wherein the powers are quite equally divided between the two organizations, the county on the one hand, and the township, as it is called, on the other. This system seems, on the whole, to be the most acceptable, inasmuch as the new states, as soon as they reach a sufficient population to warrant, have adopted it one after another, while the southern states are constantly tending toward it.

Various classes of municipalities are incorporated or chartered, the name carried in the charter, and the delegated powers, differing in different parts of the country. In certain states all incorporated bodies are known as cities of one grade or another; in others, cities, towns, and villages are chartered; in yet others, boroughs, etc. The following table shows the number of civil divisions of the United States in 1890, the nearest date to which reference can be made:

CIVIL DIVISIONS OF THE UNITED STATES IN 1890

States	44
Territories	5
Federal district	1
Counties, including parishes of Louisiana	2,772
Towns and townships	20,371
Other subdivisions of the county	12,000
Cities	1,623
Chartered towns, villages, boroughs, etc.	8,000

According to this table there is a total of about 44,800 governments of various kinds existing under and tributary to the federal government. All these work in harmony one with another. Rarely does any conflict of jurisdiction arise, and in all such cases decisions are easily reached through the judiciary and readily accepted.

GOVERNMENT DEBTS

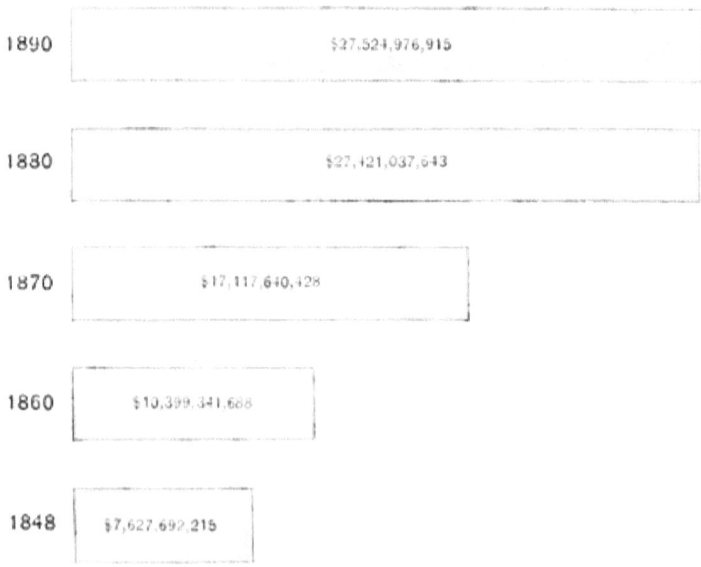

1890	$27,524,976,915
1880	$27,421,037,643
1870	$17,117,640,428
1860	$10,399,341,688
1848	$7,627,692,215

NATIONAL DEBT OF THE WORLD, 1848 TO 1890

THE BUILDING OF A NATION

PLATE 1

NET PUBLIC DEBT, BY CLASSES OF
ORGANIZATIONS, IN 1890

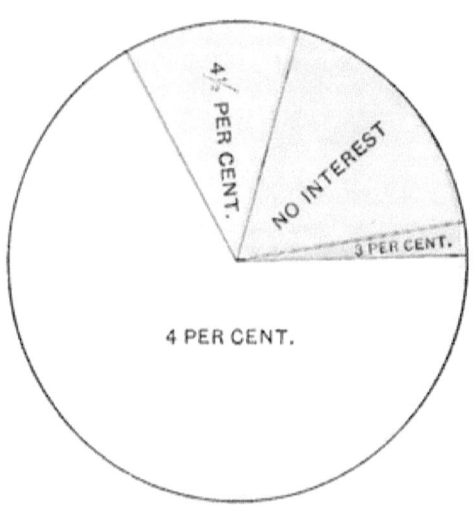

NET NATIONAL DEBT, BY RATES OF
INTEREST, IN 1890

The following table, and the upper diagram on Plate I, facing page 32, show the national debt of the United States, and the debts of states, of counties, and of the subdivisions of counties, including municipalities and school districts, in 1890. In the table these amounts are compared with the corresponding figures for 1880:

GOVERNMENT DEBTS IN 1880 AND 1890

Character of Debt	Debt less Sinking Fund		Per Capita	
	1890	1880	1890	1880
National	$891,960,104	$1,922,517,364	$14.24	$38.33
State	228,997,389	297,244,095	3.66	5.93
County	145,048,045	124,105,027	2.32	2.47
Municipal	724,463,060	684,318,843	11.57	13.64
School district	36,701,918	17,580,682	0.59	0.35

National Debt.— December 31, 1892, the national debt, less the cash in the Treasury, was $835,000,000, having been reduced in the last two and one-half years to the extent of $56,000,000, as appears from a comparison with the above table. This debt when analyzed is found to consist (a) of $585,000,000 represented by interest-bearing bonds, of which all but $25,000,000 are at four per cent., and (b) non-interest-bearing debts amounting to $250,000,000, as shown in the lower diagram on Plate I, facing page 32. This non-interest-bearing debt is composed almost entirely of legal tender notes, the gold and silver certificates so common in circulation being issued upon an equivalent amount of coin or bullion on deposit in the Treasury, and it is therefore offset by the item, "Cash in the Treasury."

The national debt of this country, prior to the civil war, was never of great magnitude. From the beginning of our history down to 1825 it oscillated from $45,000,000 to $127,000,000, with an average of about $75,000,000. Then it was reduced in 1835–36, and we were in the rare position among nations of having no debt; but subsequently our obligations were increased greatly, and in 1851 they reached $68,000,000, diminishing again until 1857, when they were less than $29,000,000. At

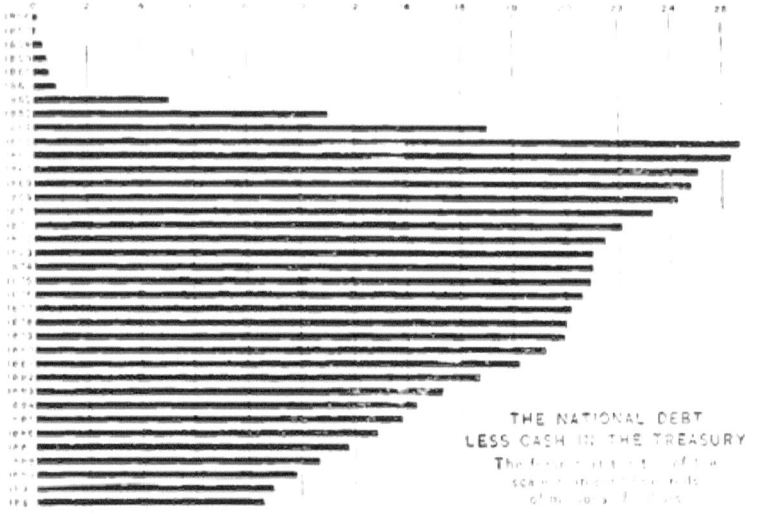

THE NATIONAL DEBT
LESS CASH IN THE TREASURY

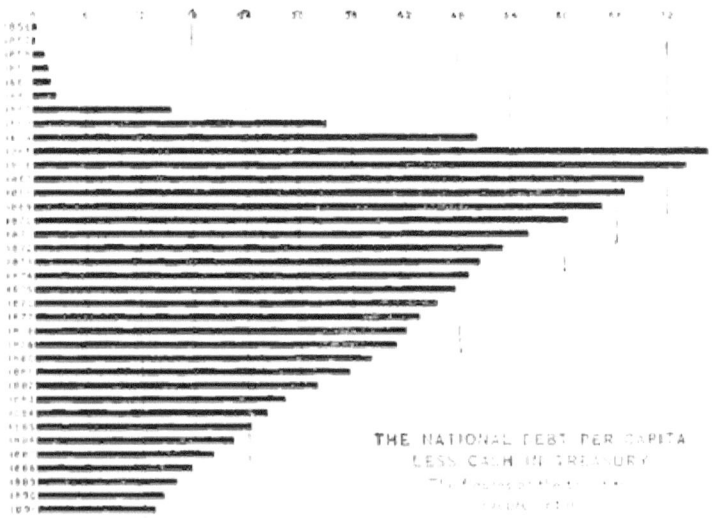

THE NATIONAL DEBT PER CAPITA
LESS CASH IN TREASURY

THE NATIONAL DEBT 1856 TO 1891

GOVERNMENT

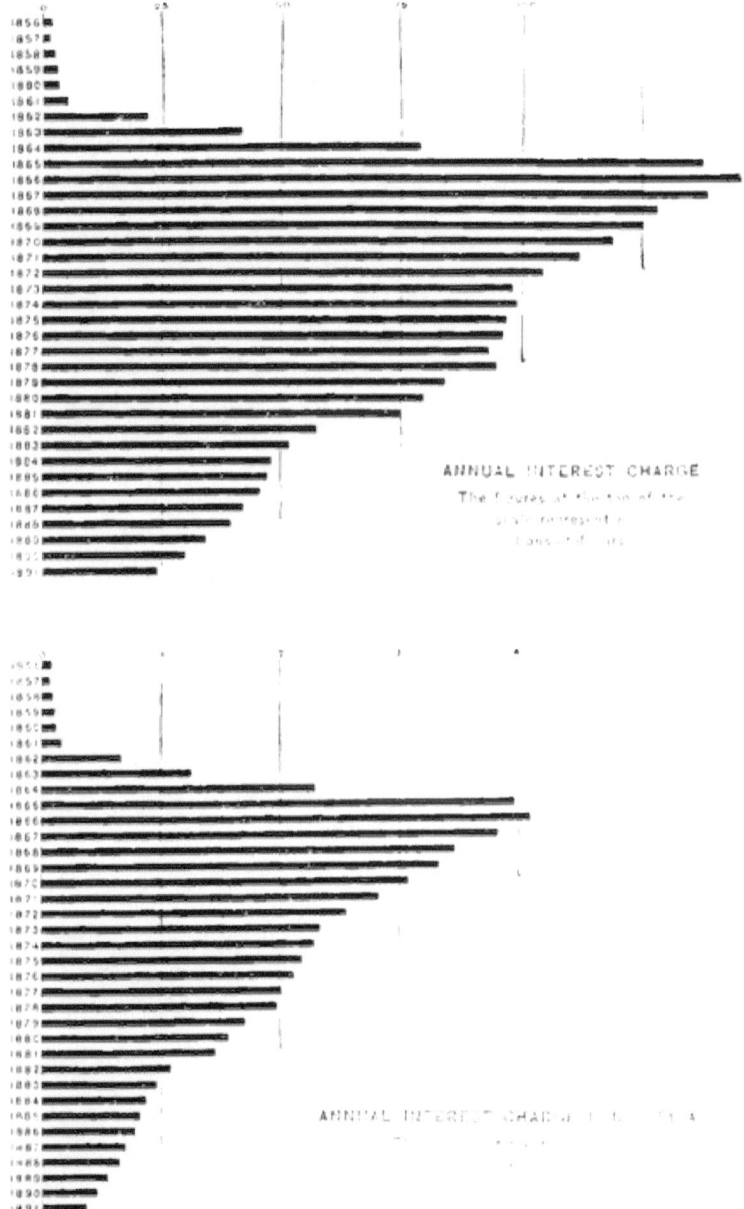

ANNUAL INTEREST CHARGE

THE NATIONAL DEBT, 1856 TO 1891

the opening of the war in 1861 the national debt was $90,000,-
000. From that date to 1866 the debt increased by enormous
strides, and in the latter year it reached the overwhelming amount
of $2,773,000,000, an average of $80 per capita of the population.
Upon this there was due each year the sum of $143,000,000
in interest, or more than $4 per annum to each inhabitant.

With the close of the war the nation set itself to paying off
this enormous burden, and, aided by wise management of its
finances and unexampled prosperity, it has done this at a rate
which the world had never before witnessed. In twenty-seven
years it has reduced the debt by the sum of $1,938,000,000, or
at the average rate per annum of over $72,000,000. It is now
less than one-third what it was in 1866, and with the increase of
population during the last part of the century, the burden upon
each inhabitant has been reduced to $13.

The interest has been reduced in a still greater proportion, as
the credit of the government has risen with each additional payment of principal, until now the total annual interest is less
than $25,000,000, an average of less than forty cents to each
inhabitant, or one-tenth of what it was in 1866. To-day the credit
of the United States is the highest of all nations. Its four per
cent. bonds, due in 1907, are selling at twenty-five per cent. above
par; while the three per cents., which were issued a few years
ago and have since been taken up, were sought for at par with
the greatest avidity, and quoted in financial markets at a considerable premium.

State Debts.—The debts of states aggregated, in 1890,
$228,997,389, showing a reduction of twenty-three per cent. dur-
ing the ten years preceding. The indebtedness of states, individually, is set forth in the map on Plate 2, and in the diagrams
on pages 38 and 39. They show the widest possible diversity
among the states in this regard.

In the northern states there is apparently some thought of
proportion between the amount of debt and the population and
wealth, but in the southern states no such relation exists.
This may be due to the origin of the debts of the southern
states, and their mode of treating them. In many cases these
debts were created by what were popularly known as "carpet

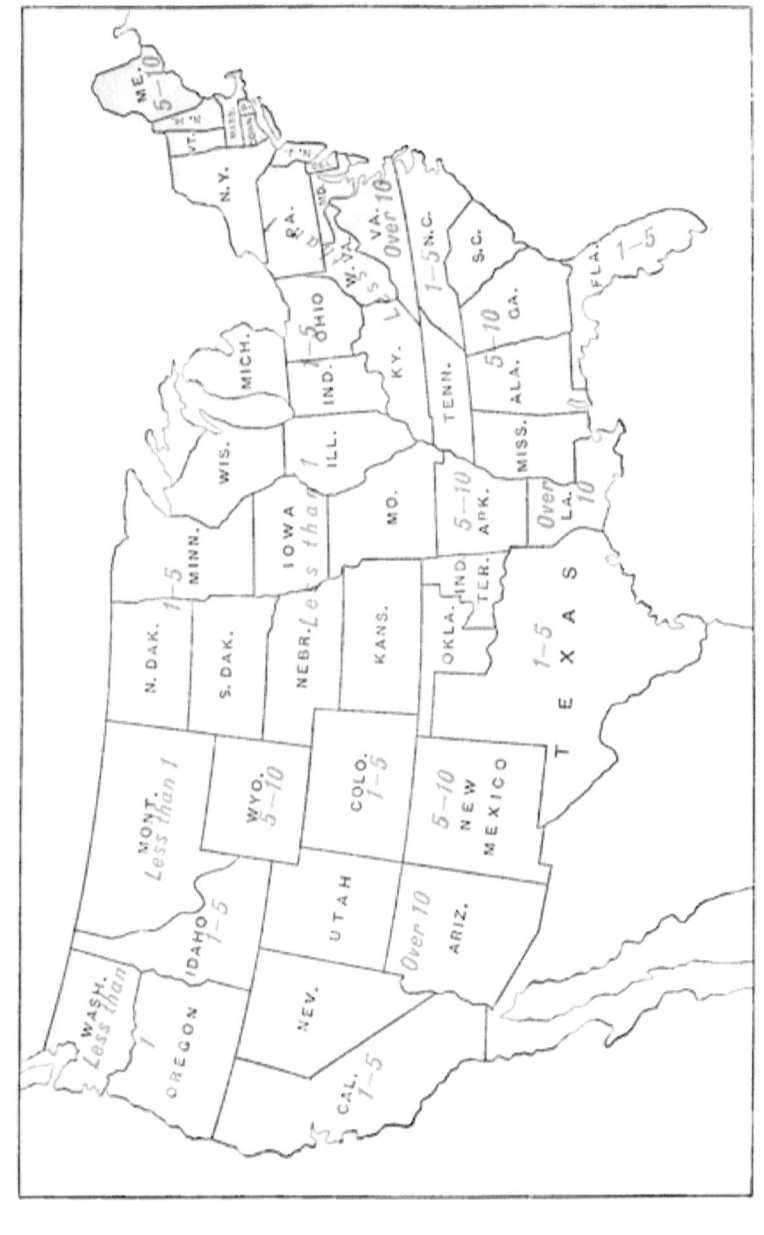

bag" governments, which had possession of the states for a period following the civil war, and sadly abused the responsibilities they had assumed, creating debt in the most reckless manner. In some cases these debts were repudiated by succeeding administrations, while in others they have been assumed by them and efforts are being made for their reduction.

The diagram on page 38 shows that of all the states Virginia has by far the heaviest debt, while she is followed by six other southern states. The states least burdened with debt are mainly the newer ones of the far west.

In most cases the debts of individual states have been reduced during the last decade, and in some instances this reduction has been enormous, when the size of the communities involved is taken into account. Thus Massachusetts has reduced her debt from $20,000,000 to $7,000,000; Pennsylvania, from nearly $14,000,000 to $4,000,000. In a few cases they have been increased, but the increase has generally occurred in states where values are increasing and to which population is flocking, and therefore the increase appears to be warranted.

There is one case not in the list which requires a special explanation, that of the District of Columbia, whose debt is by far the largest in proportion to its population. This debt amounted in 1890 to $19,781,050, and the per capita debt was not less than $85.86. It was incurred in transforming the city of Washington from a straggling country village into a beautiful city. The work was done rapidly and not in the most economical manner. The debt thus incurred, together with the interest, is shared by the people of the District and by the United States government, in equal proportions. Properly speaking, therefore, only one-half of it should be chargeable against the District.

Debts of Counties and Municipalities.—The debts of counties, which in 1890 amounted to about $145,000,000, have increased slightly during the decade, though at a much less rate than the population.

The debts of municipalities, which are proportionally large, especially in the case of the larger cities, have also increased slightly, being at the rate of less than six per cent., indicating a reduction of the per capita debt to a large extent. The municipal debt is at present probably almost the same in amount as the national debt.

The school district debt, while small in total amount, has more than doubled during the decade. Indeed, this is the only feature of the public debt of the country which has increased in proportion to the population.

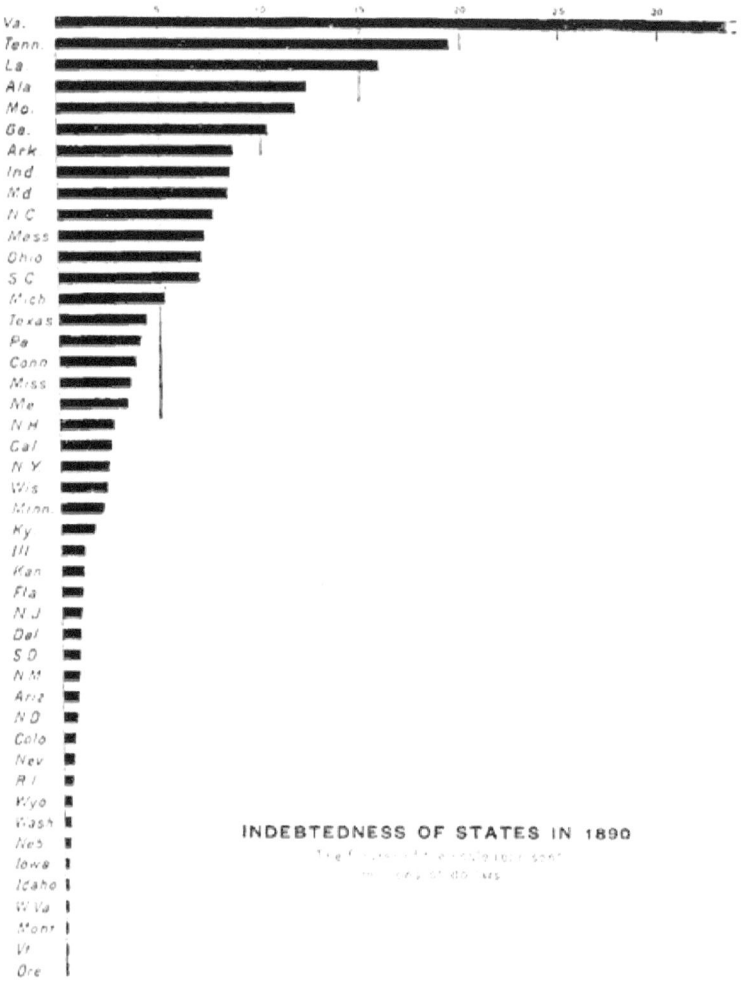

INDEBTEDNESS OF STATES IN 1890

GOVERNMENT

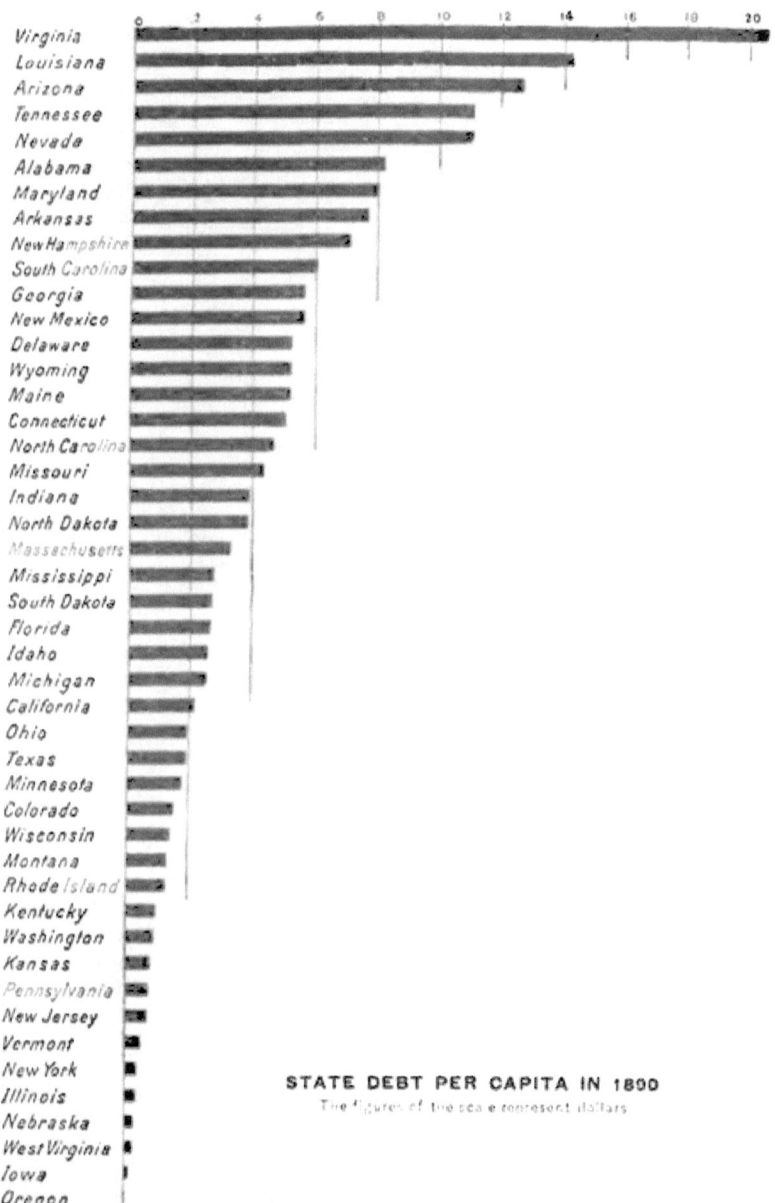

STATE DEBT PER CAPITA IN 1890

The figures of the scale represent dollars

BUDGET

The income of the general government is derived almost entirely from two forms of taxation—customs duties on imported articles, and internal revenue from the taxation of spirits and tobacco. The receipts of the government for the year 1890 were $362,600,000, or $6.14 per capita of the population, of which $219,500,000 was derived from customs duties, $145,700,000 from internal revenue, and $4,000,000 from sales of public lands. The expenditures for that year amounted to $355,400,000, or $5.55 per capita of the population, distributed as follows:

PRINCIPAL ITEMS OF EXPENDITURE

Maintenance of the army..........................$48,700,000
Maintenance of the navy............................26,100,000
Support of Indian tribes............................8,500,000
Pensions...124,400,000
Interest on the public debt........................37,500,000
Miscellaneous, including civil expenses...........110,000,000

It is popularly supposed that the cost of maintenance of the general government, in proportion to population, has steadily and gradually increased in recent years. This is not the case, as is shown by the following table, which gives the receipts and expenditures per capita for the past twenty years:

RECEIPTS AND EXPENDITURES PER CAPITA, 1872 TO 1891

Year	Receipts per Capita	Payments per Capita	Year	Receipts per Capita	Payments per Capita
1872	$9.22	$6.84	1882	$7.64	$4.89
1873	8.01	6.97	1883	7.37	4.90
1874	7.13	7.07	1884	6.27	4.39
1875	6.55	6.25	1885	5.67	4.56
1876	6.52	5.87	1886	5.76	4.15
1877	6.07	5.21	1887	6.20	4.47
1878	5.41	4.98	1888	6.32	4.33
1879	5.60	5.16	1889	6.01	4.38
1880	6.65	5.34	1890	6.14	4.75
1881	7.01	5.07	1891	6.14	5.55

From the foregoing table it appears that during the last ten years, from 1882 to 1892, neither the receipts nor the expenditures have been as great per capita as in the ten years between 1872 and 1882, and furthermore, that this reduction is not due alone to the reduction in the interest on the public debt, as that has been fully offset by the increase in the pensions.

MILITARY FORCES

The Regular Army.—Situated as we are, with a broad ocean upon either side separating our country from any nation which could for a moment pretend to cope with us, we have little need of a standing army. Occasionally there is an Indian outbreak in the far west, and its services are required to quell the trouble and protect the settlers. Occasionally, too, a labor strike develops into a mob, and troops are called on to uphold the arm of the law; but these are petty matters, and order is usually restored by the aid of one or two thousand men.

The regular army is limited by law to 25,000 non-commissioned officers and privates. It contains in addition 2,169 officers, the number being considerably in excess of that required for commanding the troops, so as to admit of easy and rapid expansion should occasion arise. The following table shows the classification and disposition of the troops:

CLASSIFICATION OF THE REGULAR ARMY

	Commissioned Officers	Non-commissioned Officers and Privates
General staff	100	....
Ordnance corps	58	450
Engineer corps	113	500
10 regiments of cavalry	432	6,050
5 regiments of artillery	289	3,675
25 regiments of infantry	877	12,125
Indian scouts, etc.	...	2,200
	2,169	25,000

Organized Militia.—In addition to the regular army, most of the states maintain a militia force, as an aid to the civil authorities in case of need. This militia is under the direct authority of the governor of the state, and can be called out at his discretion.

The following table shows the strength of the organized militia of the several states:

DISTRIBUTION OF ORGANIZED STATE MILITIA

State	Number	State	Number
Alabama	2,766	Montana	646
Arizona	288	Nebraska	1,956
Arkansas	2,322	Nevada	533
California	4,227	New Hampshire	1,060
Colorado	781	New Jersey	3,377
Connecticut	3,089	New Mexico	752
Delaware	606	New York	13,063
District of Columbia	984	North Carolina	1,982
Florida	1,603	North Dakota	131
Georgia	3,067	Ohio	4,708
Idaho	313	Oregon	1,243
Illinois	3,651	Pennsylvania	8,120
Indiana	1,972	Rhode Island	1,815
Iowa	2,558	South Carolina	4,906
Kansas	3,143	South Dakota	421
Kentucky	1,120	Tennessee	1,607
Louisiana	1,653	Texas	3,162
Maine	987	Vermont	711
Maryland	1,934	Virginia	2,746
Massachusetts	5,365	Washington	1,015
Michigan	2,341	West Virginia	872
Minnesota	1,803	Wisconsin	2,238
Mississippi	2,828	Wyoming	298
Missouri	1,579		

The total organized militia numbers 104,477, of which 9,099 are commissioned officers, and 95,378 non-commissioned officers and privates. The forces are classified as follows:

CLASSIFICATION OF THE MILITIA

Infantry	86,570
Cavalry	1,574
Artillery	4,234

Potential Militia.—The potential militia includes all males between the ages of eighteen and forty-five years. In 1890 this class numbered 13,230,168, of which it is estimated that two-thirds might be made available in the event of war; in 1880 it numbered 10,231,239, showing an increase of 29.31 per cent., which is much larger than that of the total population.

This is due to the excessive immigration of the preceding decade, as is proven by the fact that the increase in the native born militia from 1880 to 1890 is approximately equal to the increase among the native born of the total population—viz., 26.04 per cent.—while the increase of the foreign born militia is not less than 43.10 per cent.

The native born militia number 10,424,086, or 78.79 per cent. of the whole number, and the foreign born 2,806,082, or 21.21 per cent. This may be contrasted with similar elements of the total population, of which 85.23 per cent. were native born, and 14.77 were foreign born.

Of the total potential militia, 68.01 per cent., or more than two-thirds, were native whites, while 73.03 per cent. of the total population were native whites. Of the militia, 10.78 per cent. were colored, and of the total population 12.20 per cent. were colored.

Of the total militia a little more than one-half—namely, 51.20 per cent.—were whites of native extraction (that is, native whites of native parentage), while 48.80 were foreign born, native born of foreign parentage, or colored.

The following table shows the proportion of the potential militia in each of the five divisions of the country, in 1890, contrasted with similar proportions of the total population:

PROPORTIONS OF POTENTIAL MILITIA AND POPULATION

	Militia	Population
North Atlantic Division	28.74	27.79
South Atlantic Division	12.23	14.14
North Central Division	36.55	35.71
South Central Division	15.58	17.52
Western Division	6.93	4.84

Thus it will be seen that in the northern and western states the proportion of potential militia is greater than that of the population, showing a preponderance of the mature male element; while in the southern states the proportion of militia is less than that of the population, showing the reverse.

THE NAVY

Next to that of its industrial achievements, the naval history of the United States has been its most brilliant record. From the time of John Paul Jones to the civil war, the navy has played more than its part in our difficulties.

The outbreak of the civil war found the navy in a neglected condition. We had few war-ships, and fewer still in condition for service. But with marvelous rapidity we built a navy, and at the close of the war we ranked among the first of the powers of the world upon the sea. More than that, by our boldness of invention we revolutionized the building and fighting of war-ships.

The war being over, the navy was rapidly reduced, until eight years ago little was left of our magnificent fleet, and that little had been distanced in the march of progress. We were left practically defenseless against a naval power. Then we commenced to restore the navy by the construction of new and modern types of vessels, and will soon have ample protection for our seaports, and strength to spare for offensive operations.

Of armored and protected vessels, we have now twenty-two completed and sixteen in process of building, including a number of monitors which are undergoing reconstruction. The displacement of these ships ranges from 1,875 to 10,231 tons, and their horse-power from 340 to 21,000. Their speed ranges from 6 to 21 knots per hour.

Of unarmored vessels, twenty-five have been built and six are under construction. Their displacements range from 420 to 4,413 tons, and their speed from 8 to 23 knots. Besides these, a number of torpedo boats and dynamite cruisers have been constructed, and there are still several sailing vessels in commission.

The present naval force consists of 726 officers, 8,250 enlisted men and boys, and a marine corps of 2,177 officers and men. Here again, as in the case of the regular army, is seen a great disproportion of officers, to admit of rapid and efficient expansion of the force in case of war.

PENSIONS

It has remained for the United States to prove the fallacy of the claim that "republics are ungrateful." Certainly in its treatment of the veterans of the late civil war the government has proved itself the most generous on which the sun ever shone.

Since the close of the war the pension laws have been amended many times, each amendment making them more and more liberal. Money has been poured out like water upon the country's defenders. More money is paid out annually to its pensioners than is expended by many of the great nations of Europe upon their armaments. Regarded purely as an investment, without considering its sentimental aspect, this money has been wisely spent; although, perhaps, the time is approaching when it will become necessary to call a halt. Surely a nation which has provided so munificently for its defenders in the past, cannot fail of defenders should necessity arise in the future.

The money expended thus far for pensions since 1861, is $1,418,000,000. This vast sum would far more than pay off the balance of the national debt. In the year 1892 alone, $141,000,000 was thus disbursed. The number of invalid pensioners upon the rolls was 536,821, and the number of widows and orphans was 139,339. The total number of pensioners was 876,068.

PUBLIC LANDS

When the United States had shaken off the yoke of the mother country, the territory of which it found itself possessed was limited on the west by the Mississippi River, and on the south by the thirty-first parallel of latitude, practically the northern boundary of Florida; the limits on the north and east being about the same as at present. The area contained within these limits is estimated at 827,844 square miles. Besides the thirteen original states, this area comprised a large tract known as the Northwest territory, over which the claims of several of the states extended, these claims overlapping one another in the most perplexing manner.

State Cessions.—As a simple method of settling these complicated claims, the states transferred their interests in this territory to the general government, and thus the government became a large land-owner. The territory so ceded now constitutes the states of Ohio, Indiana, Illinois, Michigan, Wisconsin, and the eastern part of Minnesota. Again, in the south the state of Georgia laid claim to the present area of Alabama and Mississippi, which it also ceded to the general government, in consideration of $6,209,000. At that time nearly all of it was an uninhabited wilderness, only a trifling part being owned by individuals.

The states of Kentucky and Tennessee were constituted respectively from parts of Virginia and North Carolina, and none of their lands ever belonged to the general government.

Annexation of Territory.—At various times additions have been made to the territory of the United States by treaty and purchase. These are set forth in the following table, and are represented on the map, Plate 3.

COST AND AREA OF ACQUIRED TERRITORY

Date		Area	Cost
1803	Louisiana purchase	1,171,931 square miles.	$12,000,000
1821	Florida purchase	59,268 " "	5,000,000
1845	Annexation of Texas	375,239 " "	
1848	Mexican cession	545,783 " "	15,000,000
1853	Gadsden purchase	45,535 " "	10,000,000
1867	Purchase of Alaska	570,000 "	7,200,000

In the statement of area of the Louisiana purchase is included the area of Oregon territory, comprising the present states of Washington, Oregon, and Idaho. This region was acquired, however, not as a part of the Louisiana purchase, which extended only to the summit of the Rocky mountains in Montana; but as a direct and almost immediate result of it by occupation and settlement.

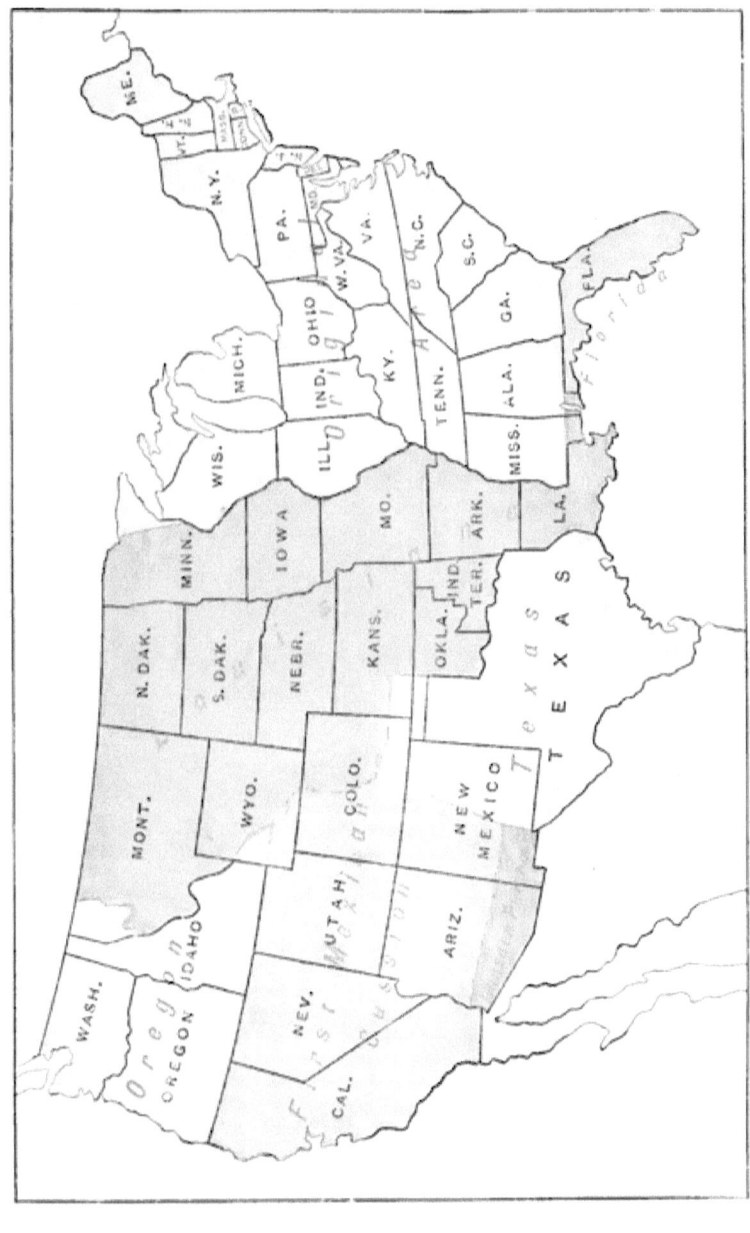

ACCESSIONS OF TERRITORY (EXCEPT ALASKA)

All the above additions to our territory increased the public lands owned by the general government, excepting in the case of Texas. That state, which had achieved its independence of Mexico, voluntarily joined the sisterhood of states and retained control of its public lands, with the exception of certain areas in the north and west which it sold to the United States for the sum of $16,000,000; these now form parts of New Mexico, Colorado, and Kansas.

Within the areas thus added to the country were, taken collectively, considerable bodies of land owned by private parties, including grants which had been made by the Mexican or Spanish government to individuals. All lands thus held in fee simple were of course retained under such ownership, but the balance of the territory, forming vastly the greater proportion of it, became the property of the government.

The rules to be observed by the government in the disposal of its empire, early commanded the attention of legislators. A liberal and enlightened policy was soon developed; though accompanied perhaps by certain abuses, it has proved, on the whole, a most beneficial one for the people of the country.

Method of Survey.—The land was first cut up into parcels convenient for sale or other form of disposal, and the plan adopted early in the present century has been pursued up to the present time with but slight changes. It consists essentially in a subdivision of the land into tracts six miles on a side, known as townships; the subdivision of each of these townships into sections, each approximately one mile on a side; and the further subdivision of these sections into quarter sections, or even smaller fractions. The north and south lines of the townships are theoretically true meridians, and hence, while six miles apart at the points of beginning, they converge northward. At a distance of twenty-four or thirty-six miles a fresh start is made, and these lines are again set at intervals of six miles; the line along which this fresh start is made is known as a correction line. The section lines are set one mile apart on the south line of each township, and the shortage in the breadth of the township is thrown entirely into the western tier of sections.

These surveys have been initiated at various points in the

country, independently of one another, the first step being to select an initial point and to run through that point a north and south line known as a principal meridian, and an east and west line known as a base line. The townships are numbered north or south from the base line to which they appertain; and the ranges, as the north and south tiers of townships are called, are numbered east or west from the principal meridian.

To a resident of any of the Land Office states, *i. e.*, those states in which there is or has been public land, these methods of description are as familiar as the alphabet; and the statement that one owns the northwest quarter of section 23, in township 10 north, range 15 west of the sixth principal meridian, defines that square half mile with precision and much more clearly than a statement of the latitude and longitude of the place would convey.

In this way the government has subdivided nearly all of its possessions.

Out of a total area of public lands, excluding Alaska, of 1,440,000,000 acres, there remained unsurveyed in 1890, 460,-000,000 acres. This consisted, with the exception of certain Indian reservations, of tracts of desert and mountain land, which under present conditions of climate and altitude are practically uninhabitable.

Methods of Disposal.—The idea of disposing of the public land for the purpose of making pecuniary profit, was early abandoned; instead thereof the purpose of all legislation, excepting perhaps the earliest, has been to use the public land as a means of inducing the spread of settlement and the development of the country.

In legislation concerning the disposal of land to private individuals, whatever the terms, one provision has always existed, to wit, that title should pass from the government to actual settlers. This provision forms the characteristic feature of the various preëmption, homestead, timber claim, and desert land acts. Under the preëmption acts, a man was permitted to settle upon the public land, laying claim to a quarter section, and after keeping it a certain length of time he obtained a patent for it, upon the payment of $1.25 per acre.

For many years this was the only general law under which title to the public lands could be secured by individuals. Later a homestead law was enacted; under its provisions an actual settler, after occupying a quarter section for a certain term of years, obtained a patent therefor at no further expense than the fees of the Land Office. Moreover, the fact that he had homesteaded a claim did not prevent him from taking up an adjoining claim, so that under the laws a *bona fide* settler could thus obtain two quarter sections by paying for one of them.

Still later, when the desirability of tree-planting upon the plains and deserts became apparent, what is known as the Timber Culture Act was passed, which enabled a settler to obtain a third quarter section, upon furnishing proof that he had planted and maintained for a certain term of years upon this quarter section a certain number of trees.

In recent years another act, known as the Desert Land Act, has still further increased the ability of the settler to avail himself of the public land. This act, which is intended to apply only to those regions in which the rainfall is insufficient for farming, provides in effect that any settler may take up a full section, 640 acres, of desert land, provided he conducts water to it and puts it under irrigation.

Amount Alienated.—The total area of the public land in all the states and territories, excluding Alaska, was approximately 1,440,000,000 acres. Of this area the United States had, up to June 30, 1892, alienated by means of grants, patents, etc., 873,000,000 acres; leaving 567,000,000 acres, or much less than one-half. Of the area thus alienated, the principal items are:

DISPOSITION MADE OF PUBLIC LANDS

Homesteads	130,000,000 acres.
Cash sales	224,000,000 "
Railway land grants patented	79,000,000 "
Swamp lands to States	70,000,000 "
Land bounties for military services	61,000,000 "

Of the remainder still left in the hands of the government, estimated at 567,000,000 acres, a large part, say 100,000,000 acres, consists of Indian reservations. Another large part, estimated at 103,000,000 acres, has been granted to railroads, but has not yet been patented to them; while yet another considerable area, impossible to estimate, has been filed upon as homestead, preëmption, or timber culture claims, the titles for which have not yet passed.

With trifling exceptions the public lands that are desirable to the agriculturist have now passed from the possession of the government into private hands. Those which remain are mountainous or arid lands, not suitable under present conditions for the support of population. The wave of westward migration will ere long cease for want of a motive, and perhaps a reflex wave may be substituted, and abandoned farms in the east again be occupied.

POPULATION

Early Settlements.—Original settlements within our territory were effected mainly under charters granted by the English government. Many charters were given which were without effect so far as settlement was concerned, and these it is unnecessary to mention. Again, some settlements were made by Europeans other than English, in defiance of the English claims to the territory, but these were afterward conquered and annexed.

The first permanent settlement made upon our soil was at Jamestown, Virginia, in 1607, under a charter of James I., of England, granting to one of the so-called Virginia companies a strip of land, extending along the sea-coast from the 34th to the 41st parallel of latitude. At the same time a charter was given to a second company, of a strip extending along the sea-coast from the 38th to the 45th parallel; but under this charter no attempt at colonization was made. The company possessing this charter was reorganized in 1620, under the name of the Plymouth Company, and obtained a new charter granting to it the land between the 40th and 48th parallels, and extending from the Atlantic to the South Sea, as the Pacific Ocean was then called.

Under this charter the Plymouth colony was started in 1620, and under a sub-grant from the Plymouth Company, the Massachusetts colony was established, the first settlers coming over in 1628. From these colonies, by the aid of sub-grants of territory, settlements were effected in Maine, New Hampshire, Rhode Island, and Connecticut; besides being extended over the seaboard of Massachusetts, and far into the interior of the State. Later, changes were made in the charters of all these New England colonies, bringing each of them directly under the crown of England.

New York was first colonized by the Dutch, who settled upon Manhattan island in 1623-24, under a claim based on a right of discovery by Hendrick Hudson. The settlements thus begun grew rapidly, and remained in the hands of the Dutch until 1664, when they were taken by the English. They were recaptured by the Dutch in 1673, but in 1674 were restored to the English by treaty. Settlements in New Jersey were made at Elizabeth in 1664, but prior to that the Dutch had spread slightly from Manhattan island into that state.

The settlement of Pennsylvania commenced in 1681, under a charter granted in that year to William Penn, whose enlightened policy toward the Indians saved his people from many of the ills suffered by other colonies, and this one grew with great rapidity from the start. The settlement of Maryland was commenced by a colony planted at St. Mary in 1634, under a charter issued two years previously to Lord Baltimore. The permanent settlement of the Carolinas was begun by extension from Virginia. In 1664 colonists from Barbadoes settled at Clarendon, on the Cape Fear river, and six years after a colony was formed on the Ashley river. The settlement of Georgia commenced much later; the first colony was started by Oglethorpe at Savannah in 1733, under a charter granted by the crown the previous year, and spread slowly up the Savannah river and to the neighboring islands on the coast.

Statistics concerning the growth of the colonies prior to the first census in 1790, are wanting. Our only knowledge as to the population is derived from estimates, and the best are those given by Bancroft, which are summarized in the following table:

ESTIMATED POPULATION PRIOR TO 1790

Year	White	Black	Total
1688	200,000	......	200,000
1750	1,040,000	220,000	1,260,000
1754	1,165,000	260,000	1,425,000
1760	1,385,000	310,000	1,695,000
1770	1,850,000	462,000	2,312,000
1780	2,383,000	562,000	2,945,000

Thus, at the outbreak of the Revolution the population of the colonies was probably not far from 2,500,000, of which it is estimated that 2,000,000 were whites and 500,000 blacks.

Increase of Population.—The first census of the United States was taken in 1790. From that time to the present a census has been taken every ten years. For a century, therefore, we have a trustworthy record of our numbers. Starting a hundred years ago with 3,929,214 inhabitants, we have advanced with such tremendous strides that 62,622,250 was the constitutional population of the country, June 1, 1890, as returned by the last census. This did not include the inhabitants of Alaska or the Indian territory, nor did it embrace Indians still remaining in tribal relations or living upon reservations. Including all these classes, the number of human beings within the limits of the country, was about 63,000,000.

POPULATION AND RATE OF INCREASE BY DECADES

Census Years	Population	Per cent. of Increase
1790	3,929,214	
1800	5,308,483	35.10
1810	7,239,881	36.38
1820	9,633,822	33.07
1830	12,866,020	33.55
1840	17,069,453	32.67
1850	23,191,876	35.87
1860	31,443,321	35.58
1870	38,558,371	22.63
1880	50,155,783	30.08
1890	62,622,250	24.86

The above table shows the constitutional population as returned at each census during the past century, with the percentage of increase during each decennial period. Although the population as returned by the census of 1870 is known to have been incorrect to a considerable extent, it is here given as returned; and the rates of increase between 1860 and 1870, and between 1870 and 1880, since they were computed from it, are also necessarily incorrect, being too small in the former case, and too large in the latter.

It will be seen that the rate of increase in the early decades, when it was dependent almost entirely upon natural causes, ran from 32 to 36 per cent., generally diminishing as the population increased. Between 1840 and 1850 the natural increase was reinforced by a heavy immigration, and accordingly the rate advanced decidedly at that time; since then it has diminished rapidly, as the full effect of immigration in reducing natural increase has become felt. In the first twenty-five years the population doubled; in the second twenty-five years it doubled again, the population in 1840 being four times that in 1790. But in recent years the rate of increase has diminished. Instead of doubling in the last quarter of a century, as it did in the first twenty-five years of our history, it has required thirty years, the population in 1890 being almost exactly double that in 1860.

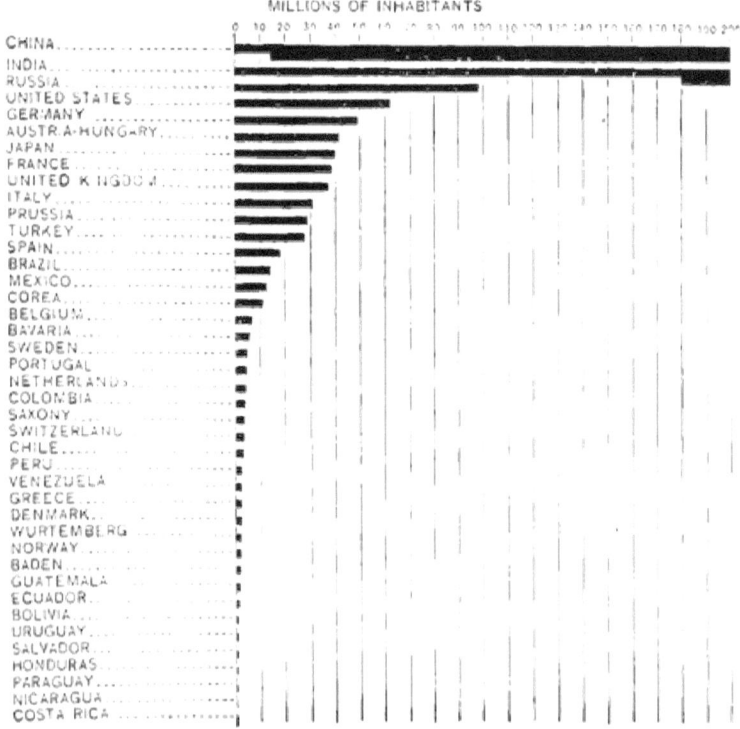

POPULATION OF COUNTRIES OF THE GLOBE IN 1890

These rates of increase are extremely large as compared with those of European nations; many times larger than the rate of France, several times larger than that of Great Britain, and greatly in excess of that of Germany. Indeed, in rapidity of growth, no other civilized nation has ever approached this country. While the United States has doubled its population in the last thirty years, France during the same period has increased but 3 per cent., Great Britain and Ireland but 29 per cent., and Prussia but 62 per cent. Since 1797 Prussia has increased in population from 8,700,000 to 30,000,000, while the population of this country has increased from 4,000,000 or 5,000,000 to 62,-622,250; nor is this tremendous advance due in any great degree to immigration, since in all probability, as is shown later, the earlier rates of increase would have been nearly maintained by the excess of births over deaths had there been no immigration.

TOTAL POPULATION BY STATES IN 1890

STATES AND TERRITORIES	POPULATION	STATES AND TERRITORIES	POPULATION
The United States	62,622,250	Minnesota	1,301,826
		Iowa	1,911,896
North Atlantic Division	17,401,545	Missouri	2,679,184
Maine	661,086	North Dakota	182,719
New Hampshire	376,530	South Dakota	328,808
Vermont	332,422	Nebraska	1,058,910
Massachusetts	2,238,943	Kansas	1,427,096
Rhode Island	345,506	South Central Division	10,972,893
Connecticut	746,258		
New York	5,997,853	Kentucky	1,858,635
New Jersey	1,444,933	Tennessee	1,767,518
Pennsylvania	5,258,014	Alabama	1,513,017
		Mississippi	1,289,600
South Atlantic Division	8,857,920	Louisiana	1,118,587
Delaware	168,493	Texas	2,235,523
Maryland	1,042,390	Oklahoma	61,834
District of Columbia	230,392	Arkansas	1,128,179
Virginia	1,655,980	Western Division	3,027,613
West Virginia	762,794		
North Carolina	1,617,947	Montana	132,159
South Carolina	1,151,149	Wyoming	60,705
Georgia	1,837,353	Colorado	412,198
Florida	391,422	New Mexico	153,593
		Arizona	59,620
North Central Division	22,362,279	Utah	207,905
Ohio	3,672,316	Nevada	45,761
Indiana	2,192,404	Idaho	84,385
Illinois	3,826,351	Washington	349,390
Michigan	2,093,889	Oregon	313,767
Wisconsin	1,686,880	California	1,208,130

Population of States. The preceding table shows the total population of each state, and of each group of states, in 1890, arranged in geographical order; and the following diagram presents the same facts, the states being arranged in the order of their population, with the smallest at the top.

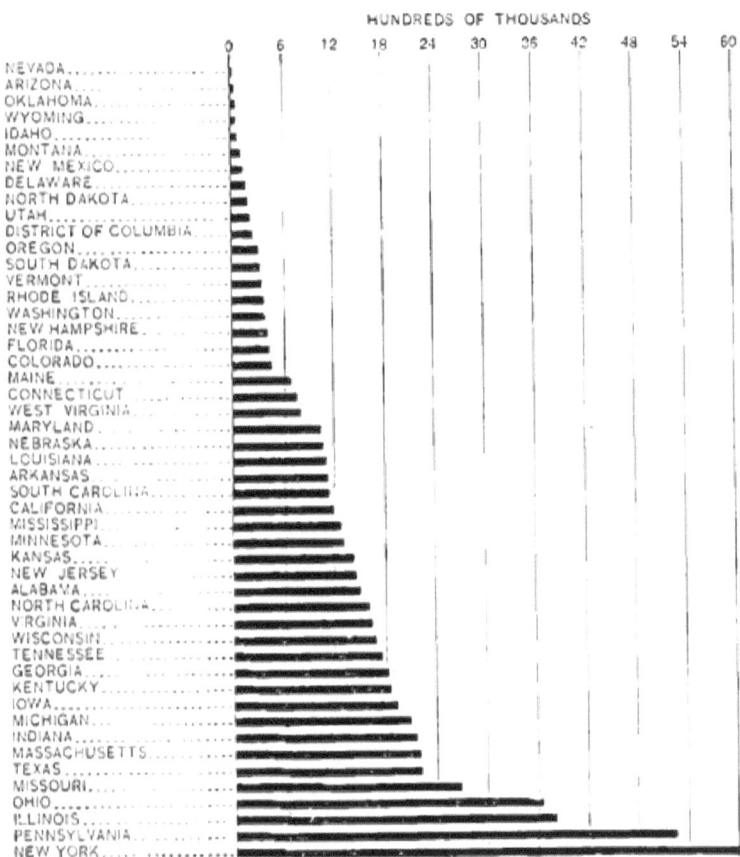

POPULATION OF EACH STATE AND TERRITORY IN 1890

Rate of Increase of Population of States.—The next table shows the percentage of increase of each state, and each group of states, during each ten year period, from the time of the formation of the state.

PERCENTAGE OF INCREASE OF POPULATION, BY DECADES

STATES AND TERRITORIES	1880 to 1890	1870 to 1880	1860 to 1870	1850 to 1860	1840 to 1850	1830 to 1840	1820 to 1830	1810 to 1820	1800 to 1810	1790 to 1800
The United States	24.86	30.08	22.63	35.58	35.87	32.67	33.55	33.07	36.38	35.10
North Atlantic Division	19.95	17.96	16.09	22.81	27.60	21.99	27.22	21.95	32.29	33.92
Maine	1.87	3.54	60.22	7.74	16.22	25.62	33.92	30.42	50.74	57.16
New Hampshire	8.51	9.01	2.38	2.55	11.54	5.99	10.37	13.78	16.64	29.58
Vermont	0.04	0.52	4.86	0.31	7.50	4.02	18.94	8.29	41.06	80.82
Massachusetts	25.57	22.35	18.35	23.79	34.81	20.85	16.68	10.83	11.65	11.63
Rhode Island	24.94	27.23	21.47	18.35	35.57	11.95	17.09	7.91	11.30	0.43
Connecticut	19.84	15.86	16.80	21.10	19.62	4.13	8.19	5.04	4.36	5.49
New York	18.00	15.97	12.94	25.29	27.52	26.60	39.83	43.07	62.84	73.19
New Jersey	27.74	24.83	34.83	37.27	31.14	16.36	15.64	12.98	16.30	14.67
Pennsylvania	22.77	21.61	21.19	25.71	34.00	27.87	28.71	29.31	34.40	38.67
South Atlantic Division	16.59	20.79	9.11	14.65	19.20	7.67	19.11	14.43	16.99	23.47
Delaware	14.96	17.27	11.41	22.00	17.32	1.74	5.30	0.10	13.07	8.76
Maryland	11.40	19.73	13.66	17.84	24.04	5.14	9.74	7.04	11.42	6.82
District of Columbia	29.71	34.87	75.41	45.26	18.24	9.74	20.57	37.53	20.46	
Virginia	9.48	23.46	4.41	12.29	14.67	2.34	13.73	9.29	10.72	17.74
West Virginia	23.34	39.92								
North Carolina	15.59	30.65	7.98	14.22	15.35	2.09	15.52	15.00	16.19	21.43
South Carolina	15.63	41.10	0.27	5.27	12.47	2.27	15.60	21.11	20.12	38.75
Georgia	19.14	30.21	12.06	16.67	31.07	33.78	51.57	35.08	55.17	97.08
Florida	45.24	43.54	33.70	60.59	60.52	56.86				
North Central Division	28.78	33.76	42.70	68.35	61.23	108.11	87.49	192.99	474.77	
Ohio	14.83	19.96	13.92	18.14	30.33	62.01	61.35	151.90	408.67	
Indiana	10.82	17.71	24.45	36.63	44.11	99.94	133.07	500.24	384.67	
Illinois	24.32	21.18	48.36	101.06	78.84	202.44	185.42	349.13		
Michigan	27.92	38.25	58.06	88.38	87.34	570.80	260.97	84.06		
Wisconsin	28.23	24.73	35.93	154.06	886.88					
Minnesota	66.74	77.57	155.61	2,730.72						
Iowa	17.68	36.06	76.91	251.13	345.85					
Missouri	23.56	25.93	45.62	73.30	77.75	173.19	111.03	219.29		
North Dakota	278.41	853.23	193.18							
South Dakota										
Nebraska	134.96	267.83	326.45							
Kansas	43.27	173.35	239.91							
South Central Division	23.02	38.62	11.54	34.05	42.24	46.72	54.91	72.89	134.09	246.68
Kentucky	12.73	24.81	14.31	17.64	25.18	13.36	21.94	38.57	83.98	159.90
Tennessee	14.60	22.55	13.40	10.68	20.92	21.00	61.28	61.53	147.84	195.88
Alabama	19.81	26.63	3.40	24.96	30.62	90.86	142.01			
Mississippi	13.96	36.68	4.63	30.17	61.46	174.96	81.08	86.97	355.95	
Louisiana	19.01	29.31	2.67	36.74	46.92	63.35	41.08	99.55		
Texas	40.14	94.45	35.48	184.21						
Oklahoma										
Arkansas	40.58	65.65	11.26	107.46	115.12	221.09	113.17			
Western Division	71.27	78.16	69.02	246.15						
Montana	237.49	50.14								
Wyoming	192.01	128.00								
Colorado	112.12	387.47	16.30							
New Mexico	28.66	30.14	*1.76	54.91						
Arizona	47.43	348.72								
Utah	44.62	65.88	115.49	253.89						
Nevada	*26.54	46.54	519.67							
Idaho	158.77	117.41								
Washington	365.13	213.57	106.62							
Oregon	70.53	92.22	73.50	294.65						
California	39.72	54.34	47.44	310.37						

* Decrease.

The thirteen original states, which comprise practically the North Atlantic and South Atlantic divisions, were at the time of the first census, in 1790, to a large extent settled communities, and their rates of increase in the early decades were in no case very great, while in certain cases they were very small indeed.

From the beginning of the century these states have been the source of supply of a great westward migration. Their children have peopled the Mississippi valley, the lake region, and the vast territory farther west. Indeed, for nearly a century these eastern states have been the hive from which millions have swarmed westward to subdue the plains and deserts.

In the North Atlantic states these enormous drafts have been largely made good in numbers, especially during the past forty years, by foreign immigration, which has to a great extent replaced the original stock. This is not the case, however, with the South Atlantic states, which thus far have received no foreign immigration, owing partly to climatic conditions and partly to the presence of the colored race, with which the foreign element either cannot or will not compete. In the Central and Western states the rate of increase, which in the first stage of settlement was excessively large, has diminished greatly as the population has become denser.

Considerations Affecting Increase.—It is a well-recognized general law governing the matter, that unless disturbed by extraneous causes, such as wars, pestilence, immigration, emigration, change of occupations, and so on, increase of population goes on at a constantly diminishing rate. The operation of this law in the United States has been disturbed in recent years by the civil war, which not only destroyed a vast number of lives, but decreased the birth rate materially during its progress. Again, the war was followed by an increased birth rate, as is invariably the case under like circumstances, and to an extent that it is impossible to estimate, since its effects are very complicated.

Within the United States, too, there is an enormous movement of population, which is mainly conducted westward along parallels of latitude. This also interferes with the operation of the law of increase in individual states and sections of the country. Moreover, changes in occupations and industries have affected in the past and are now affecting the rate of increase and the operation of this general law.

In the settlement of a region, the ruling occupations of the people usually follow one another in a certain order, depending largely upon the density of settlement. Thus, after the pioneers, hunters, trappers, and prospectors, follow the graziers and cattle men, who support themselves from the products of large herds of cattle and sheep, and naturally require great areas of country for their support. As the population becomes less sparse and land for grazing purposes is no longer to be had, the farmer, who derives his living from smaller areas of land, gradually takes the place of the grazier. Under ordinary circumstances, the limit of density of a purely agricultural community is in turn ultimately reached, and as that limit is approached, manufactures acquire more and more prominence; and since this class of industries requires limited space and a close association of people, cities spring up and grow with the increase of manufacturing.

As a community passes from one to another of these stages, and especially as it passes from the agricultural to the manufacturing stage, there is generally a considerable reduction in the rate of increase. Indeed, the growth of population in certain cases has for a time stopped entirely; to go on, however, at an increasing rate when the new class of industries had been established. Thus we find that southern New England, New York, New Jersey, and Pennsylvania have passed the agricultural stage; their principal industries are now trade and manufactures, and they are growing at a rate much more rapid than a quarter of a century ago, when they were beginning to emerge from the agricultural stage. On the other hand, Ohio, Indiana, Illinois, and Iowa have nearly reached the limit of agricultural settlement, and are now developing manufacturing industries; but the latter have not yet reached a stage sufficiently advanced to induce a rapid increase of population. Thus the growth of a state consists in a series of waves representing the rate of increase of its population, the summit of each wave being coincident with the maximum development of a group of industries, and each depression between two waves marking the period of change from industry to industry.

The northeastern states are primarily manufacturing centers, and as a necessary result of this preponderance of the manufacturing element, there is a corresponding preponderance of urban population. Consequently, more than half the population is grouped in cities. Agriculture is the primary industry of the Upper Mississippi valley and the Lake states, but in many of them manufactures are now acquiring prominence. The industries of the southern states are almost entirely agricultural, while in the western states and territories the leading industries are grazing, agriculture, and mining.

Recent Changes.—Maine and Vermont are practically at a standstill as regards increase of population; New Hampshire has passed the lowest point of its rate of increase and is now making rapid strides, owing to the stimulus of manufacturing industries. The other northeastern states are increasing rapidly, more so than for several decades.

Among the southern states, comparison of the growth during the past decade with the growth of those immediately preceding, is practically impossible, because the omissions of the census of 1870 vitiate the results. As nearly as can be judged, these states are holding their own; while certain of them, notably Florida, Texas, and Arkansas, are growing rapidly.

Of the North Central states, Ohio, Indiana, and Iowa show a decided reduction in the rate of increase, and this is true of Illinois also, if the city of Chicago be not considered. Michigan, in spite of its extensive frontier, has not advanced as rapidly as hitherto; while Wisconsin has added to its rate of increase. Missouri has nearly maintained its former rate, and Minnesota has not lost materially.

The Plains states, North and South Dakota, Nebraska, and Kansas, have had a very rapid growth during the past decade, although the rate of increase as expressed in percentages has diminished. A succession of rainy seasons in the early part of the decade attracted hundreds of thousands of settlers to their fertile plains, and the states filled up rapidly, reaching their maximum in 1887-88, when they had a population in excess of that given by the census of 1890, three years later.

Then followed a series of dry seasons in which the rainfall was insufficient for the needs of crops, and the discouraged settlers retreated eastward in large numbers. The state censuses of Kansas taken in 1885, 1886, 1887, 1888, 1889, showed an increase up to 1888, and from that time a diminution of over 90,000. It is probable that there has been a similar movement in the Dakotas and Nebraska, since their state censuses, taken in 1885, gave a population very nearly as great as that returned by the census of 1890.

The states and territories of the Western division show rather violent oscillations in population, due to the discoveries and the exhaustion of mines in various parts of this region. Thus Montana has had a tremendous growth, owing primarily to the discovery of the mines at Butte, which have not only attracted a considerable population to that neighborhood, but have induced the building of railways and the settlement of agricultural regions. Wyoming also has grown with unusual rapidity, and this without the stimulus of mines, its increase being due to the opening up of rich agricultural regions in the northern part of the state, near the foot of the Bighorn mountains. The growth of Colorado in the last decade has been in its agricultural regions and in its cities, while the mining regions have suffered a positive decline; the last census but one was taken on the top wave of a mining excitement occasioned by the Leadville discoveries. The growth in New Mexico, Arizona, and Utah has been comparatively slow; while Nevada, owing to the exhaustion of the Comstock and other mines, has suffered a loss of population during the decade amounting to more than one-third its numbers.

Idaho has filled up rapidly, the increase being mainly in the northern part of the state, where rich agricultural lands, requiring little irrigation, have invited settlers. Washington has had an exceedingly rapid growth, due entirely to agricultural and commercial interests. The increase of settlement has been mainly in the eastern part and in the valley of Puget sound. Oregon also has filled up rapidly, the increase being mainly in the Willamette valley; and, finally, California has maintained a steady rate of increase, its development of agricultural and commercial interests having much more than offset the losses from the exhaustion of its mines.

Relative Standing of States.—In 1790 Virginia was the most populous State in the Union, and it continued at the head of the list for three decades, when New York came to the front and has since remained first in population. In 1790, and also in 1800, Pennsylvania occupied the second position; in 1810 this position was taken by New York, and in 1820 by Virginia. In 1830 Pennsylvania resumed the second position, and has held it continuously since that time. The third position was occupied in 1790 by North Carolina, in 1800 by New York, in 1810 and 1820 by Pennsylvania, and in 1830 by Virginia; while between 1840 and 1880 it was held by Ohio. In 1890 Illinois in her upward progress reached and secured third place.

DENSITY OF POPULATION

The following table gives the area of the country, and the average number of inhabitants to the square mile, at the date of each census:

AREA AND DENSITY OF POPULATION AT EACH CENSUS

Census Years	Area	Density
1790	827,844	4.75
1800	827,844	6.41
1810	1,999,775	3.62
1820	1,999,775	4.82
1830	2,059,043	6.25
1840	2,059,043	8.29
1850	2,980,959	7.78
1860	3,025,600	10.39
1870	3,603,884	10.70
1880	3,603,884	13.92
1890	3,603,884	17.37

This table shows that in spite of successive acquisitions of territory, which have increased our domain from 827,844 to

3,603,884 square miles, the density of population has increased within the century from 4.75 to 17.37 inhabitants per square mile. This increase is also strikingly shown in the annexed diagram:

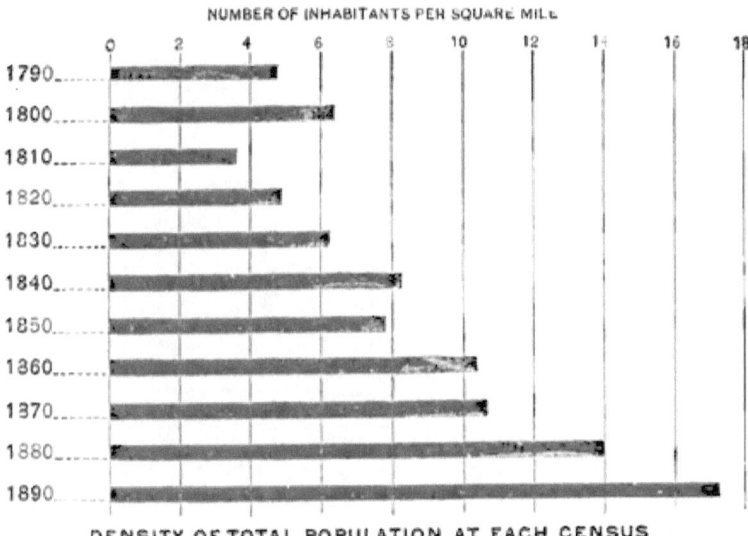

DENSITY OF TOTAL POPULATION AT EACH CENSUS

The diagram on page 64, showing the density of population of various countries in 1890, is inserted for purposes of comparison. It will be seen that the United States is a comparatively sparsely settled country, being exceeded in density of population by every country of Europe, excepting Russia and Norway.

Extent of Settlement.—In order to distinguish between settled and unsettled areas, it is necessary to adopt a certain arbitrary definition. Accordingly we will regard as settled those areas having two or more inhabitants to a square mile, and, conversely, those areas having a smaller number of inhabitants will be regarded as unsettled.

Under this definition, let us watch the spread of settlement as its advancing wave has swept across the continent. At the end of each decade opportunity is given to witness the progress made.

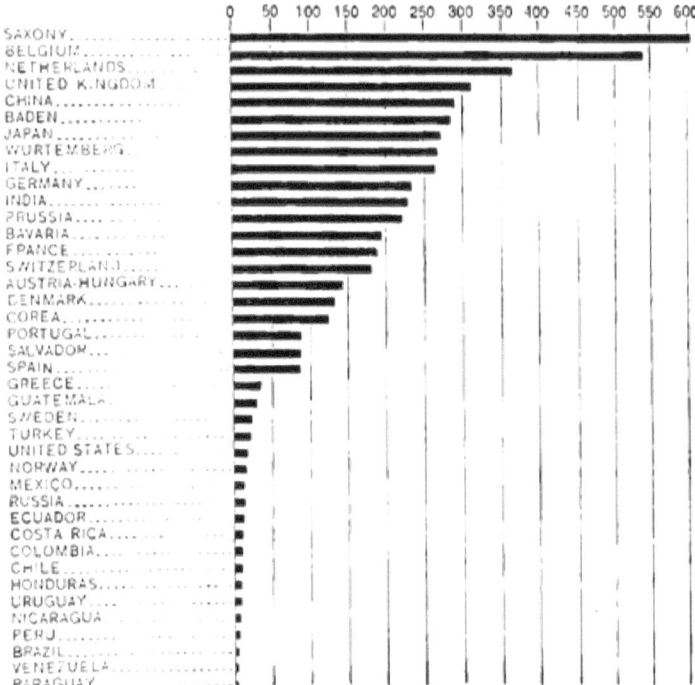

NUMBER OF INHABITANTS PER SQUARE MILE
IN VARIOUS COUNTRIES IN 1890

The maps on Plate 4 represent the status of settlement at the beginning and at the end of the century. The colored portions show the settled area of the country at each date, respectively.

In 1790 settlement stretched continuously along the Atlantic coast from Maine to Georgia, and occupied the greater part of the Atlantic plain. At several points it reached feebly westward, up the Mohawk river in New York, and down the Appalachian valley in east Tennessee; while in northern Kentucky, in the neighborhood of Cincinnati, quite a body of settlement appeared, isolated from the rest. Each decade has seen the frontier line pushed westward, crossing the Appalachians, stretching gradually across the great valley of the Mississippi, and climbing the plains beyond.

With every succeeding census there were new isolated bodies

PLATE 4

THE SETTLED AREA IN 1790

THE SETTLED AREA IN 1890

of settlement beyond the frontier, at points where the exceeding
fertility of the soil, facilities for Indian trading, or valuable
mines, had attracted the pioneers. These centers have grown
and spread until their margins have touched the main frontier
line and they have become merged in the great body of population. In two or three cases settlements that grew up under
foreign powers, have fallen under our jurisdiction by the acqui-
sition of territory. Among these are the old French-Spanish
settlements of southern Louisiana, the American-Spanish settlements in Texas, and the Spanish settlements of New Mexico,
Arizona, and California.

In 1860 settlements of magnitude first appeared in the Rocky
mountains and on the Pacific coast. Those in California consisted of gold-hunters, and those in Utah of Mormons. In 1870
they had spread widely. To the gold-hunters of California had
been added thousands of farmers who were subduing the broad
acres of the Sacramento valley. The Mormons had increased
and multiplied, and gold-hunters had spread into Idaho and
Montana.

Settlement in 1890.—The last decade has witnessed an
unprecedented development of the public domain. With the
exception of a few isolated areas of small extent, the eastern
half of the United States had long ago been subjugated, and the
extension of settlement has been confined practically to the far
west, which has been the scene of tremendous changes during
the decade.

Ten years ago there was a well-defined frontier line stretching
down the plains not far from the 100th meridian, the limit of
settlement being here a degree or two east, and there a degree or
two west of this line; while beyond it were scattered and isolated bodies of settlement—some of them, it is true, of considerable extent. During ten years this frontier line moved westward, while the isolated bodies of settlement have spread out
east and west, north and south, and joined themselves together,
and in turn have been joined by the advancing frontier line; so
that to-day there is in this region no longer a frontier line, but
rather a continuous body of settlement, interspersed by a few
unoccupied areas, like islands, some large, some small, which

either by reason of their elevation and consequent rigorous climate, or the absence of water for irrigation, have thus far been passed by in the selective development of the great west.

The Settled Area.—The following table presents the total settled area and the unsettled area at the date of each census, with the proportion which the settled area bears to the total area of the country:

SETTLED AND UNSETTLED AREA AT EACH CENSUS

Census Years	Total area of settlement; 2 or more to the square mile	Unsettled area	Proportion of settled to total area
1790	239,935	587,909	29.
1800	305,708	522,136	37.
1810	407,945	1,590,830	20.
1820	508,717	1,491,058	25.
1830	632,717	1,426,326	31.
1840	807,292	1,251,751	39.
1850	979,249	2,001,710	33.
1860	1,194,754	1,831,746.	39.
1870	1,272,239	2,331,645	35.
1880	1,568,570	2,034,314	44.
1890	1,947,285	1,656,599	54.

Thus it is shown that, under the definition given, the settled area in 1790 comprised nearly one-third of the total area of the United States, and that, in spite of the enormous additions which have increased the national domain to nearly four and a half times its original area, the proportion of settled area has increased within a century, until at present it exceeds one-half of the total area, including Alaska. Excluding this territory of 570,000 square miles, nearly two-thirds of the total area of the country is now classed as settled.

This table shows also that except in very few cases the settled area has constantly and rapidly increased; but by no means at a uniform rate, or at rates proportional to the increase of population. To illustrate these facts, the following table is appended, showing in juxtaposition the rates of increase of the settled area and of the population:

RATES OF INCREASE OF SETTLED AREA AND OF POPULATION

Decade	Per Cent. of Increase	
	Settled Area	Population
1790–1800	27.41	35.10
1800–1810	33.44	36.38
1810–1820	24.70	33.07
1820–1830	24.38	33.55
1830–1840	27.59	32.67
1840–1850	21.30	35.87
1850–1860	22.01	35.58
1860–1870	6.49	22.63
1870–1880	23.37	30.08
1880–1890	24.06	24.86

At the last census the population was nearly sixteen times as great as at the first census, while during the century the settled area has increased only about eightfold. On the whole, the increase of population has been twice as rapid as that of settled area.

Density of Population by Groups.—Let us now glance at the distribution of the population more in detail, and discover those areas which are densely settled and those which are sparsely settled, using the following classification—it being understood that all cities of 8,000 inhabitants or upwards have been separated from the remainder of the population and dropped from consideration:

CLASSIFICATION OF SETTLED AREA

(a) Less than 2 inhabitants to a square mile.
(b) 2 to 6 inhabitants to a square mile.
(c) 6 to 18 inhabitants to a square mile.
(d) 18 to 45 inhabitants to a square mile.
(e) 45 to 90 inhabitants to a square mile.
(f) More than 90 inhabitants to a square mile.

The first of the above groups, (a), that in which the population averages less than two inhabitants to a square mile, is regarded as unsettled country.

These limits define in a general way the prevalence of differ-cut groups of industries. Group (b), two to six to a square mile, indicates a population mainly occupied with the grazing industry; or, at best, a widely scattered farming population. Group (c) indicates a farming population with a systematic cultivation of the soil, but in rather an early stage of settlement, or in an unproductive region. Group (d) indicates a highly successful agricultural stage, while in some localities the commencement of the manufacturing stage has arrived.

Generally speaking, agriculture is not so highly developed in this country as to afford employment and support to a population greater than forty-five to a square mile. The last two groups, therefore, (e) and (f), where the density of population is forty-five inhabitants or more to a square mile, appear only as commerce and manufactures are developed, and personal and professional services are therefore in demand.

The following table gives the area included at the time of each census, in each of the five groups which collectively comprise the settled area:

AREA IN SQUARE MILES OF THE DIFFERENT CLASSES OF SETTLEMENT

Census	B 2 to 6 to a square mile	C 6 to 18 to a square mile	D 18 to 45 to a square mile	E 45 to 90 to a square mile	F 90 and over to a square mile
1790	83,436	83,346	59,282	13,051	820
1800	81,040	123,267	82,504	17,734	1,193
1810	116,629	154,419	108,155	27,499	1,243
1820	140,827	177,153	150,390	39,004	1,343
1830	151,460	225,894	186,503	65,446	3,414
1840	183,607	291,819	241,587	84,451	5,828
1850	233,697	294,608	338,796	100,794	11,264
1860	260,866	353,344	431,601	134,722	14,224
1870	245,897	363,475	470,529	174,636	18,302
1880	384,820	373,890	554,300	231,410	25,150
1890	592,037	393,943	701,845	235,148	24,312

Density of Population of States.—The table on page 69 gives the number of inhabitants of each state, and group of states, per square mile, in 1890:

POPULATION PER SQUARE MILE, BY STATES, IN 1890

States and Territories		States and Territories	
The United States (excluding Alaska)	21.3	Wisconsin	31.0
		Minnesota	16.4
		Iowa	34.5
North Atlantic Division	107.4	Missouri	39.0
		North Dakota	2.6
Maine	22.1	South Dakota	4.3
New Hampshire	41.8	Nebraska	13.8
Vermont	36.4	Kansas	17.5
Massachusetts	278.5		
Rhode Island	318.4	South Central Division	18.9
Connecticut	150.4		
New York	126.0	Kentucky	46.5
New Jersey	193.0	Tennessee	42.3
Pennsylvania	116.9	Alabama	29.4
		Mississippi	27.8
South Atlantic Division	33.0	Louisiana	24.6
		Texas	8.5
Delaware	86.0	Oklahoma	1.6
Maryland	105.7	Arkansas	21.3
District of Columbia	3,839.8		
Virginia	41.3	Western Division	2.6
West Virginia	31.0		
North Carolina	33.3	Montana	0.9
South Carolina	38.2	Wyoming	0.6
Georgia	31.2	Colorado	4.0
Florida	7.2	New Mexico	1.3
		Arizona	0.5
North Central Division	29.7	Utah	2.5
		Nevada	0.4
Ohio	90.1	Idaho	1.0
Indiana	61.0	Washington	5.2
Illinois	68.3	Oregon	3.3
Michigan	36.5	California	7.7

This table shows that, with the exception of the District of Columbia, which is to all intents and purposes a municipality, the most densely settled state is Rhode Island, with three hundred and eighteen inhabitants per square mile, and following that is Massachusetts, with two hundred and seventy-eight per square mile. In these states the density of population is as great as in many of the most thickly settled European countries. Indeed, the entire North Atlantic Division, which is preëminently the manufacturing section, has a dense population, the average being more than one hundred inhabitants to the square mile.

The South Atlantic and South Central Divisions, which are preeminently farming regions, are much less densely peopled; and the scattered character of the population of the western states and territories, with their mixed industries, which consist largely of grazing and mining with some agriculture, is illustrated by its low density.

The density of population of each state in 1890, is graphically shown by the following diagram and also by the map, Plate 5.

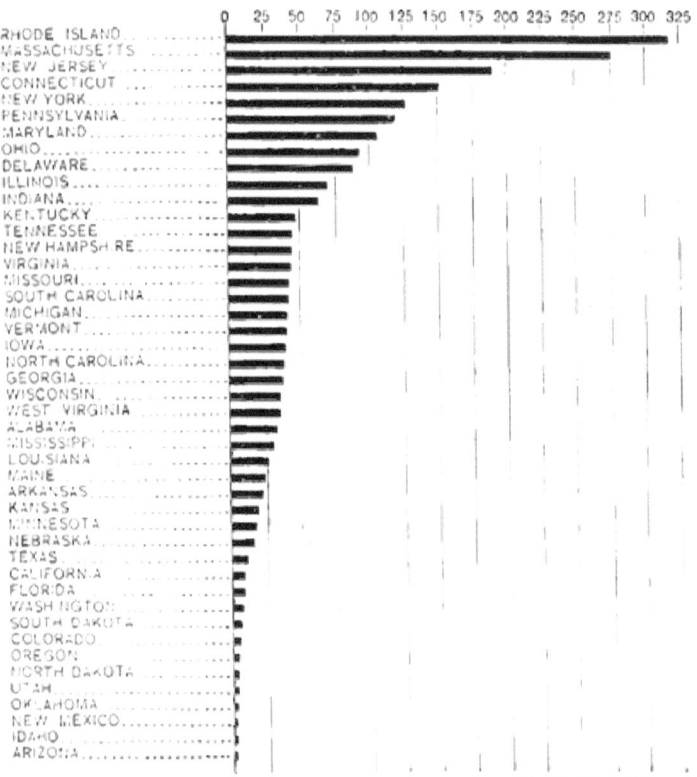

NUMBER OF INHABITANTS PER SQUARE MILE IN 1890

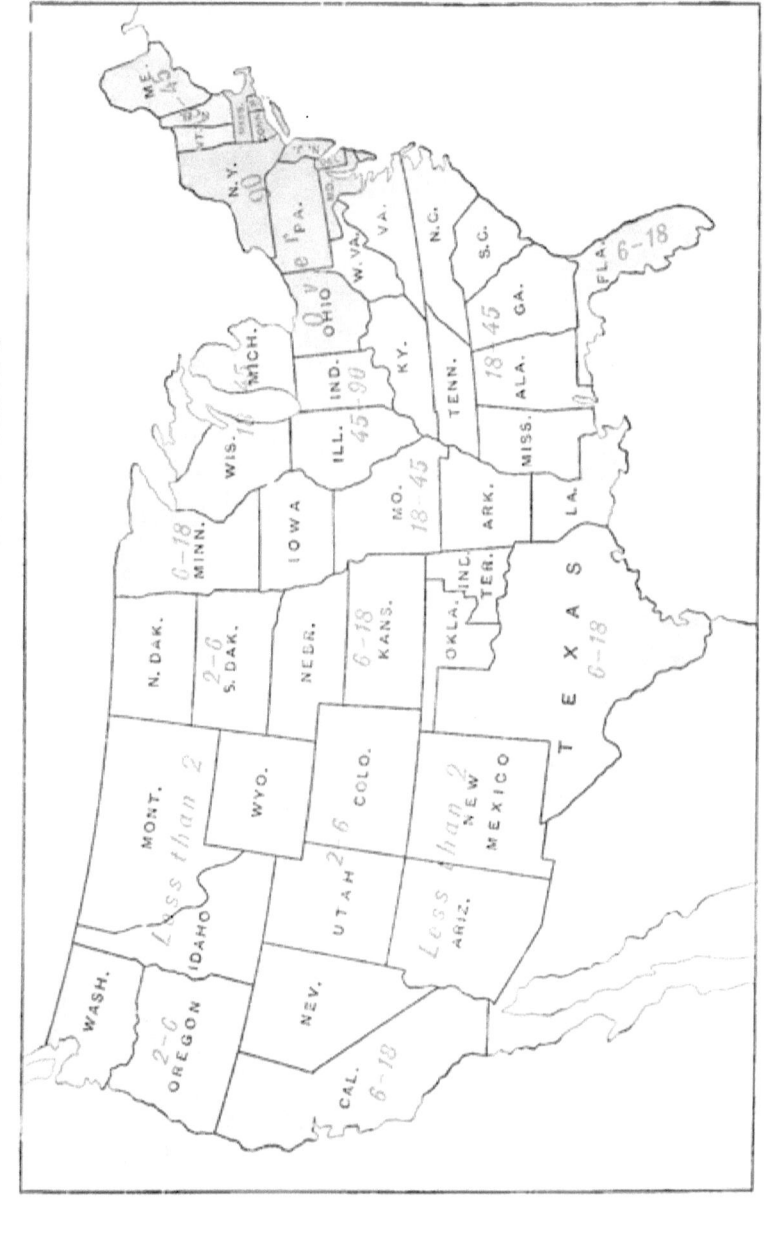

THE BUILDING OF A NATION—PLATE 5

NUMBER OF INHABITANTS TO A SQUARE MILE IN 1890

CENTER OF POPULATION

The center of population is the center of gravity of the inhabitants of the country; each person being supposed to have the same weight, and to press downwards with a force proportional to his distance from this center. The movement of the center of population from decade to decade expresses the net resultant of all the movements of population which have taken place. The following table, and the map on page 73, show its position at each census from the beginning:

POSITION OF THE CENTER OF POPULATION

CENSUS YEAR	North Latitude	West Longitude
1790	39° 16.5′	76° 11.2′
1800	39° 16.1′	76° 56.5′
1810	39° 11.5′	77° 37.2′
1820	39° 5.7′	78° 33.0′
1830	38° 57.9′	79° 16.9′
1840	39° 2.0′	80° 18.0′
1850	38° 59.0′	81° 19.0′
1860	39° 0.4′	82° 48.8′
1870	39° 12.0′	83° 35.7′
1880	39° 4.1′	84° 39.7′
1890	39° 11.9′	85° 32.9′

Movements of the Center.—In 1790 the center of population was about twenty-three miles east of Baltimore, Maryland. During the next decade it moved almost due west to a point about eighteen miles west of Baltimore, the westward movement being about forty-one miles. Between 1800 and 1810 it moved thirty-six miles to the westward and made a little southing, being then, in 1810, about forty miles northwest by west from Washington. The southward movement during this decade was probably due to the annexation of Louisiana, which added quite a body of population in the vicinity of New Orleans.

Between 1810 and 1820 it moved fifty miles to the westward and again slightly southward, being found in 1820 about sixteen miles north of Woodstock, Virginia. The southward component of its motion was probably due to the extension of settlement in Mississippi, Alabama, and eastern Georgia. Between 1820 and 1830 it moved thirty-nine miles to the westward and again slightly southward, to a point about nineteen miles west southwest of Moorefield, West Virginia.

This southward movement was due to the accession of Florida and to the rapid extension of settlements in Mississippi, Louisiana, and Arkansas. Between 1830 and 1840 its westward movement amounted to fifty-five miles, while, instead of bearing southward, it bore slightly northward to a point sixteen miles south of Clarksburg, West Virginia, the extension of settlement in Michigan and Wisconsin having apparently overbalanced that in the far south. Between 1840 and 1850 it again made fifty-five miles of westing and turned slightly southward, being found at a point twenty-three miles southeast of Parkersburg, West Virginia. The change to the southward was probably due to the annexation of Texas, which embraced a considerable population.

From 1850 to 1860 it moved eighty-one miles to the westward and turned slightly northward, reaching a point twenty miles south of Chillicothe, Ohio. From 1860 to 1870 it moved westward forty-two miles, besides making a considerable northing, being in 1870 forty-eight miles east by north of Cincinnati, Ohio. This northing was doubtless due in part to the waste and destruction attendant on the civil war at the south, and in part to the rapid extension of settlement in the northwest, and, furthermore, to the omissions of the census of 1870.

In 1880 the center had returned southward to nearly the same latitude it occupied in 1860, and at the same time it had marched westward fifty-eight miles, being found eight miles west by south of Cincinnati, Ohio. During the past decade the center of population has moved to practically the same latitude reached in 1870, and has made a westing of forty-eight miles, being in 1890 twenty miles east of Columbus, Indiana.

While the increase of population has been rapid in many parts of the south, notably in Florida and Texas, still it has been far overbalanced by the increase in the Dakotas, Montana, Wash-

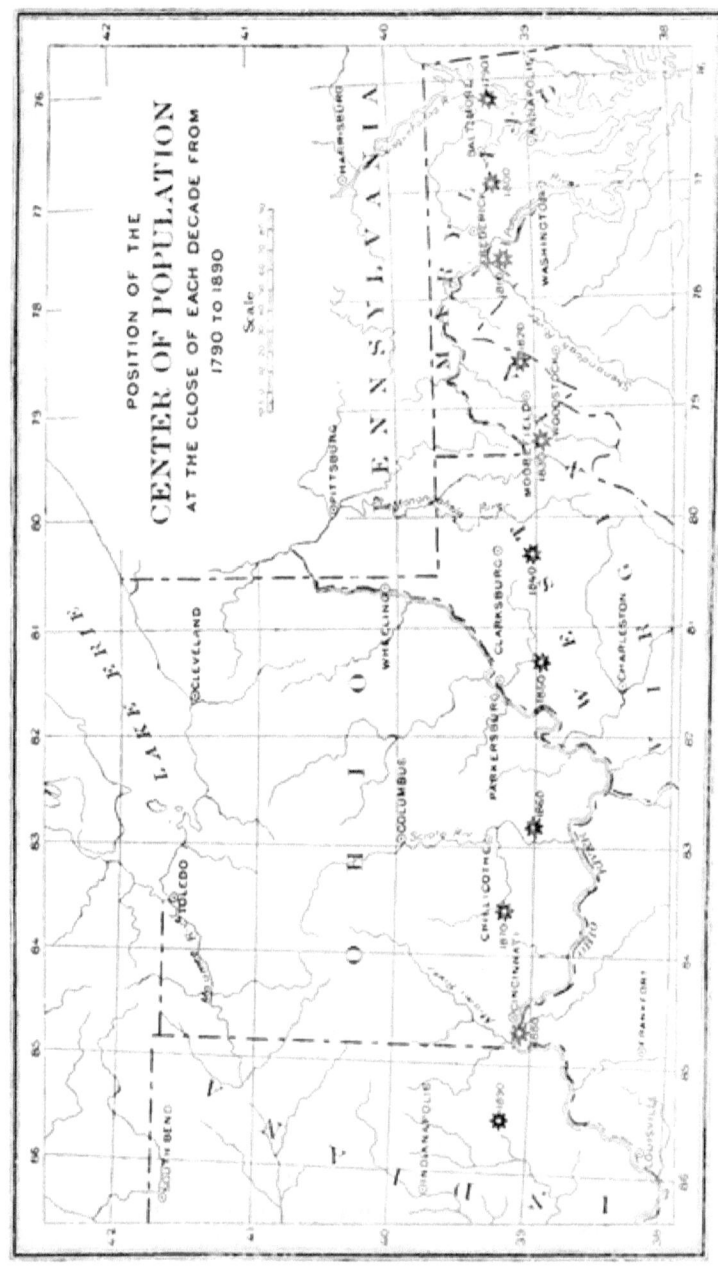

ington, and Oregon, in the northwest, which accounts for the northward component of its movement. On the other hand, the reduction in the rate of its westward movement is doubtless due to the rapid growth in the northeastern manufacturing states, which has tended toward retarding the center in its westward march.

The progress of the nation in population and spread of settlement is epitomized in the following statement: The center of population has moved westward within the century 9° 22' of longitude, or a distance of five hundred and five miles. It has remained during this period in almost precisely the same latitude, the extreme range in latitude among the positions which it has assumed being only 18'.6, or about twenty-five miles.

The center of population in 1890 was in latitude 39° 11'.9, and longitude 85° 32'.9. On the other hand, the center of area of the country, excluding Alaska, is in the northern part of Kansas, in approximate latitude 39° 55', and approximate longitude 98° 50'. The center of population is therefore about three-fourths of a degree south, and more than seventeen degrees east, of the center of area.

URBAN POPULATION

The population of the country may be classed as urban and rural; the rural element being engaged mainly in agricultural occupations, while the urban element is engaged in manufactures, transportation, commerce, and personal services of one sort or another. These two elements are closely allied with the groups of occupations as here noted, so that as manufactures and commerce increase, the urban element increases correspondingly.

For obvious reasons it is impossible to make a complete distinction between these two elements, although it is easy to make an approximate classification. Many cities contain, within their corporate limits, extensive suburbs which are practically rural communities; and, on the other hand, there are scattered all through the country small bodies of population closely aggregated, which cannot be distinguished from the scattered rural population among which they dwell. Such cases are extremely common in the New England towns and cities, which comprise considerable areas, and which consist in varying parts of urban and rural population, that cannot be separated from one another, owing to the fact that the town is the smallest political unit returned by the census. The Census Office maintains the iron rule of regarding as urban all concentrated bodies of population exceeding eight thousand in number, and this rule has been observed in the following discussion.

The annexed table shows the urban and rural population of the country, under the above definition, at each census, together with the proportion which the urban population bears to the total population. The urban and rural population is shown also in the diagram on page 76.

URBAN AND RURAL ELEMENTS OF POPULATION

Census Years	Urban Population.	Rural Population.	Urban to total Population.
1790	131,472	3,797,742	3.35
1800	210,873	5,097,610	3.97
1810	356,920	6,882,961	4.93
1820	475,135	9,158,687	4.93
1830	864,509	12,001,511	6.72
1840	1,453,994	15,615,459	8.52
1850	2,897,586	20,294,290	12.49
1860	5,072,256	26,374,065	16.13
1870	8,071,875	30,486,406	20.93
1880	11,318,547	38,837,236	22.57
1890	18,284,385	44,367,865	29.20

A century ago this country contained but six cities having a population of more than 8,000 each, and the urban population constituted but 3.35 per cent., or about one-thirty-third, of the entire population of the country. To-day the number of such cities is 443, and their population 18,284,385, which is 29.20 per cent., or not very much less than one-third of the entire population. The total population is about sixteen times as great as it was a hundred years ago, while the urban population is one hundred and thirty-nine times as great.

This aggregation of the people in cities is a natural and

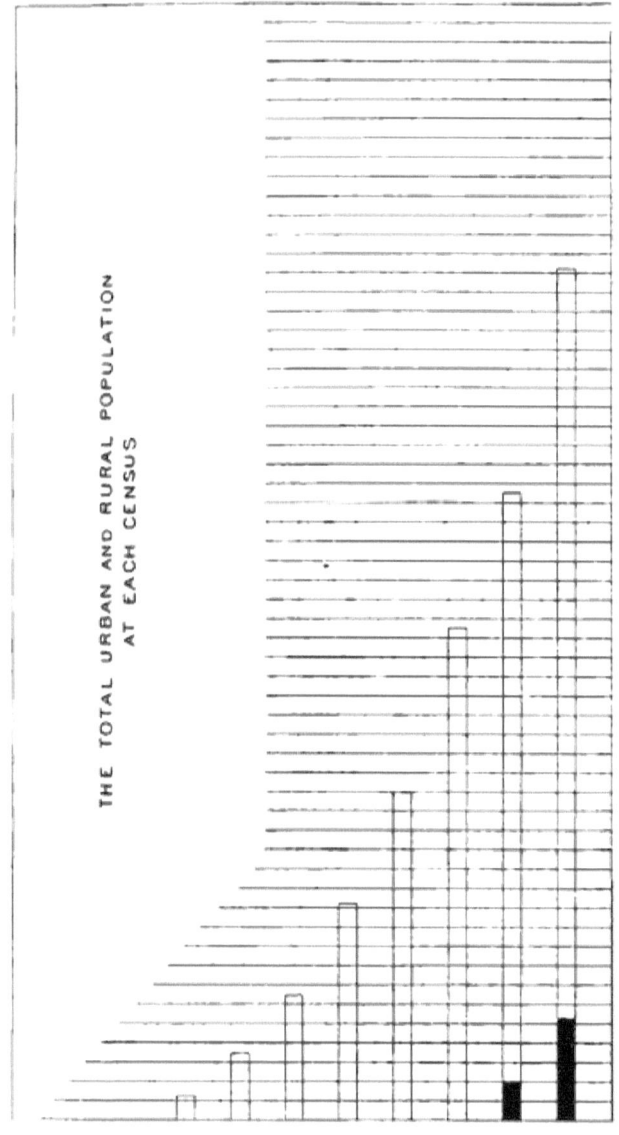

necessary result of the increasing density of population and of the consequent change in avocations, as has already been stated. It has gone on in this country at a constantly accelerating rate, and the acceleration will probably be even more marked in the future than in the past, as a greater part of our domain reaches and passes in density of population the limit of successful agriculture.

The following table shows the rate of increase of the urban and rural elements during each decade:

URBAN AND RURAL INCREASE, BY DECADES

Decade	Per Cent. of Increase	
	Urban	Rural
1790–1800	60	34
1800–1810	70	35
1810–1820	34	33
1820–1830	82	31
1830–1840	68	30
1840–1850	99	30
1850–1860	75	30
1860–1870	59	15
1870–1880	40	27
1880–1890	61	15

The increase of the rural element appears to be quite regular, having diminished gradually from thirty-four or thirty-five per cent. to fifteen. Between 1860 and 1870 the rate of increase of this element was reduced, and between 1870 and 1880 it was increased, by the omissions of the census of 1870. It is presumable that if the correct figures of that census could be obtained, they would eliminate these apparent irregularities.

The rate of increase of the urban element has been greater in each decade than that of the rural element, and in most cases has been much greater, even doubling or trebling it.

Distribution of the Urban Element.—The urban element is distributed very unequally over the country, as is shown in the table on page 78, which gives the number and proportion of this element in each geographic division of the country. This distribution is shown further and more in detail by the map, Plate 6.

URBAN POPULATION BY GEOGRAPHIC DIVISIONS

Geographic Divisions	Urban Population	Per cent. of entire Urban Population
Total	18,284,385	100.00
North Atlantic Division	9,015,383	49.31
South Atlantic Division	1,419,964	7.76
North Central Division	5,793,896	31.69
South Central Division	1,147,089	6.27
Western Division	908,053	4.97

Thus it appears that the North Atlantic states contain nearly one-half of the urban population of the country, and that the North Atlantic and North Central states together contain nearly five-sixths of it.

Of the total population of the North Atlantic states, 51.81 per cent., or more than one-half, is contained in cities of 8,000 or more inhabitants. During the past decade the urban element of these states has increased 43.53 per cent., while the entire population has increased but 19.95 per cent. This rapid growth of the urban element is due to the rapid extension of manufactures and commerce.

In several of these states the urban element greatly exceeds the rural. Thus in Rhode Island the urban population forms 78.80 per cent., in Massachusetts 69.90, in New York 59.50, in New Jersey 54.05; while in Connecticut the population is almost equally divided between the rural and urban elements.

Of the population of the North Central states, 25.9 per cent., or a trifle more than a quarter of the inhabitants, was, under our definition, classed as urban. In the past decade the urban element has nearly doubled in numbers, while the population has increased but 28.78 per cent. Although the number of cities has increased from 95 in 1880 to 152 in 1890, the greater part of the increase in the urban element has consisted in additions to a few large cities. Indeed, the increase in the eleven largest cities of these states, whose population comprised a trifle more

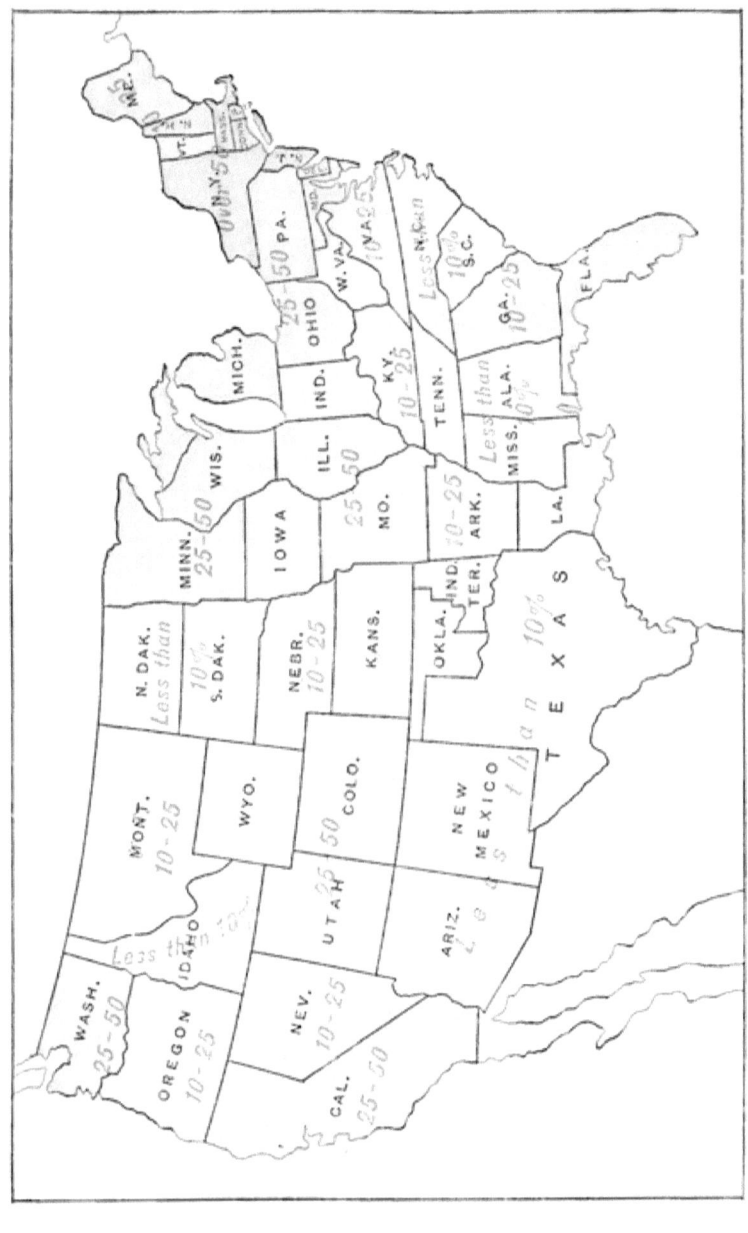

THE BUILDING OF A NATION—PLATE 6

PROPORTION OF URBAN TO TOTAL POPULATION IN 1890

than half their total urban population, amounted to more than half the entire gain in urban population in this group of states.

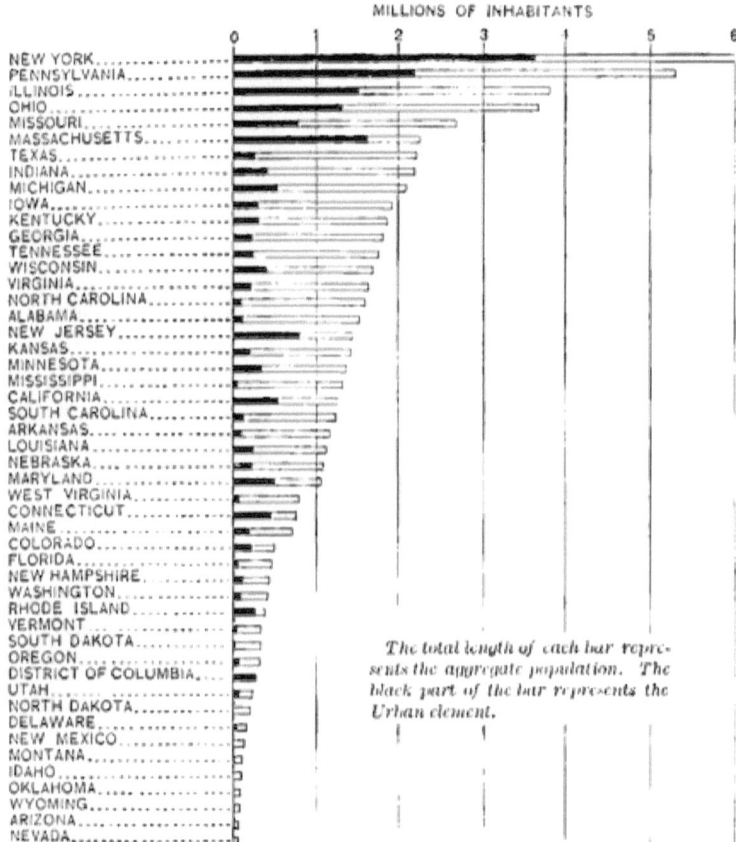

AGGREGATE POPULATION AND URBAN ELEMENT IN CITIES OF 8,000 OR MORE INHABITANTS, BY STATES, IN 1890

In the southern states the proportion of urban population is small, being less than 13 per cent. The industries of these States are mainly agricultural, and while manufacturing and mining are making some progress they are still in their infancy. The growth of these branches of industry may be measured roughly by the growth of the urban element. During the past decade the urban element of the south increased 58.58 per cent., while the entire population had increased but 20.07 per cent. In certain of the southern states the proportion of the urban element is still absolutely trifling. Thus, in Mississippi it constitutes but 2.64 per cent., in North Carolina but 3.87, and in Arkansas only 4.89 per cent. of the total population.

In the western states mining, commerce, and manufactures are in a much more advanced stage than at the south, as is shown by the greater proportion of the urban element. In 1880 it constituted 23.97 per cent. of the population, and in 1890 29.74 per cent., showing that it had gained more rapidly than the total population.

Great Cities.—In 1880 there was but one city, New York, which had a population of more than a million. In 1890 there were three—New York, Chicago, and Philadelphia. In 1870 there were only 14 cities of more than 100,000 inhabitants each. In 1880 this number had increased to 20, and in 1890 to 28. They are as follows:

CITIES OF OVER 100,000 POPULATION IN 1890

Cities	Population	Cities	Population
New York	1,515,301	Detroit	205,876
Chicago	1,099,850	Milwaukee	204,468
Philadelphia	1,046,964	Newark	181,830
Brooklyn	806,343	Minneapolis	164,738
St. Louis	451,770	Jersey City	163,003
Boston	448,477	Louisville	161,129
Baltimore	434,439	Omaha	140,452
San Francisco	298,997	Rochester	133,896
Cincinnati	296,908	St. Paul	133,156
Cleveland	261,353	Kansas City	132,716
Buffalo	255,664	Providence	132,146
New Orleans	242,039	Denver	106,713
Pittsburg	238,617	Indianapolis	105,436
Washington	230,392	Allegheny	105,287

The population of these 28 cities was 9,788,150, which formed not less than 15.6 per cent. of the entire population of the country.

The following table shows the number of cities, classified according to population, at the date of each census:

NUMBER OF CITIES, CLASSIFIED ACCORDING TO POPULATION

Census Years	Total	8,000 to 12,000	12,000 to 20,000	20,000 to 40,000	40,000 to 75,000	75,000 to 125,000	125,000 to 250,000	250,000 to 500,000	500,000 to 1,000,000	1,000,000 and above
1790	6	1	3	1	1					
1800	6	1		3	2					
1810	11	4	2	3		2				
1820	13	3	4	4	2					
1830	26	12	7	3	1	1	2			
1840	44	17	11	10	1	3	1	1		
1850	85	36	20	14	7	3	3	1	1	
1860	141	62	34	23	12	2	5	1	2	
1870	226	92	63	39	14	8	3	5	2	
1880	286	110	76	55	21	9	7	4	3	1
1890	443	173	105	91	45	14	14	7	1	3

The Greater New York.—While the only defined limits which can be given to a city are those described in its charter, and within which it has jurisdiction, still it is easy to see that in many cases large bodies of population, to all intents and purposes portions of the city, may not be credited to it, because they happen to lie without its charter limits. There are many cases of large and populous suburbs, whose inhabitants are connected with the adjoining city through their business and personal interests, which, lying without the corporate limits, are not parts of it, either legally or in the view of the Census Office.

By far the most important of such cases is that of New York, whose charter limits comprise only Manhattan island and a small area upon the mainland to the north. Within a radius of fifteen miles of the City Hall are included not only all of New York city proper, but Brooklyn, and indeed all of Kings county which is practically one continuous city, and a large part of Queens county which contains a number of populous towns. On the north this radius includes Yonkers and an immense suburban population in Westchester county, while across the Hudson river, in New Jersey, are Jersey City, Hoboken, Passaic, and Paterson, with numerous large villages. Now, all this territory is in the truest sense tributary to New York. The ferries and suburban trains carry a hundred thousand people into the metropolis every morning to their business and return them to their homes at night. It is the greater New York in as true a sense as the metropolitan district is the greater London.

Within this greater New York live three and a quarter millions of human beings, making a city two-thirds the size of London, and second only to it upon the globe.

GEOGRAPHIC DISTRIBUTION

Although civilized man has made himself independent of his environment to a considerable extent, still that environment retains a decided influence over him. It consists mainly of geographic conditions, such as climate, soil, and altitude. The influences of these factors in determining his migrations and his welfare are of great interest.

The elements of climate which it is worth while to consider in connection with man's distribution in this country, are temperature and rainfall. These elements have been discussed in earlier pages with reference to the surface of the country. Let us now see in what proportions the population is distributed with reference to them.

Distribution according to Temperature.—The following table shows the proportional parts of the total population, the foreign born, and the colored, living at the date of the last census within the designated belts of temperature. The population at each census is supposed to be one hundred, and the proportional parts are expressed in percentages thereof. Each temperature belt comprises five degrees.

DISTRIBUTION OF POPULATION AS TO MEAN ANNUAL TEMPERATURE

DEGREES OF TEMPERATURE	Total	Foreign	Colored
Below 40°	1.65	3.43	.04
40° to 45°	8.18	14.43	.21
45° to 50°	27.42	40.94	2.16
50° to 55°	31.58	31.25	10.20
55° to 60°	13.78	6.04	24.16
60° to 65°	9.87	1.27	36.43
65° to 70°	6.28	1.49	23.57
70° to 75°	1.21	1.03	3.15
Above 75°	.03	.12	.08

Thus it appears that more than half the population live where the mean annual temperature ranges from 45 to 55 degrees. Nearly three-fourths live between 45 and 60, and between 40 and 70 degrees practically the entire population is found.

The foreign population live under colder conditions than the total population. Forty per cent. are found where the temperature averages between 45 and 50 degrees, and between 40 and 55 degrees are found nearly 87 per cent. of the entire foreign element, while at the higher temperatures the proportion of this element is trifling.

On the other hand, the colored population are found under conditions of temperature much higher than either the total population or the foreign born. The maximum proportion—namely, 36 per cent.—live between the temperatures of 60 and 65 degrees, while between 55 and 70 degrees are no less than 84 per cent. of the entire colored element. Where the maximum of the foreign element is found, there exists but two per cent. of the colored.

The average annual temperature of the territory of the United States, excluding Alaska from consideration, is 53 degrees. The average annual temperature under which the people of the country live, taking into account the density of settlement, is practically the same.

The average temperature under which the foreign born element exist is 5 degrees lower—namely, 48 degrees—whilst that under which the colored people live is 61 degrees, being 8 degrees higher than that of the total population, and no less than 13 degrees higher than that of the foreign element.

Distribution under Rainfall Conditions. — The amount of rainfall has a direct influence upon most industries, and especially upon agriculture, in which the majority of the population are occupied. Where the rainfall ranges from 30 to 50 inches annually, there, other things being equal, the conditions are most favorable for the agricultural industry, and within that range of annual rainfall is found, as was to have been expected, the greater portion of the population. Indeed, nearly three-fourths of the population occupy this region, as shown in the following table:

DISTRIBUTION OF POPULATION AS TO MEAN ANNUAL RAINFALL

Inches of Rainfall	Total	Foreign	Colored
Below 10	.30	.55	.03
10 to 20	2.61	3.98	.23
20 to 30	6.04	10.32	.39
30 to 40	34.11	41.64	5.15
40 to 50	39.16	41.08	31.49
50 to 60	16.16	1.56	59.99
60 to 70	1.27	.75	2.73
Above 70	.06	.12	....

In the region where the rainfall is greater than 20 inches, are found 97 per cent. of all the inhabitants, the remaining 3 per cent. being scattered over the region where irrigation is required.

The average annual rainfall on the surface of the United States, excluding Alaska, is 26.7 inches. The average rainfall with reference to the population, deduced by giving a weight to each area of country in proportion to the number of its inhabitants, was, in 1870, 42.5 inches. In 1880 it had diminished to 42 inches, and in 1890 to 41.4 inches, this progressive diminution being caused by the settlement of the great plains and the arid regions of the west.

The distribution of the foreign born with respect to rainfall conditions does not differ materially from that of the total population. On the whole, the foreigners inhabit a slightly dryer climate. Nearly all of them live where the rainfall ranges from 30 to 50 inches annually.

The habitat of the colored people with reference to rainfall conditions is more characteristic than that of the foreign born. They affect regions having a greater rainfall than either the foreign element or the total population. The maximum proportion of this element—namely, 60 per cent.—is found where the rainfall ranges from 50 to 60 inches, and between 40 and 60 inches are over nine-tenths of all the colored.

Distribution in Altitude.—The distribution of the population with its elements, in altitude above sea level, is another matter of geographic interest. In the following table is given the proportion of the population and of its elements, expressed in percentages of the total, found living in 1890 at various elevations ranging from sea level to more than ten thousand feet:

DISTRIBUTION OF POPULATION AS TO ALTITUDE

	Total	Foreign Born	Colored
0 to 100	16.59	25.08	22.86
100 to 500	22.10	11.28	17.34
500 to 1,000	38.24	37.84	24.34
1,000 to 1,500	15.10	14.92	3.74
1,500 to 2,000	3.76	3.44	.80
2,000 to 3,000	1.84	1.29	.58
3,000 to 4,000	.61	.52	.20
4,000 to 5,000	.47	.62	.05
5,000 to 6,000	.78	1.23	.08
6,000 to 7,000	.26	.37	.03
7,000 to 8,000	.16	.18	.01
8,000 to 9,000	.07	.10	.....
9,000 to 10,000	.06	.11	.....
Above 10,000	.02	.03	.....

From this table it appears that the great body of the population, indeed more than three-fourths of them, live at elevations less than one thousand feet above the level of the sea, and that more than nine-tenths of them are found below the contour of fifteen hundred feet. At greater elevations the population is scattering.

The distribution of the foreign born in this respect does not differ materially from that of the total population. A much larger proportion is found below one hundred feet than in the case of the total population, while below one thousand feet and fifteen hundred feet the proportions are very nearly the same.

The chief characteristic of the colored element is its indisposition to seek great altitudes: 23 per cent. are found below one hundred feet, 68 per cent. below five hundred feet, and no less than 94 per cent. below one thousand feet; while above eight thousand feet no measurable number are found.

The average elevation of the United States, excluding Alaska, is estimated at about two thousand five hundred feet. The average elevation at which all the inhabitants live is seven hundred and eighty-eight feet. That of the foreign element is somewhat greater, being eight hundred and ninety feet, while the colored population live much nearer the sea level, their mean elevation being only four hundred and twenty-seven feet, a fact which serves to emphasize the tendency of this element toward the low, hot sections of the country.

Size of Families.—The average size of families has diminished continuously since 1850, when statistics on this point were first obtained by the census. The following little table shows the average number of persons per family at each census since that date:

SIZE OF FAMILIES AT EACH CENSUS

CENSUS YEAR	PERSONS PER FAMILY
1850	5.55
1860	5.28
1870	5.09
1880	5.04
1890	4.93

The family has diminished in average size, from 5.55 persons in 1850 to 4.93 persons in 1890, a diminution of over eleven per cent. in the past forty years.

In 1890 the smallest families were found in northern New England, where the number of children has steadily diminished, and in the states and territories of the far west, where, owing to the unsettled conditions, the proportion of women and children is small. The average family of the southern states, although diminishing in size, is still much larger than in other parts of the country. This is due in no small degree to the large proportion of the colored in these states, among which the birth-rate is exceptionally great. The families of the whites in the south are also larger than the average of the country, indeed quite as large as in the north central states, where the large proportion of Germans, Norwegians, and Swedes, with their large families, increases the average of this group of states. This distribution is shown in the following diagram:

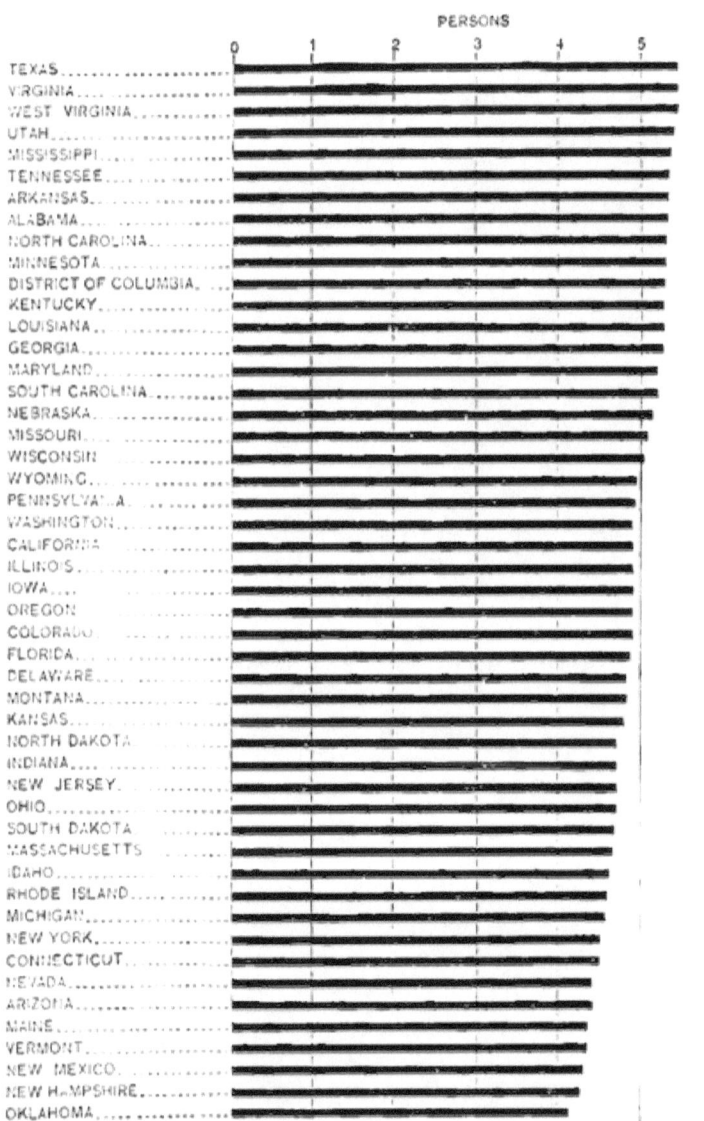

AVERAGE NUMBER OF PERSONS TO A FAMILY IN 1890

SEX

Of the total population in 1890, 32,067,880 were males and 30,554,370 were females. The following table shows the proportion which the number of each sex bore to the total population at each census, from 1850 to 1890:

PROPORTION OF THE SEXES, 1850 TO 1890.

CENSUS YEARS	SEX	
	Male	Female
	Per cent	Per cent
1890	51.21	48.79
1880	50.88	49.12
1870	50.56	49.44
1860	51.16	48.84
1850	51.04	48.96

From this it appears that the proportion of males has been in excess of females continuously since 1850, and that this proportion has tended to increase, but that such tendency received a set-back during the civil war, from which it is now recovering.

Distribution of the Sexes in European Countries.—Under normal conditions the numbers of the two sexes are very nearly equal, the preponderance, if any, being in favor of the female. This is true among the nations of Europe, and is illustrated in the following table showing the proportions of the sexes in the population of the countries named:

PROPORTIONS OF THE SEXES IN FOREIGN COUNTRIES

	PERCENTAGE OF	
	Males	Females
United Kingdom	48.54	51.46
Austria	48.91	51.09
Denmark	48.75	51.25
Germany	48.94	51.06
Netherlands	49.42	50.58
Spain	49.04	50.96
Sweden	48.44	51.56
Norway	47.90	52.10

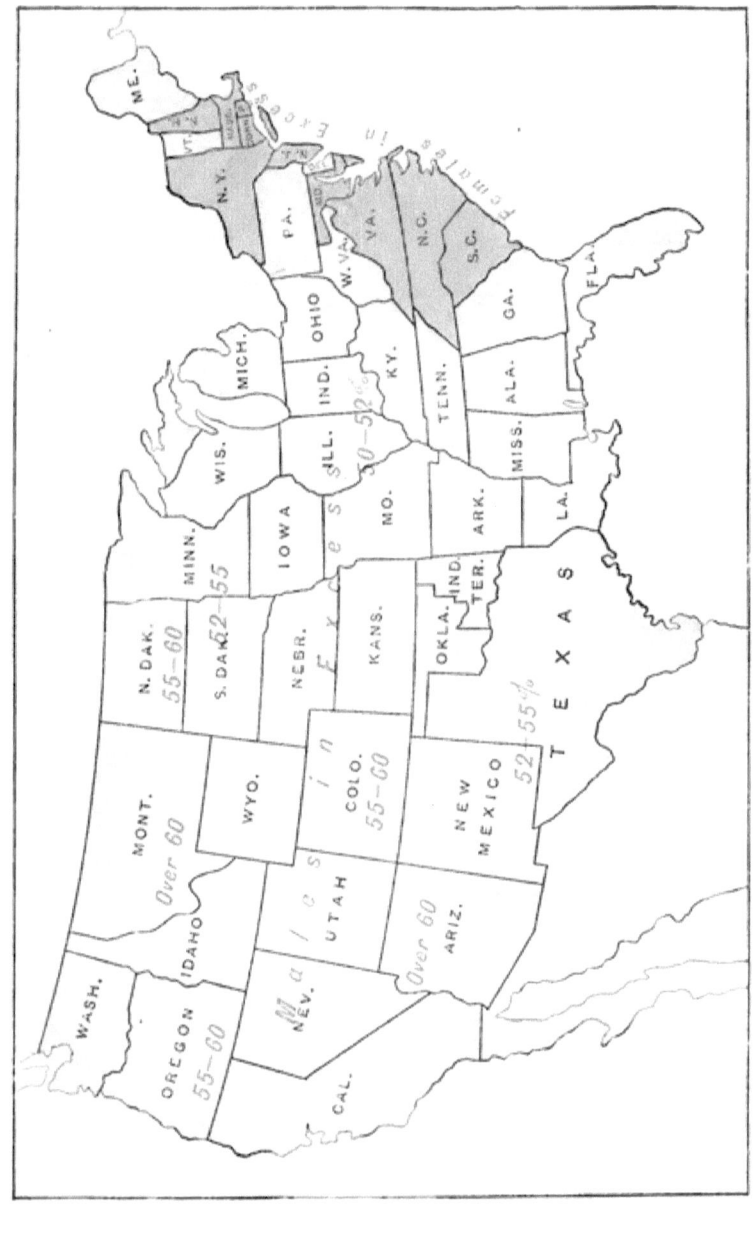

PROPORTION OF SEX TO TOTAL POPULATION, 1890

In every one of these countries females are in excess, the proportion ranging from 50.58 to 52.10. The preponderance of males in the United States is doubtless due to immigration, of which males constitute a decided majority. Of the European countries mentioned in the foregoing table, the excess of females in the United Kingdom, Denmark, Germany, Sweden, and Norway may be accounted for by the emigration from these countries; but in the cases of Austria, the Netherlands, and Spain there has been little either of immigration or emigration, and therefore the figures given for them present the result of comparatively undisturbed natural increase.

Distribution of the Sexes by States.—The following table shows the proportions of males and females in each state, and in each group of states, in 1890. This is illustrated also by the map, Plate 7, facing page 88.

PERCENTAGE OF THE SEXES TO TOTAL POPULATION IN 1890

STATES AND TERRITORIES	Males	Females	STATES AND TERRITORIES	Males	Females
The United States	51.24	48.79	Wisconsin	51.87	48.13
			Minnesota	53.41	46.59
			Iowa	52.01	47.99
North Atlantic Division	49.87	50.13	Missouri	51.70	48.30
			North Dakota	55.60	44.40
Maine	50.31	49.69	South Dakota	54.82	45.18
New Hampshire	49.55	50.45	Nebraska	54.10	45.90
Vermont	50.94	49.06	Kansas	52.70	47.30
Massachusetts	48.58	51.42			
Rhode Island	48.63	51.37	South Central Division	50.98	49.02
Connecticut	49.52	50.48			
New York	49.63	50.37	Kentucky	50.72	49.28
New Jersey	49.89	50.11	Tennessee	50.44	49.56
Pennsylvania	50.71	49.29	Alabama	50.06	49.94
			Mississippi	50.38	49.62
South Atlantic Division	49.88	50.12	Louisiana	50.01	49.99
			Texas	52.45	47.55
Delaware	50.79	49.21	Oklahoma	56.17	43.83
Maryland	49.47	50.53	Arkansas	51.92	48.08
District of Columbia	47.56	52.44			
Virginia	49.78	50.22	Western Division	58.88	41.12
West Virginia	51.17	48.83			
North Carolina	49.39	50.61	Montana	66.50	33.50
South Carolina	49.72	50.28	Wyoming	64.81	35.19
Georgia	50.07	49.93	Colorado	59.70	40.30
Florida	51.59	48.41	New Mexico	54.05	45.95
			Arizona	61.34	38.66
North Central Division	51.85	48.15	Utah	52.13	46.87
			Nevada	63.84	36.16
Ohio	50.53	49.47	Idaho	60.78	39.22
Indiana	51.01	48.99	Washington	62.27	37.73
Illinois	51.55	48.45	Oregon	57.95	42.05
Michigan	52.14	47.86	California	57.95	42.05

Various states show a wide range in the proportion of the sexes. In the states bordering on the Atlantic, with the exception of

Maine, Vermont, Pennsylvania, Delaware, Georgia, and Florida, females are in excess; this excess is greatest in the District of Columbia, where they constitute no less than 52.44 per cent. of the population, and next greatest in Massachusetts, where the corresponding proportion is 51.42 per cent. In all the other states males are in excess; and, speaking broadly, the excess of males increases with the longitude, until in the states and territories of the far west, where settlement commenced more recently, the proportion of females is smallest. Thus in Montana there are two males to one female, and in Wyoming the proportion of males is nearly as great.

This condition of things is easy of explanation. The Atlantic states constitute an old and settled region, from which for many decades a stream of emigration has flowed westward, and this stream has consisted mainly of males. To a certain extent their place has been taken by foreign immigration; otherwise the disproportion of the sexes on the Atlantic border would be greater than it is. The manufacturing centers of the northeastern states have attracted large numbers of female as well as male operatives, and thus have tended to maintain the disproportion of the former sex.

RACES

Out of a total population in 1890 of 62,622,250, there were 7,470,040 of negro or mixed blood, 107,745 Chinese, 2,039 Japanese, and 58,806 Indians enumerated as of the constitutional population. Persons of negro blood were classified according to shades of color, as follows: Blacks, 6,337,980; mulattoes, 956,989; quadroons, 105,135; and octoroons, 69,936. It is needless to say that these latter figures are utterly worthless and misleading. It is not to be supposed for a moment that six-sevenths of the colored race are of unmixed negro blood, or that the mulattoes number less than a million. As for the quadroons and octoroons, the numbers given are too absurdly small to require comment.

The Africans present the spectacle of an inferior race existing in close juxtaposition with the whites, and, since the early part of the century, unaided by additions to their numbers from abroad. For seventy years they existed in a state of slavery; for the last thirty, more or less, in a state of freedom. It is most interesting to watch the progress of this race and compare it with that of the whites.

History of the Races.—Throwing together all these classes of colored, the population is made up of 87.8 per cent. of whites, and 12.2 per cent. of colored. Ten years before there were 6,580,793 colored persons in the country, and the proportion of the two races was 86.54 per cent. white, and 13.12 per cent. colored. The following table shows the number of white and colored during the past century as returned by the censuses:

WHITE AND COLORED POPULATION AT EACH CENSUS

Census Years	White	Colored
1790	3,172,006	757,208
1800	4,306,446	1,002,037
1810	5,862,073	1,377,808
1820	7,862,166	1,771,656
1830	10,537,378	2,328,642
1840	14,195,805	2,873,648
1850	19,553,068	3,638,808
1860	26,922,537	4,441,830
1870	33,589,377	4,880,009
1880	43,402,970	6,580,793
1890	54,983,968	7,638,282

The annexed table, derived from the above, shows the proportions of the two races, given in percentages of the total, at each census during the past century:

PROPORTION OF WHITE AND COLORED BY DECADES

Census Years	White	Colored
	Per cent.	Per cent.
1790	80.73	19.27
1800	81.13	18.87
1810	80.97	19.03
1820	81.61	18.39
1830	81.90	18.10
1840	83.17	16.83
1850	84.31	15.69
1860	85.62	14.13
1870	87.11	12.65
1880	86.54	13.12
1890	87.80	12.20

Relative Diminution of the Colored Element.— It appears from the foregoing table that in this period of one hundred years the proportion of whites has increased from 80.73 to 87.80 per cent., and that the colored people have correspondingly diminished from 19.27 to 12.20 per cent. In 1790 the first census showed that the colored race formed nearly one-fifth of the population. In 1840, after a lapse of fifty years, during which time the country had received practically no increase from immigration, the proportion of colored had fallen to about one-sixth of the whole. In the next half century, ending with 1890, during which the white race had received great additions from immigration, that proportion had fallen to less than one-eighth of the whole population. The present proportion of the colored element is less than two-thirds what it was at the beginning of the century. Indeed, the results of each census show a diminution in the proportion of colored, with the exception of the third and tenth censuses, and the latter was undoubtedly due to the deficient enumeration of the census preceding.

The annexed table and the diagram on page 93 give the percentages of increase of the two races:

INCREASE OF WHITE AND COLORED, BY DECADES

Decades	Percentage of Increase	
	White	Colored
1790–1800	35.76	32.38
1800–1810	36.13	37.16
1810–1820	34.12	28.57
1820–1830	34.03	31.41
1830–1840	34.72	23.28
1840–1850	37.74	26.61
1850–1860	37.69	22.06
1860–1870	24.76	9.86
1870–1880	29.91	34.85
1880–1890	26.68	13.41

This table shows that with two exceptions, one of which is due to the faulty enumeration in 1870, the rate of increase of the white element has been greater than that of the colored element, while during the past ten years the increase has been apparently more than twice as rapid. Throughout our history the colored race has almost continuously lost ground in proportion to the white. Although the birth rate of the colored race is decidedly larger than that of the whites, its death rate, as is shown by the mortality records of large southern cities, is still greater, being little less on an average than double the death rate of the whites.

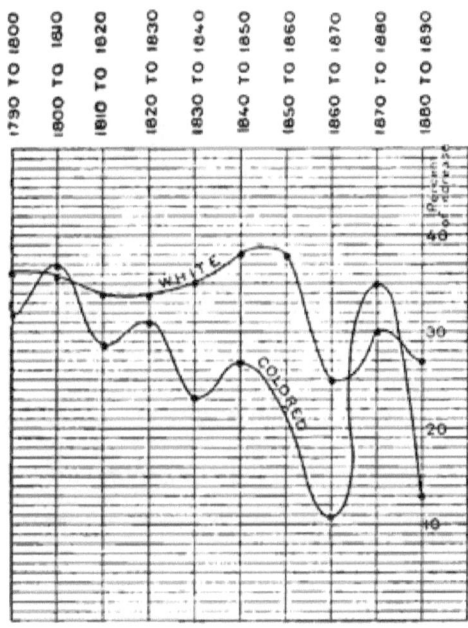

RATE OF INCREASE—WHITE AND COLORED

The relative rate of increase of the colored people has been, especially since the war, a matter of great interest. The exaggerated rate which was given to it between 1870 and 1880, because of the omissions of the census of 1870, aroused much anxiety concerning the future of the two races. In spite of the known weakness of the evidence—for at that time the faulty character of the ninth census had been fully established—the matter created wide-spread uneasiness, and various projects were suggested for averting the evils threatened by the expected numerical preponderance of the colored race. It is now apparent that all this anxiety was unwarranted.

The facts developed by the returns of the eleventh census fully corroborate the past history of the race and fit in with the probabilities of the case. During the seventy years following 1790, while the colored race was in a condition of slavery, its increase was much less rapid than that of the whites, and in this time the proportion of the colored element diminished from 19.27 per cent. of the total population to 14.13 per cent. Within the past thirty years, during most of which period it has been in a state of freedom, it has still further diminished, the proportion having fallen from 14.13 to 12.20 per cent. The country is now much more interested in preserving the laboring population of the south than in getting rid of it.

The colored element is not only increasing less rapidly than the whites in the country at large, but in nearly every state, as will be seen hereafter; and in all probability the relative rates of increase of the two races in the southern states will differ more and more widely, as time goes on and the industries of these states change from an agricultural to a manufacturing character and thus attract the foreign labor element. In the border states and in the Appalachian mountains manufacturing industries are rapidly developing, and in these regions foreign born labor is encroaching. This movement threatens to become of great importance in the near future.

The question has been asked, "Has the condition of slavery or of freedom proved the most favorable to the numerical increase of the colored people?" The figures of the census give a ready answer. Their increase has been more rapid under conditions of freedom. In the thirty years preceding 1860, they increased 48 per cent., while in the following thirty years, during only twenty-seven of which they were free, and which included the disturbed period of the civil war and of reconstruction, they increased not less than 68 per cent.

Distribution of the Races by States.—The following table shows the white and colored population in 1890 by states and groups of states:

WHITE AND COLORED POPULATION IN 1890

STATES AND TERRITORIES	White	Colored	STATES AND TERRITORIES	White	Colored
The United States	54,983,890	7,638,360	Wisconsin	1,680,473	6,107
			Minnesota	1,296,159	5,067
			Iowa	1,901,086	10,810
North Atlantic Division	17,121,984	279,564	Missouri	2,528,458	150,726
			North Dakota	182,123	506
Maine	659,263	1,823	South Dakota	327,290	1,548
New Hampshire	375,840	620	Nebraska	1,046,888	12,022
Vermont	331,418	1,004	Kansas	1,376,553	50,513
Massachusetts	2,215,373	23,570			
Rhode Island	337,859	7,617	South Central Division	7,487,526	3,185,317
Connecticut	733,438	12,820			
New York	5,923,952	73,963	Kentucky	1,590,162	268,173
New Jersey	1,396,581	48,352	Tennessee	1,336,637	430,881
Pennsylvania	5,148,257	109,757	Alabama	833,718	679,299
			Mississippi	544,851	744,749
South Atlantic Division	5,592,149	3,263,774	Louisiana	558,395	560,192
			Texas	1,745,935	488,788
Delaware	140,063	28,127	Oklahoma	78,890	3,008
Maryland	826,193	215,897	Arkansas	818,752	309,427
District of Columbia	154,695	75,696			
Virginia	1,020,122	635,858	Western Division	2,870,257	157,356
West Virginia	730,077	32,717			
North Carolina	1,055,382	562,565	Montana	127,271	1,888
South Carolina	462,008	689,141	Wyoming	59,275	1,430
Georgia	978,357	858,999	Colorado	404,408	7,330
Florida	224,949	166,673	New Mexico	142,719	10,874
			Arizona	55,580	1,040
North Central Division	21,911,987	170,352	Utah	205,899	2,066
			Nevada	39,084	6,677
Ohio	3,584,805	87,511	Idaho	82,018	2,367
Indiana	2,146,736	45,668	Washington	340,513	8,877
Illinois	3,768,472	57,879	Oregon	301,758	12,069
Michigan	2,072,884	21,005	California	1,111,672	96,158

The maps on Plate 8, facing page 96, give the number of colored persons to a square mile in each state, in 1890, and also the proportion of colored to total population.

In the South Atlantic and South Central states are found no less than 88 per cent., or seven-eighths of the entire colored element of the country. In these states, as a whole, the colored form very nearly one-third of the entire population, while in several of them they greatly exceed this proportion. In Louisiana they constitute just about one-half the inhabitants, and in Mississippi and South Carolina, nearly three-fifths of the population are colored. In every state on the Atlantic and Gulf coast, from Virginia to Louisiana, more than one-third of the inhabitants are colored.

The following table shows the proportion, expressed in percentages, of the colored element to the total population at each census in the southern states, where it is of importance:

PERCENTAGE OF COLORED (a) TO TOTAL POPULATION

STATES AND TERRITORIES	1880	1880	1870	1860	1850	1840	1830	1820	1810	1800	1790
South Atlantic Division	36.83	38.51	37.38	38.35	38.77	40.89	41.95	41.00	40	41.5	36.87
Delaware	16.85	18.01	18.23	19.27	22.45	25.00	24.95	24.01	23.82	22.41	21.94
Maryland	20.40	22.40	22.46	24.90	28.32	32.20	34.88	36.12	38.22	36.09	34.74
District of Columbia	32.80	33.57	32.96	19.07	26.56	28.82	30.81	31.35	32.62	28.57	
Virginia	38.36	41.76	41.89	41.39	37.06	40.23	42.40	43.38	43.41	41.57	40.86
West Virginia	4.20	4.19	4.07								
North Carolina	34.87	37.96	36.56	36.42	36.36	35.64	35.90	34.28	32.24	29.85	26.84
South Carolina	59.85	60.70	58.92	58.59	58.86	56.44	55.63	52.77	48.40	43.21	43.72
Georgia	46.74	47.02	46.01	44.05	42.44	41.03	42.57	44.40	42.49	37.14	35.93
Florida	42.46	47.01	48.84	44.63	46.02	48.74	47.06				

South Central Division	34.75	33.78	34.25	35.34	34.65	34.54	30.58	27.30	23.93	17.40	14.92
Kentucky	14.42	16.46	16.82	20.42	22.49	23.31	24.12	22.95	20.24	18.30	17.03
Tennessee	24.35	26.14	25.60	25.50	24.52	22.74	21.43	19.60	17.52	14.16	10.50
Alabama	44.84	47.54	47.69	45.40	44.73	43.26	38.48	31.19			
Mississippi	57.58	57.47	53.65	55.28	51.24	52.33	48.44	44.10	42.91	41.48	
Louisiana	49.99	51.46	50.10	49.49	50.65	55.04	58.54	52.64	56.18		
Texas	24.84	24.74	30.96	30.27	27.51						
Oklahoma	4.81										
Arkansas	27.40	26.25	25.22	25.55	22.73	20.91	15.52	11.30			

a Persons of African descent only.

In the South Atlantic states the colored race comprised in 1790, 36.37 per cent., and a century later it formed 36.87 per cent. of the entire population, the proportion at the beginning and ending of the century being almost identical. During this period, however, it has oscillated within wide limits, increasing up to 1830, when it was 41.95 per cent., and then diminishing to its present proportion. In the South Central states, on the other hand, the proportion at the beginning of the century was small, for the reason that these states were first settled mainly by whites. As their settlement progressed, however, the proportion of colored people increased, reaching its maximum in 1860, when it was 35.36 per cent. From that time it has diminished, and now stands at 34.76. Taking the south as a whole, the proportion of the colored element increased up to 1840 or 1850, while since that date it has diminished.

The above statement regarding these groups of states, holds good in the case of individual states. Thus in Delaware the proportion of the colored element increased up to 1840 and then diminished. In Maryland the maximum was reached in 1810, and during the past eighty years there has been a proportional

THE BUILDING OF A NATION
PLATE 8

NUMBER OF COLORED PERSONS TO A SQUARE MILE IN 1890

PROPORTION OF COLORED TO TOTAL POPULATION IN 1890

diminution. The colored element of the District of Columbia also reached a maximum proportion in 1810, and from that point diminished until the opening of the civil war. During the war the colored people flocked to the capital for protection, and the proportion increased until it reached about one-third of the entire population. For the past twenty years it has continued to hold practically this proportion. In Virginia the maximum was reached in 1820 and has since diminished. In Kentucky the maximum was reached in 1840. All these are border states, and all show a similar history.

In the states farther south, the proportion of the colored population continued to increase until a much more recent date. Thus, in North and South Carolina, Georgia and Tennessee, it increased until 1880, and only during the past decade has the proportion suffered any diminution. In Alabama the corner was turned in 1870, while in Mississippi and Arkansas the proportion has continued to increase to the present time. In Louisiana the maximum was reached in 1880. In Texas and Florida, which have received within the past twenty years considerable immigration, both from the north and from foreign countries, the proportion of the colored race has notably diminished.

The table and the foregoing statements show that there has been a perceptible southward movement of the colored race. This movement was pointed out long ago by Judge Tourgee, in his "Appeal to Cæsar;" but he greatly exaggerated its extent, and failed to take into account the fact that the rate of increase of the race as a whole was much less than that of the whites, which is a vital point. Indeed, the greater rate of increase of the whites has overcome the increase of blacks, not only in the border states, but also in the southern states where this massing is taking place.

The following table gives the proportion of the entire colored element which at each census was contained in each of the five divisions of the country, and serves to emphasize still more strongly what has been previously pointed out—that an increase is found only in the far southern states, and that the main movement of that element has been southward:

PROPORTION OF THE COLORED ELEMENT AT EACH CENSUS

CENSUS YEARS	North Atlantic Division	South Atlantic Division	North Central Division	South Central Division	Western Division
1890	3.66	42.75	5.90	45.63	2.06
1880	3.46	43.59	5.96	44.69	2.50
1870	3.65	41.65	5.69	44.40	1.61
1860	3.46	45.56	4.35	15.12	1.51
1850	4.12	51.14	3.73	10.98	0.03
1840	4.95	55.59	3.41	36.35	....
1830	5.38	65.67	1.78	27.47	....
1820	6.25	71.88	1.03	20.84	....
1810	7.42	78.45	0.51	13.62	....
1800	8.29	85.79	0.07	5.85	....
1790	8.90	88.94	....	2.16	....

THE CHINESE

The immigration of Chinese commenced in 1854, and continued with an annual average of 4,000 to 5,000 for fifteen years. About 1869 or 1870, the annual increase became more rapid, and aroused considerable alarm, especially upon the Pacific coast. The agitation thus produced brought about the passage in 1882 of the Chinese Exclusion Act, which has practically put a stop to the immigration of that element.

The total number of Chinese immigrants from the beginning was 290,655. The following figures show the number of Chinese found in the country at the date of each census:

THE CHINESE POPULATION, BY DECADES

1850	758
1860	35,565
1870	63,042
1880	104,468
1890	106,462

As will be seen, the number increased with considerable rapidity up to 1880. Since that time the increase has been only about two thousand, showing that the Exclusion Act has practically put a stop to their immigration.

In 1880 the Chinese were contained almost entirely in California and Nevada, with a few in the other Pacific coast states,

In 1890, while the great majority of them were still living upon the coast, they were much more scattered, some being found in nearly every state in the Union.

THE INDIANS

When the whites settled upon the Atlantic coast, they found the country sparsely inhabited by red men. It is impossible to estimate the number who lived at that time within the present limits of the United States. They were formerly supposed to have been extremely numerous, but recent investigations have indicated that their number was probably never much larger than at present. They were for the most part nomadic, but their ranges were limited by the confines of neighboring hostile tribes. Certain of them were sedentary, such as the Moki and Pueblo Indians. They were grouped in tribes, differing widely in numbers and in power. Socially their status ranged from savagery to barbarism.

Intertribal wars were frequent. Although it is scarcely fair to say that the normal condition of the Indians was one of warfare, still their code of morals reflected that condition very forcibly. For instance, it was regarded as right to steal from or to kill a member of a neighboring tribe, while similar offences against members of their own tribe were wrong.

The Indian tribes of this country may be broadly divided, according to language, into the following classes: Algonquin, Iroquois, Muskogee, Sioux, Caddo, Kiowa, Shoshone, Athabascan, Yuma, and Pima, besides numerous smaller subdivisions which it is not necessary to enumerate. Of these the Algonquins inhabited New England and the northeastern part of the Mississippi Valley. The Iroquois, or the Six Nations, ranged over New York, much of Pennsylvania, and the southern Appalachian region. The Muskogees, including the Cherokees and Creeks, occupied the Gulf states east of the Mississippi.

The Sioux, including the Dakotas, Cheyennes, and Arapahoes, ranged over the Great Plains. The Caddoes were found mainly in eastern Texas; while the Shoshones, including the tribe of that name, the Bannocks, and other allied tribes, were scattered over the Great Basin, Colorado, and central Texas. A branch of the Athabascans, who are mainly northern Indians, was found far from the body of this stock, in Arizona, New Mexico, and western Texas, where they are known to-day as Apaches. The Pimas are found in southern Arizona, the Yumas in western Arizona and southern California, and the Kiowas in southern Nebraska and southeastern Wyoming.

As the whites have spread over the country, the advancing wave of civilization has driven these Indians westward before its front, so that to-day most of them are found far from their original homes.

Treatment of the Indians.—The policy of the government toward the Indian tribes, as a rule, has been that of a protectorate. It has treated with the tribes as one power might with another under its jurisdiction. As land has been required for the use of settlers, the government has, in most cases, purchased it from the tribes, the payments commonly taking the form of annuities. In this way the Indians have been gradually dispossessed of the enormous areas over which they formerly ranged, and now such of them as still remain under tribal organizations are confined to reservations.

The Indian population of the United States in 1890, as appears from the returns of the census, was 249,273. There were then living upon reservations 216,706 Indians. The reservations have a total area of 98,145,788 acres, thus giving to each Indian about 450 acres. Of the Indians upon reservations, 133,382, or nearly two-thirds, are supported wholly or partially by the general government. The remainder, while under the control of the government, are self-supporting, and all are self-governing.

First in importance of those not supported by the government are what are known as the five civilized tribes—namely, the Cherokees, Chickasaws, Choctaws, Creeks, and Seminoles—comprising a total number of 52,065, who occupy reservations which practically comprise Indian territory. These Indians have made great progress in civilization. Most of them are educated, live in houses, and maintain forms of government quite similar to those of states. There are also the Pueblos of New Mexico, numbering 8,278; the remnant of the Six Nations now living on reservations in New York, and now numbering 5,304; and the Cherokees of North Carolina, numbering 2,885. The latter are located upon a reservation in a mountainous section of the state, where they have reached a degree of civilization that compares favorably with that of the neighboring whites.

For the support of Indians during the year 1892, the general government appropriated the sum of $11,150,578, equivalent to about $84 per head of those supported.

The work of civilizing the Indians has been greatly hampered by this policy of supporting them, and thus removing all incentive to labor. Indeed, those who have had their wants supplied have made little or no advance in civilization. Such progress as has been made has been confined almost entirely to the Indians who have had little or no assistance from the government, but have been thrown upon their own resources.

Indeed, the history of the Indians who have been fed and clothed by the government, forms a striking illustration of the probable effect upon mankind of the application of the Bellamy theories. The situation is precisely such as Mr. Bellamy advocates— every man entitled to support from the State and receiving it. There is little likelihood that the white man, under similar circumstances, would behave better than the red man has done.

Within the last few years the policy in regard to ration Indians—the name applied to those supported by the government—has been so modified, in the case of a number of tribes, that lands have been allotted in severalty, and rations have been issued only to those Indians who work the land, thus giving them a motive for working. Altogether the outlook for the civilization of the Indians is brighter at present than ever before.

NATIVITY

It has often been stated that the strongest and most virile nations are the composite ones, those made up from a mixture of blood. If this be true, we should easily distance all others, ancient or modern, since the blood of immigrants from every country of Europe, from the Mediterranean to the Arctic, to say nothing of the negroes, Chinese, and Indians within our borders, bids fair to make of us the most thoroughly composite nation that ever existed.

Of a total population of 62,622,250, the eleventh census reported that 9,249,547 were of foreign, and 53,372,703 of native birth. Of the persons of native birth 7,638,360 were colored, including those of African blood, Chinese, Japanese, and "constitutional Indians," leaving as native whites 45,862,023. The following table shows the nativity of the population at each census since and including that of 1850:

NATIVITY OF THE POPULATION, 1850 TO 1890

Census Years	Native	Native White	Foreign
1850	20,947,274	17,273,804	2,244,602
1860	27,304,624	22,862,794	4,138,697
1870	32,991,142	28,111,133	5,567,229
1880	40,475,840	36,895,047	6,679,943
1890	53,372,703	45,862,023	9,249,547

In the next table are given the proportions which each of these elements of the population bore to the total at each census:

RATIO OF NATIVE AND FOREIGN POPULATION, 1850 TO 1890

Census Years	Native	Native White	Foreign
1850	90.32	73.24	9.68
1860	86.84	73.46	13.16
1870	85.56	72.94	14.44
1880	86.68	73.56	13.32
1890	85.23	73.24	14.77

Thus it appears that the proportion of foreign birth, which was 9.68 per cent. of the population in 1850, rose in ten years to 13.16 per cent., and since then has more than retained this proportion, being in 1890 14.77 per cent.

IMMIGRATION

During the early decades of our history immigration was slight. The attractions offered to Europeans were not sufficiently great at that early stage of our development to induce them to undergo the expense and hardships of a voyage across the Atlantic. Prior to 1820 immigration was trifling in amount, and it was not until the succession of famines in Ireland, between 1840 and 1850, coupled with political troubles in Germany, that immigration upon a large scale set in. During the past forty or forty-five years, however, there has been a migration of peoples across the Atlantic to these shores, the equal of which in any quarter the world had probably never seen before. Immigration statistics were first obtained in 1820, and have been kept continuously since that time. The total number of immigrants in the seventy years which have since elapsed is not less than 15,376,986. The following table shows the accessions to its population by immigration which this country has received in each ten year period since 1820:

IMMIGRATION, 1821 TO 1890, BY DECADES

1821–1830	143,439
1831–1840	599,125
1841–1850	1,713,251
1851–1860	2,579,580
1861–1870	2,282,787
1871–1880	2,812,191
1881–1890	5,246,613
Total	15,376,986

Of this enormous number it will be seen that more than one-third have arrived during the past ten years, almost double the number which came between 1870 and 1880, and more than double that of any preceding decade. The next table shows the immigration, by decades, from the countries whence it was mainly derived:

PRINCIPAL CONSTITUENTS OF THE IMMIGRATION

NATIONALITY	1821 to 1830	1831 to 1840	1841 to 1850	1851 to 1860	1861 to 1870	1871 to 1880	1881 to 1890
Canada	2,277	13,624	41,723	59,309	153,878	383,926	392,802*a*
Ireland	50,724	207,381	780,719	914,119	435,778	436,871	655,482
b England and Wales	22,167	73,143	263,332	385,643	568,128	400,470	657,488
Scotland	2,912	2,667	3,712	38,331	38,769	87,564	149,869
Norway and Sweden	91	1,201	13,903	20,931	109,298	211,245	568,992
Denmark	169	1,063	539	3,749	17,004	31,771	88,132
Russia and Poland	91	646	656	1,621	4,536	52,254	265,088
Hungary					7,800	72,969	525,339
Italy	408	2,253	1,870	9,231	11,728	55,759	307,309
Germany	6,761	152,454	434,626	951,667	787,468	418,182	1,452,970
France	8,497	45,575	77,262	76,358	35,984	72,206	50,464
Netherlands	1,078	1,412	8,251	10,789	9,102	16,541	53,701

a Five years only.   *b* Including Great Britain, not specified.

From this it appears that, of the total immigration, 40.5 per cent., or more than two-fifths, have been derived from the United Kingdom, the majority of which came from Ireland, and 28.3 per cent. from Germany. The United Kingdom and Germany together have supplied over two-thirds of the entire immigration to the United States, while the other countries have severally contributed but a trifling proportion.

The character of the immigration has changed greatly since the beginning. In the late forties and early fifties it was mainly composed of Irish. Later the German element assumed prominence; while in recent years, mainly during the past decade, other and far less desirable elements have increased with great rapidity. Thus it will be seen by the table that nearly all the Hungarians, Italians, Russians, and Poles have arrived since 1880. This unpleasant picture is relieved to some extent by the immigration of Norwegians and Swedes, than whom no more desirable element has joined us; but altogether the changes wrought in the character of the foreign influx during the past ten or fifteen years have tended to lower the standard of American citizenship, and to make it a serious question whether steps should not be taken to limit immigration henceforth.

The diagram on page 106 is interesting as showing by comparison the constituents of the total immigration and the immigration between 1880 and 1890.

Distribution of the Foreign Born.—The maps on Plate 9, facing page 106, portray the distribution of the foreign born over the country, expressed in the number to a square mile and in percentages of the total population, state by state. It will be seen that the home of this element is in the north and west. The foreign born have never invaded the south to compete in labor with the colored element. Indeed, the northern and western states are found to contain no less than ninety-six per cent. of the entire foreign born element of the country.

The following table shows the number of native and foreign born, by states and groups of states, in 1890:

NATIVE AND FOREIGN BORN POPULATION IN 1890

STATES AND TERRITORIES	Native	Foreign	STATES AND TERRITORIES	Native	Foreign
The United States	53,372,703	9,249,547	Wisconsin	1,167,380	519,199
			Minnesota	841,170	467,356
			Iowa	1,587,827	324,069
North Atlantic Division	14,513,164	3,888,084	Missouri	2,441,315	234,869
			North Dakota	101,258	81,461
Maine	582,125	78,961	South Dakota	237,751	91,055
New Hampshire	304,190	72,340	Nebraska	856,398	202,542
Vermont	288,334	44,088	Kansas	1,279,358	147,828
Massachusetts	1,581,806	657,107			
Rhode Island	239,291	106,305	South Central Division	10,654,085	324,808
Connecticut	562,730	183,708			
New York	1,436,803	1,574,090	Kentucky	1,799,279	59,176
New Jersey	1,115,168	328,975	Tennessee	1,714,180	20,024
Pennsylvania	4,112,294	845,720	Alabama	1,498,210	14,777
			Mississippi	1,281,618	7,952
South Atlantic Division	8,619,414	308,706	Louisiana	1,068,854	49,474
			Texas	2,082,767	152,896
Delaware	155,322	13,164	Oklahoma	59,024	2,740
Maryland	948,091	91,236	Arkansas	1,113,905	14,264
District of Columbia	211,622	18,770			
Virginia	1,637,606	18,371	Western Division	2,356,503	750,940
West Virginia	743,911	18,883			
North Carolina	1,614,245	3,702	Montana	80,067	43,096
South Carolina	1,141,879	6,250	Wyoming	45,792	14,913
Georgia	1,825,235	12,118	Colorado	328,398	83,990
Florida	368,190	22,362	New Mexico	142,314	11,259
			Arizona	40,825	18,795
North Central Division	18,963,055	4,660,236	Utah	154,841	53,064
			Nevada	31,055	14,706
Ohio	3,214,051	458,268	Idaho	66,929	17,456
Indiana	2,046,190	146,205	Washington	259,385	90,065
Illinois	2,981,892	841,150	Oregon	256,450	57,317
Michigan	1,536,062	543,880	California	811,821	366,309

The next table gives the proportion which these elements bore to the total population, by states and groups of states, in 1890:

PERCENTAGE OF NATIVE AND FOREIGN BORN TO TOTAL POPULATION, 1890

STATES AND TERRITORIES	1890 Native	1890 Foreign	STATES AND TERRITORIES	1890 Native	1890 Foreign
The United States	85.23	14.77	Wisconsin	69.22	30.78
			Minnesota	64.10	35.80
			Iowa	83.05	16.95
North Atlantic Division	77.66	22.34	Missouri	91.23	8.77
			North Dakota	55.42	14.58
Maine	88.06	11.94	South Dakota	72.81	27.19
New Hampshire	80.79	19.21	Nebraska	80.87	19.13
Vermont	86.71	13.29	Kansas	89.64	10.36
Massachusetts	70.65	29.35			
Rhode Island	69.23	30.77	South Central Division	97.07	2.93
Connecticut	75.40	24.60			
New York	74.81	25.19	Kentucky	96.81	3.19
New Jersey	77.23	22.77	Tennessee	98.87	1.13
Pennsylvania	83.92	16.08	Arkansas	98.74	1.26
			Oklahoma	96.57	1.43
South Atlantic Division	97.65	2.35	Alabama	99.02	0.98
			Mississippi	99.38	0.62
Delaware	92.19	7.81	Louisiana	95.55	4.45
Maryland	90.95	9.05	Texas	93.16	6.84
District of Columbia	91.85	8.15			
Virginia	98.89	1.11	Western Division	74.54	25.46
West Virginia	97.82	2.18			
North Carolina	99.77	0.23	Montana	67.39	32.61
South Carolina	99.46	0.54	Wyoming	75.43	24.57
Georgia	99.34	0.66	Colorado	79.62	20.38
Florida	94.14	5.86	New Mexico	92.67	7.34
			Arizona	68.48	31.52
North Central Division	81.84	18.16	Utah	74.48	25.52
			Nevada	67.86	32.14
Ohio	87.49	12.51	Idaho	79.34	20.69
Indiana	96.93	6.07	Washington	74.24	25.76
Illinois	77.99	22.01	Oregon	81.73	18.27
Michigan	74.64	25.36	California	69.68	30.32

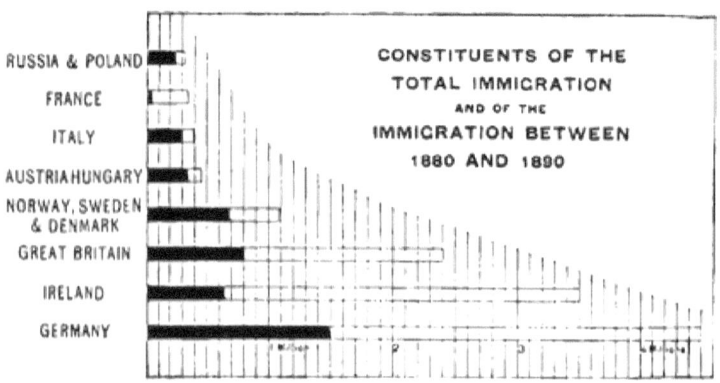

THE BUILDING OF A NATION

PLATE 9

NUMBER OF FOREIGN BORN TO A SQUARE MILE IN 1890

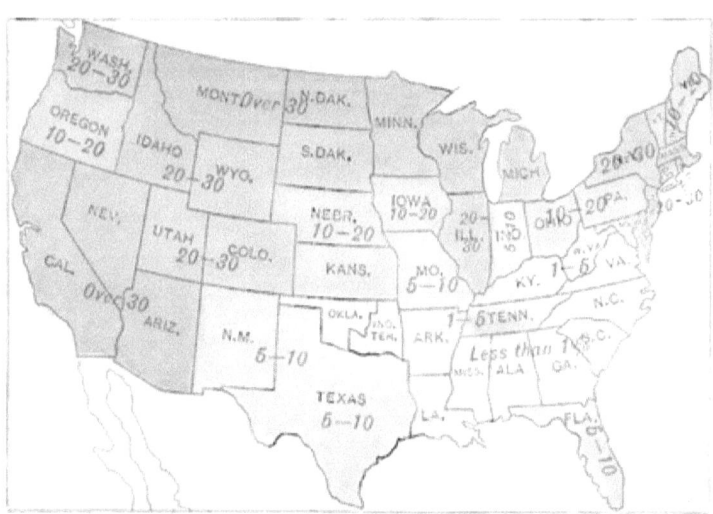

PROPORTION OF FOREIGN BORN TO TOTAL POPULATION IN 1890

This table shows also the distribution of the foreign born element. In the North Atlantic states nearly one-fourth of the inhabitants are of foreign birth; the proportion ranging among the states, individually, from 11.90 per cent. in Maine to 30.69 per cent. in Rhode Island, while Massachusetts has 29.19 per cent., and in Connecticut and New York about one-fourth of the inhabitants are of foreign birth.

In the North Central states the proportion of the foreign born is 18.13, while in individual states the range is very wide, extending from 6.66 per cent. in Indiana to 44.52 per cent. in North Dakota. More than a third of the inhabitants of Minnesota are of foreign birth, and nearly one-third of those of Wisconsin, while in Michigan and South Dakota more than a fourth are foreign born.

In the Western states, as a whole, the proportion of the foreign born is 22.22, ranging in individual states from 7.07 in New Mexico, to 30.52 in Montana. In many of these states the proportion of foreign born is not far from one-fourth.

The South Atlantic states, on the other hand, contain an average of but 2.28 per cent. of foreign born, and the South Central states but 2.90 per cent. The state having the smallest proportion of inhabitants of foreign birth is North Carolina, where it is but 0.23 of one per cent., or about one person in four hundred.

The following table shows the percentage of the whole foreign element in each of these five groups of states, at each census:

PERCENTAGE OF THE FOREIGN ELEMENT, 1850-1890.

Census Year	North Atlantic Division	South Atlantic Division	North Central Division	South Central Division	Western Division
1890	42.04	2.25	43.90	3.18	8.33
1880	42.13	2.61	43.67	4.10	7.49
1870	45.28	3.00	41.90	4.19	5.63
1860	48.90	3.93	37.29	5.55	1.33
1850	59.06	4.67	28.98	6.09	1.20

It appears from this table that the Northeastern and North Central states contained in 1890 not less than 85.94 per cent. of the entire foreign element, and adding the Western states and territories, 96.27 per cent. are accounted for, leaving only about one-twenty-fifth of the entire foreign element for the Southern states.

Constituents of the Foreign Born Element.—What are the principal nativities composing this element of the foreign born? First and foremost are the Germans, numbering nearly three millions, or thirty per cent. of all. Next in order are the natives of Ireland, numbering nearly two millions, and constituting one fifth of the entire number. Then come the British with a million and a quarter, followed by the natives of Canada and of the Scandinavian countries, with nearly a million each. The British, Irish, and Canadians together number four and one-tenth millions, constituting about two-fifths of the entire element of foreign birth. These, with the Germans and Scandinavians, constitute not less than five-sixths of the foreign born.

From these imposing figures there is a sudden drop to the Italians and Russians, each of whom number about one hundred and eighty-two thousand, the Poles one hundred and forty-seven thousand, and so on. The exact data as to these and all other nationalities of importance, are set forth in the following table, and graphically in the diagram on page 109, showing the nativities of the foreign born population in 1890.

FOREIGN BORN BY PRINCIPAL NATIONALITIES, 1890

Germany	2,784,894
Ireland	1,871,168
England, Scotland, and Wales	1,251,397
Norway, Sweden, and Denmark	933,249
Canada and Newfoundland	980,941
Italy	182,580
Russia	182,645
Poland	147,440
Austria	123,271
Bohemia	118,106
France	113,174
Switzerland	104,069
China	106,462
Hungary	62,435

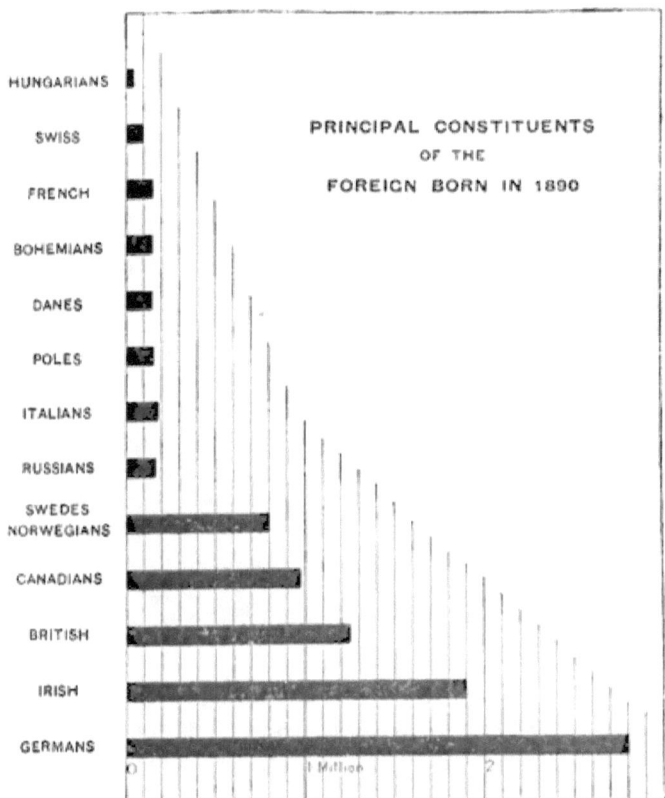

History of the Several Elements.—What has been the history of these several nativities of the foreign element in the past? This is summarized in the tersest possible form by the following table, and is also graphically presented in the diagrams, Plate 10, facing page 110. In the table the strength of the delegation from each country is represented by the proportion which its numbers bore to the total population at each census from 1850 to 1890.

In the diagram the total number of the foreign born at each census is represented by the area of the circle, while the number of each nationality is represented by the various sectors into which it is divided.

PERCENTAGES OF TOTAL POPULATION

	1850	1860	1870	1880	1890
Great Britain	1.63	1.87	1.99	1.83	2.00
Ireland	4.15	5.12	4.81	3.70	3.00
Germany	2.52	4.06	4.38	3.92	4.45
France	.23	.35	.30	.24	.18
Canada	.64	.79	1.28	1.43	1.56
Norway, Sweden, and Denmark	.08	.23	.63	.88	1.49
Italy	.01	.03	.04	.09	.29
Russia	....	.01	.01	.07	.29
Poland	....	.02	.03	.10	.23
Austria	...	.08	.08	.08	.20
Bohemia	....	....	.10	.17	.19
Switzerland	.06	.17	.20	.17	.17
China	....	.11	.17	.24	.17
Hungary	....	....	....	...	.10

In 1850 two-fifths of the entire foreign element was composed of Irish, which far outnumbered any other nationality; Germany was second and Great Britain third; while of the nationalities of southern Europe now coming hither in considerable and rapidly increasing numbers, there were practically none at that time.

In 1860, while Ireland still held the lead, Germany had narrowed the gap between them considerably; the proportion of British had increased also; while generally those nations whose contributions were small had increased in numbers, such as France, British America, and the Scandinavian countries. At this time natives of Russia, Poland, and Austria first appeared; and the Italians, who in 1850 were present in trifling numbers, had trebled proportionally in 1860.

In 1870 the Irish still occupied the leading position, but Germany had yet further narrowed the gap between them; the British had also gained slightly, while the Canadians and Scandinavians had increased their numbers greatly; the colonists from southern Europe had made little progress, scarcely more than holding their proportion.

In 1880 the Germans and Irish had changed positions, the Germans becoming the leading nationality; the British had slightly lost in proportion; the Canadians and Scandinavians had gained somewhat; while the Italians, Russians, Poles, and Bohemians had made great proportional gains.

THE BUILDING OF A NATION
PLATE 10

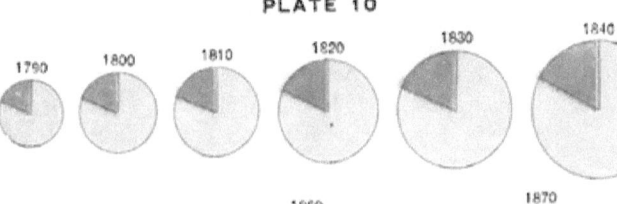
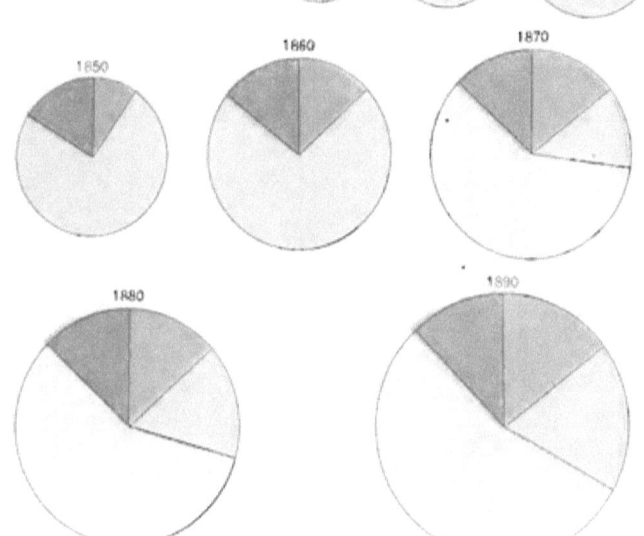

ELEMENTS OF THE POPULATION AT EACH CENSUS

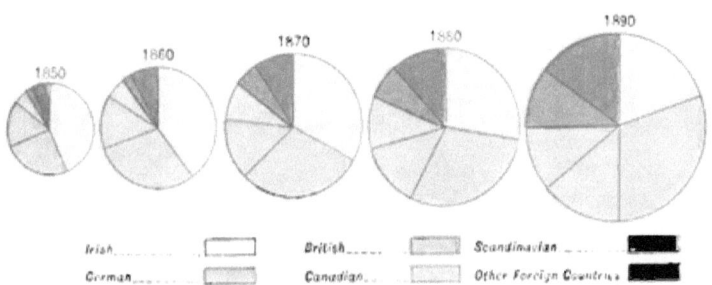

NATIONALITIES OF THE FOREIGN BORN, 1850 TO 1890

In 1890 the Germans had widened the gap between their proportion and that of the Irish, their total being nearly fifty per cent, greater, while the proportion of the Irish had greatly declined from its maximum in 1860: the British and Canadians had gained slightly; while the Scandinavians had nearly doubled their proportion, and the Italians, Poles, and Austrians had trebled their proportion to the total population. In this census the Hungarians appeared in small numbers.

How are the people of these different nationalities distributed over the country? The series of maps, Plates 11, 12, and 13, facing page 112, shows this distribution of the British, Germans and Austrians, Canadians, Irish, and Scandinavians, expressed in the form of a proportion between their numbers and the total population of the various states. It is shown also in the table on page 112, which presents the proportion that the number of each of these leading nationalities bears to the total number of the foreign born in each of the northern and western states, and in each group thereof, where the foreign born are of numerical importance.

From this table it will be seen that the Canadians form nearly two-thirds of the foreign element of Maine and New Hampshire, more than half that of Vermont, and nearly a third that of Massachusetts. In Michigan they form a third of the foreign born, and more than one-fourth that of North Dakota.

The Irish are not so concentrated. In no state do they constitute half the foreign element. The proportion is largest in Connecticut. In that state, and also in Massachusetts and Rhode Island, they number more than a third of the foreign born, and in New York and New Jersey they approach one-third.

The British are still more widely scattered. In none of the northern states do they constitute even one-fourth of the foreign element. Their highest proportion is in Rhode Island and Pennsylvania.

The Germans occupy the North Central states in force. In Ohio, Indiana, Wisconsin, and Missouri, they outnumber all other elements. In New York, New Jersey, Illinois, Iowa, Nebraska, and Kansas, they form between one-third and one-half of the foreign element.

PROPORTION OF DIFFERENT NATIONALITIES TO THE TOTAL FOREIGN POPULATION IN 1890

STATES AND TERRITORIES	Canadians	Irish	English, Scotch, and Welsh	Germans and Austrians	Norwegians, Swedes, and Danes
The United States	10.61	20.23	13.52	33.73	10.09
North Atlantic Division	12.61	31.92	15.88	25.93	3.06
Maine	65.96	14.49	12.39	1.56	3.14
New Hampshire	64.04	20.59	9.63	2.50	2.11
Vermont	56.72	22.25	14.08	2.35	2.19
Massachusetts	31.59	30.55	15.21	4.74	3.45
Rhode Island	26.27	36.61	24.54	3.48	3.60
Connecticut	11.56	42.42	14.82	16.69	6.55
New York	5.93	30.76	11.96	35.24	2.75
New Jersey	1.46	30.73	17.61	37.57	2.57
Pennsylvania	1.44	28.83	23.42	30.92	2.79
North Central Division	9.89	10.68	10.55	42.91	17.47
Ohio	3.60	15.27	16.16	55.37	.92
Indiana	3.39	14.24	10.29	62.14	3.78
Illinois	1.63	14.78	11.29	43.48	15.31
Michigan	33.35	7.48	12.55	31.88	7.63
Wisconsin	6.39	6.42	6.14	51.51	19.21
Minnesota	9.52	5.99	4.64	27.65	46.05
Iowa	5.39	11.52	11.58	43.97	22.48
Missouri	3.63	17.44	10.70	58.09	3.48
North Dakota	28.39	3.64	6.41	12.09	42.04
South Dakota	10.43	5.24	8.41	23.25	34.45
Nebraska	5.98	7.88	9.63	39.88	22.89
Kansas	8.04	10.74	17.67	36.77	14.90
Western Division	9.79	13.69	18.43	19.64	12.18
Montana	20.98	15.43	20.39	16.67	14.88
Wyoming	8.84	12.74	33.95	16.47	15.98
Colorado	10.89	14.71	24.80	23.15	14.53
New Mexico	6.05	8.58	16.13	15.90	2.18
Arizona	3.90	6.23	8.09	7.83	2.17
Utah	2.30	3.86	50.16	7.22	31.79
Nevada	11.30	17.99	18.50	14.57	4.86
Idaho	10.26	10.98	26.07	15.25	20.08
Washington	19.34	8.67	16.71	20.43	23.79
Oregon	11.27	8.53	14.47	27.44	12.80
California	7.12	17.24	12.71	20.85	6.11

The Scandinavians are highly concentrated, being found mainly in Wisconsin, Minnesota, Iowa, the Dakotas, and

PLATE 11

PROPORTION OF BRITISH TO TOTAL POPULATION IN 1890

PROPORTION OF GERMANS AND AUSTRIANS TO TOTAL POPULATION
IN 1890

THE BUILDING OF A NATION

PLATE 12

PROPORTION OF CANADIANS TO TOTAL POPULATION IN 1890

PROPORTION OF IRISH TO TOTAL POPULATION IN 1890

PLATE 13

PROPORTION OF SCANDINAVIANS TO TOTAL POPULATION IN 1890

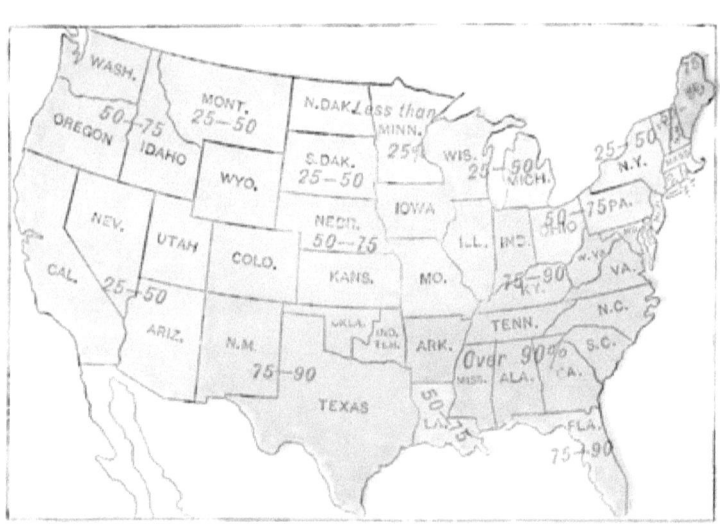

PROPORTION OF NATIVE WHITES OF NATIVE PARENTAGE TO ALL WHITES IN 1890

Nebraska. The highest proportion is in Minnesota, where they number not much less than half the total foreign element.

From the maps it will be seen that the Canadians are found mainly in northern New England, Michigan, Minnesota, and North Dakota, closely hugging the northern border. The Irish are settled mainly in New England and New York, comparatively few having wandered westward. The Germans are found from New York westward, and in the greatest body in Illinois, Michigan, and Wisconsin. The Scandinavians have settled as far north as they could and yet remain within our jurisdiction, principally in Wisconsin, Minnesota, and the Dakotas; while the British are scattered widely over the northern states.

These people are guided largely by temperature in the selection of their homes. Those from northern Europe and Canada settle in the far north. The Germans, coming from a more temperate climate, have settled mainly south of them, as have also the Irish.

The Foreign Element in Cities.—What is the distribution of the foreign element as between urban and rural life? Generally speaking, the foreign population flocks to the cities in far greater proportion than the native born. In 1890 the twenty-eight largest cities of the country contained a population of about 9,700,000, or nearly 15 per cent. of the total population of the country. The foreign born element of these cities comprised a little over 3,000,000, or almost exactly one-third of the total foreign born of the country. Putting it in another way, nearly one-third of the population of these cities is foreign born, while in the country at large only about one-sixth of it is foreign born. These cities contain, therefore, double their quota of the foreign born element.

Thus much concerning the foreign element of our cities, collectively. When analyzed, it presents results even more interesting. Not only are the foreign born as a class found in the large cities in undue proportion, but there is no contributing nationality of which this is not true. Every nationality represented contributes an undue proportion of its numbers to swell our great cities. While but 14 per cent. of the native element of the country is found in these great cities, the Canadians contribute 16 per cent. of their number, the Norwegians, Swedes, and Danes 18 per cent., the British 24 per cent., the Germans 39 per cent., the Irish 42 per cent., the Bohemians 46 per cent., the Poles 49 per cent., and the Italians and Russians each 51 per cent. Thus more than half the whole number of the two last-named nationalities found in the country are congregated in these twenty-eight cities.

Hence it appears that the most objectionable elements of the foreign-born population have flocked in the greatest proportion to our large cities, where they are in a position to do the most harm by corruption and violence.

In New York city alone are found 190,000 Irish, one-tenth of all in the United States; and 210,000 Germans, one-thirteenth of all in the United States. It contains one-fifth of all the Russians and more than one-fifth of all the Italians in the country. Over one-fourth of the total population of the metropolis is made up of persons born in Ireland or Germany.

In Chicago there are 160,000 Germans, constituting nearly one-sixth of the population of that city. It contains one-sixth of all the Poles and more than one-fifth of all the Bohemians of the country. One-sixth of the population of Boston is composed of Irish, and more than one-fourth of the population of Milwaukee is of German birth.

Occupations of the Foreign Born.—As to occupations, it may be stated broadly that the foreign born element is engaged in avocations lower in character than those of the native element, principally in such as involve skilled and unskilled labor; whereas the proportion in the learned professions is much less relative to their numbers than is the case with the native element. While in 1880 the foreign born constituted about one-seventh of the population, it was found that of lawyers, clergymen, physicians, and teachers, there were about eleven native born to one foreign born; on the other hand, among servants there was one foreign born to a little more than three native born. Among unskilled laborers, the foreign born were in the proportion of one to two native born; while of skilled laborers, such as blacksmiths, shoemakers, and carpenters, the proportion was also as one to two, and foreign born miners exceeded in total number the native born.

Illiteracy of the Foreign Born.—This flood of immigration has produced other results upon the population beyond the mere additions to our numbers and the admixture of blood. It has lowered the average intelligence and morality of the community. The illiterate of the northern states are mainly foreign born, the proportion of illiterates among them being four times as great as among the natives. Again, the criminals of foreign birth in the northern states are double their due proportion, as compared with the native born.

Effect of Immigration upon Natural Increase.— Another result of importance has been produced. It is a well-known law of population, that in a broad, general way, as the population increases the rate of increase diminishes. This is an application of the Malthusian doctrine. Now, it matters not in the least how this density of population is brought about, whether by natural increase or by immigration, the result is the same—the country is filled with people, they become more or less crowded, and the rate of natural increase is reduced thereby.

The United States is composed of two sections, the north and the south, which are sharply distinguished from one another in this regard. While the one of them has, throughout its history, depended upon natural increase for its increment of population, the other has had enormous accessions from abroad. What has been the history of the native element in these two sections, as contrasted with one another?

This question is one of interest and importance. In order to answer it intelligently and conclusively, and also for the purpose of ascertaining approximately the effect of immigration upon our rate of increase in population, a comparison is made, in the diagram on page 116, between the rates of increase of the native and white elements of the northern and southern states respectively, for each decade, the upright bars at the bottom of the diagram showing the immigration from 1830 to 1890.

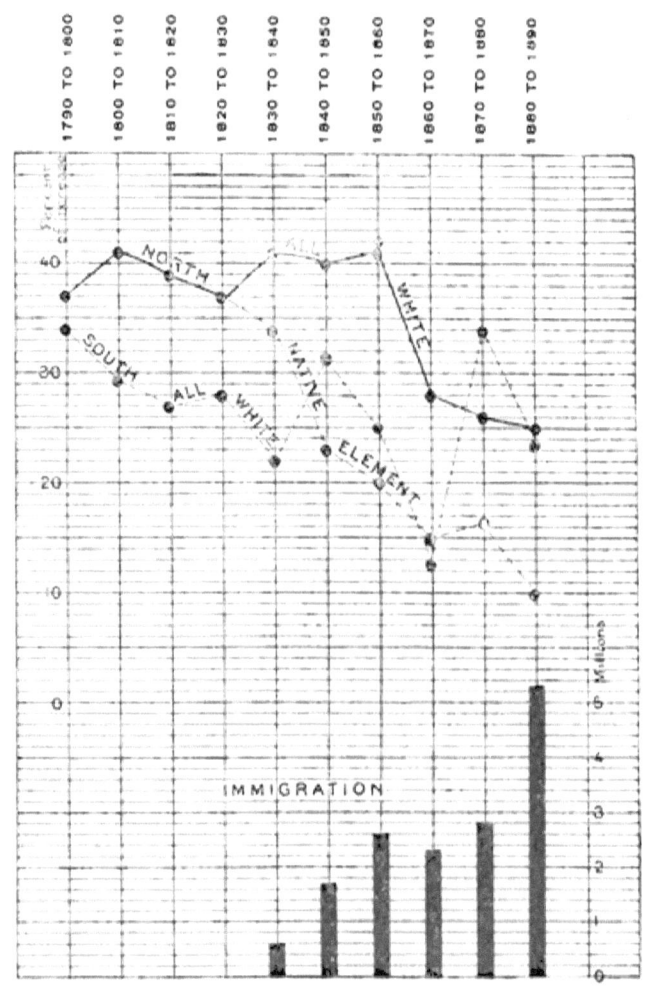

RATES OF INCREASE OF ALL WHITES
AND OF THE
NATIVE ELEMENT OF THE NORTH
AND OF
ALL WHITES OF THE SOUTH

The southern states—including in that designation all of the states east of the plains and south of Mason and Dixon's line, the Ohio river, and the southern boundary of Missouri and Kansas—have received practically no immigration. The states north of this line and east of the plains contain 86 per cent. of the foreign element, the remainder being mainly in the states and territories of the far west.

The rates of increase of the whites of the southern states, which are not complicated by immigration, are represented by the dotted line of the diagram; and, while exhibiting some oscillations, they show a general but not a great diminution from the beginning of our history to the end. Between 1790 and 1840 the white population of these states increased 239 per cent. In other words, the population of 1840 was 3.39 times that of 1790. In the succeeding fifty years the population of these states increased 204 per cent.; that is, their population in 1890 was 3.04 times as great as in 1840, the rate having thus diminished by only 35 per cent. On the other hand, how is it with the northern states?

In the first fifty years, during which there was practically no immigration, the rate of increase in each decade was considerably greater than in the southern states, and altogether during this half century the white population of these northern states increased 389 per cent.; that is, in 1840 the population was 4.89 times as great as in 1790. Between 1840 and 1890, after separating from the white population of these states the immigrants and their natural increase, and thus leaving only the native element, the rate of increase of the latter is seen to diminish remarkably. Instead of ranging from 34 up to 44 per cent. as it did in the first half century, the rates of increase by decades become 23, 20, 15, 16, and 10; while the rate of increase for this entire half century was but 112 per cent., the population in 1890 being but 2.12 times as great as that of 1840. This sudden and astonishingly rapid reduction of the rate in the north, taking place at the same time with the appearance of the flood of immigration, can be attributed to no other cause.

The rate of increase of the north is shown by the full line; the broken line—which commences at 1840 and runs up to 1890—

being the rate of increase of the native element alone, while the full line, continuing on to 1890, represents the rate of increase of the entire population of the north, including the foreign element.

Hence it is safe to conclude that the rate of our natural increase has been greatly reduced by the flood of immigration. By allowing the poor and oppressed of Europe to find homes in this country, we have substituted them for our own flesh and blood. If there had been no immigration, the rate of natural increase which prevailed before immigration commenced would have been much more nearly maintained, and our numbers would be almost as great as at present. The sudden and rapid reduction of our rate of natural increase at the north during the past forty years is surely due to this flood of immigration, and it is a question whether we have gained by the wholesale substitution of a mixture of European for American blood.

Another result has been produced by immigration which is not so apparent, but is of great and far-reaching importance in connection with this question. As has already been stated, the immigration consists, as a rule, of the lower classes, mainly of skilled and unskilled labor; and these millions of mechanics and laborers have filled and practically monopolized the lower classes of avocations at the north. In this way they forced the native American element into the higher walks of life. The head-work of the country is in the hands of Americans almost as fully as it was half a century ago. Our industrial enterprises of all sorts are under the management of Americans, and the hewing of wood and drawing of water have been assumed by the immigrant. The fact that the native is still the ruling element, probably accounts for the other fact that the foreign element, in spite of its great numerical importance, has thus far exercised but little influence upon our political, industrial, and social life.

Foreign Parentage. The effects of immigration upon our population are by no means confined to the foreign born. Although to some extent Americanized, the children of the Irish, Germans, and Scandinavians retain many of their parents' characteristics; measurably they are Irish, Germans, and Scandinavians still. It is interesting, therefore, to observe to what extent our population is composed, not only of the foreign born, but of the children of the foreign born.

In 1870 statistics were obtained for the first time concerning the nativity of parents, and the results were tabulated and published, and in 1890 similar data were obtained. In 1870 the number of persons of foreign parentage, including those of foreign birth, was 11,892,015. The number of inhabitants of native extraction at this time was, therefore, 26,666,356, and the number of whites of native extraction, 21,766,347. In 1890 the number of persons whose parents were foreign born, was 20,263,902. The native born of native parents numbered 42,358,348, and of these the whites numbered 34,720,066. In 1870 the foreign born, added to those of native birth but foreign parentage, comprised practically all of the foreign blood in the country. Only twenty-two or twenty-three years had elapsed since immigration upon a considerable scale had commenced, and it is not at all probable that there were in the country any appreciable number of persons of foreign extraction in the second generation. Nearly all the remainder of the population had been here for a series of generations, so long as to have become distinctively American. Therefore, we may treat that element of our population which in 1870 was of foreign parentage, as comprising the entire element of foreign extraction.

In 1890, forty-two or forty-three years after immigration began, the conditions were measurably changed. There were at that time, undoubtedly, a considerable number—probably quite 5,000,000—of persons of foreign extraction in the second generation.

In 1870 this element of foreign extraction comprised 31 per cent. of the entire population, and in 1890 the same element comprised 32 per cent. The element of native extraction in 1870 comprised 69 per cent., and in 1890, 68 per cent. The whites of native extraction comprised, both in 1870 and 1890, 56 per cent. of the entire population, or considerably more than one-half.

The distribution of the native born of native parentage, is illustrated in the lower map on Plate 13, facing page 112, and in the table on page 120. In the northern states east of the plains, 45 per cent., or nearly one-half of the inhabitants, are either foreign born or the children of foreigners. In Massachusetts they aggregate 56 per cent.; in Rhode Island, 58 per cent.; in Connecticut, 50 per cent.; in New York, 56 per cent.; and in New Jersey, 48 per cent.; but the heaviest proportion is found in the northwestern states. In Wisconsin and Minnesota three-fourths of the people are either foreign born or the children of foreign born, and in the new state of North Dakota four-fifths of the people are of immediate foreign extraction; only one-fifth of the inhabitants of the latter state are of American stock. The constituents of the population of states in 1890 are shown graphically by the diagram, Plate 14.

PROPORTION OF WHITE POPULATION OF NATIVE AND FOREIGN PARENTAGE

STATES AND TERRITORIES	1890		STATES AND TERRITORIES	1890	
	Native Whites of Native Parents	Having one or both Parents Foreign		Native Whites of Native Parents	Having one or both Parents Foreign
	Per cent.	Per cent.		Per cent.	Per cent.
The United States	62.49	37.51	Wisconsin	25.86	74.14
			Minnesota	23.99	76.01
			Iowa	55.97	44.03
North Atlantic Division	51.93	48.07	Missouri	73.42	26.58
			North Dakota	20.55	79.45
Maine	76.86	23.14	South Dakota	38.87	61.13
New Hampshire	67.48	32.52	Nebraska	36.76	64.24
Vermont	67.96	32.04	Kansas	72.09	27.91
Massachusetts	43.13	56.87			
Rhode Island	40.71	59.29	South Central Division	88.97	11.03
Connecticut	48.71	51.29			
New York	42.55	57.45	Kentucky	88.46	11.54
New Jersey	51.89	48.11	Tennessee	96.02	3.98
Pennsylvania	62.90	37.10	Alabama	95.83	4.17
			Mississippi	95.50	4.50
South Atlantic Division	90.62	9.38	Louisiana	73.98	26.02
			Texas	80.62	19.38
Delaware	78.07	21.93	Oklahoma	87.64	12.36
Maryland	60.73	39.27	Arkansas	95.38	4.62
District of Columbia	69.35	30.65			
Virginia	95.75	4.25	Western Division	51.83	48.17
West Virginia	91.80	8.20			
North Carolina	98.97	1.03	Montana	43.99	56.01
South Carolina	96.39	3.61	Wyoming	51.16	48.84
Georgia	96.77	3.23	Colorado	59.87	40.13
Florida	84.91	15.09	New Mexico	83.60	16.40
			Arizona	43.34	56.66
North Central Division	55.91	44.09	Utah	39.25	60.75
			Nevada	37.83	62.17
Ohio	65.12	34.88	Idaho	55.35	44.65
Indiana	79.10	20.90	Washington	54.19	45.81
Illinois	49.96	50.04	Oregon	67.59	32.41
Michigan	44.27	55.73	California	44.77	55.23

THE BUILDING OF A NATION

PLATE 14

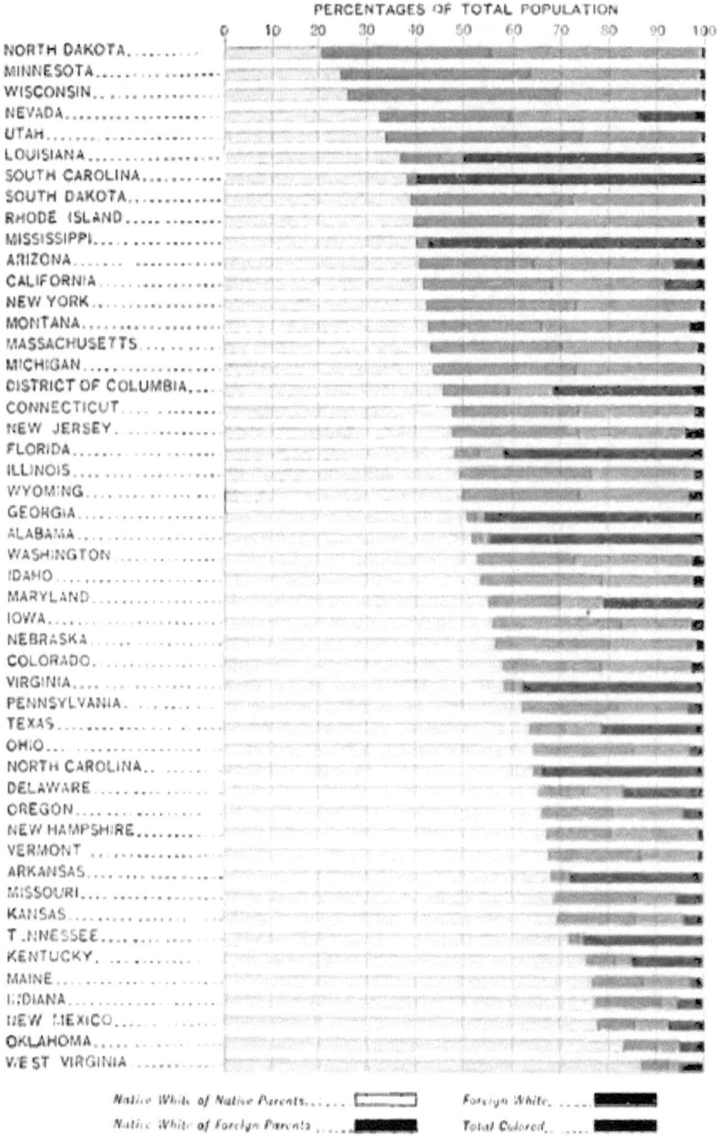

PERCENTAGES OF TOTAL POPULATION

NORTH DAKOTA
MINNESOTA
WISCONSIN
NEVADA
UTAH
LOUISIANA
SOUTH CAROLINA
SOUTH DAKOTA
RHODE ISLAND
MISSISSIPPI
ARIZONA
CALIFORNIA
NEW YORK
MONTANA
MASSACHUSETTS
MICHIGAN
DISTRICT OF COLUMBIA
CONNECTICUT
NEW JERSEY
FLORIDA
ILLINOIS
WYOMING
GEORGIA
ALABAMA
WASHINGTON
IDAHO
MARYLAND
IOWA
NEBRASKA
COLORADO
VIRGINIA
PENNSYLVANIA
TEXAS
OHIO
NORTH CAROLINA
DELAWARE
OREGON
NEW HAMPSHIRE
VERMONT
ARKANSAS
MISSOURI
KANSAS
TENNESSEE
KENTUCKY
MAINE
INDIANA
NEW MEXICO
OKLAHOMA
WEST VIRGINIA

Native White of Native Parents
Native White of Foreign Parents
Foreign White
Total Colored

CONSTITUENTS OF THE POPULATION OF THE STATES IN 1890

In our great cities the situation is even more startling, as will be seen by the diagram on Plate 15, facing page 122, and in the following table, which gives the percentage of native, foreign, and colored, to the total population.

CONSTITUENTS OF THE POPULATION OF THE GREAT CITIES

CITIES	Native of Native Parents	Native of Foreign Parents	Foreign	Colored
Milwaukee	13	48	39	0
New York	18	38	42	2
Chicago	21	56	23	0
Detroit	21	38	40	1
San Francisco	21	27	42	10
Buffalo	22	43	35	0
St. Paul	23	36	40	1
Cleveland	24	38	37	1
Jersey City	25	40	33	2
St. Louis	26	42	26	6
Cincinnati	27	45	24	4
Brooklyn	27	41	32	0
Pittsburg	29	37	31	3
Boston	30	33	35	2
Rochester	30	40	30	0
New Orleans	30	30	14	26
Newark	31	37	30	2
Minneapolis	33	30	37	0
Allegheny	36	36	25	3
Providence	37	30	30	3
Louisville	39	29	15	27
Philadelphia	40	21	35	4
Baltimore	43	26	16	15
Washington	47	12	8	33
Omaha	49	23	25	3
Denver	51	21	24	4
Indianapolis	54	23	14	9
Kansas City	55	19	15	11

Thus, in Boston the native element constitutes but 30 per cent.; in Brooklyn, 28 per cent.; in Buffalo, 22 per cent.; while New York, with only 18 per cent., is practically a foreign city so far as its population is concerned. Chicago contains a native element of but 20 per cent., and Detroit of but 21 per cent.; while among the great cities Milwaukee stands at the head (or foot), with a native element of but 13 per cent. The most extreme case, however, appears to be that of the little city of Ishpeming, in the heart of the iron region of Michigan, a city of some 11,000 people, of which only 6 per cent. are native born of native parents; the remainder, 94 per cent., being foreign born or the children of foreign born.

The following table shows the proportion in which the element of foreign birth of the great cities is made up as regards nationality, the total foreign element of each city being regarded as constituting 100 per cent.:

PROPORTION OF THE PRINCIPAL ELEMENTS OF FOREIGN BIRTH TO THE TOTAL FOREIGN BORN, IN CITIES

CITIES	Germans	Ireland	England Scotland and Wales	Canada and New-foundland	Norway, Sweden, and Denmark	Poland	Russia	Bohemia	Italy
Cincinnati	69	17	5	1	2	2	1	1	1
Milwaukee	69	4	1	2	3	12	1	4	1
Louisville	55	22	5	2	1	1	1	1	1
Baltimore	56	19	6	1	1	1	6	1	1
St. Louis	57	21	6	2	1	1	1	4	1
Indianapolis	51	24	9	3	2	1	1	1	1
Allegheny	54	24	17	1	1	1	1	2	1
Buffalo	48	13	10	12	1	10	5	1	2
Newark	18	24	14	1	1	1	2	1	5
Rochester	14	16	15	15	1	1	3	1	1
Detroit	14	9	12	55	1	1	1	1	1
Cleveland	41	14	15	2	1	3	2	11	1
Brooklyn	36	32	15	2	6	1	1	1	1
Chicago	36	16	9	2	16	5	2	6	1
Pittsburg	31	29	20	1	1	4	3	1	3
New Orleans	33	23	6	1	1	1	1	1	11
New York	34	29	8	1	1	1	8	1	6
St. Paul	31	11	7	7	32	2	1	2	1
Washington	31	38	15	1	1	1	1	1	1
Jersey City	30	42	14	2	2	2	1	1	3
Kansas City	25	25	15	5	11	1	3	1	3
Philadelphia	29	41	18	1	1	1	3	1	3
Omaha	24	22	10	6	32	2	2	2	1
Denver	21	17	29	10	17	1	1	1	2
San Francisco	21	24	11	3	5	1	1	1	4
Minneapolis	13	6	6	13	56	1	1	1	1
Boston	7	45	12	24	4	1	1	1	3
Providence	1	49	25	11	1	1	2	1	1

From this table it appears that more than two-thirds of the foreign element of Cincinnati and Milwaukee are Germans. In Cincinnati one-sixth are Irish; the Germans forming the majority of the foreign element, not only in these two cities, but also in Louisville, Baltimore, St. Louis, Indianapolis, and Allegheny. The German is the leading foreign element in nineteen out of these twenty-eight cities, and stands second in seven more. Thus in twenty-six out of the twenty-eight cities em-

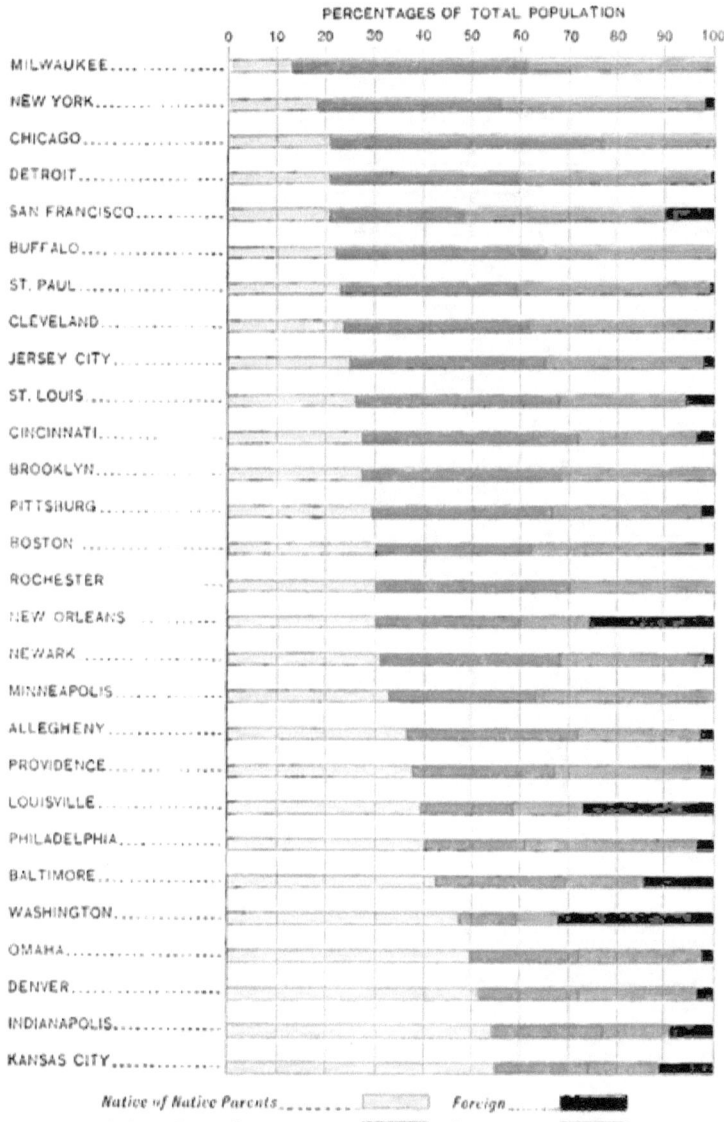

CONSTITUENTS OF THE POPULATION OF THE GREAT CITIES IN 1890

braced in this table, the Germans are either the best or the
next best represented.

The Irish form a plurality in six cities only, but stand second
in fifteen. The Scandinavians—including the Norwegians,
Swedes, and Danes—are more numerous than any other foreign
nationality in the cities of St. Paul, Minneapolis, and Omaha,
and stand second in this regard in Denver. The Italians are
somewhat prominent in New Orleans, being exceeded in numbers only by the Germans and Irish. Many other interesting
features are brought out in this table, especially concerning the
habitat of the people from the south of Europe.

Summary.—The attempt has been made to sum up, in the
diagram on Plate 16, facing page 124, many of the facts concerning the population. This consists in an effort to show the
growth of each element of the population for a century, with its
status at the end of the century.

The breadth of the diagram opposite the years is proportional
to the population at that date, and the breadth of the various
subdivisions is proportional to the numbers of the three elements—colored, native, and foreign. The immigration of each
decade is indicated by the additions between the dates. The
separation between the elements of native and foreign blood is,
of course, only an approximation. A tentative separation was
made, under the assumption that the rate of natural increase of
the foreign element was equal to that of the native element.
Under this assumption the separation was carried forward to
1870, where, as explained above, a definite separation was made
by the census enumeration. This gave a correction which
showed that the natural increase of the foreign element had
been more rapid than that of the native element. Accordingly
the earlier results were corrected, and the rates of increase of
the foreign and of the native elements, thus deduced, were projected forward to 1890. The diagram at the bottom shows
the present status of the population as regards colored, native,
and foreign blood, classifying the last by the leading nationalities.

From this showing it appears that the present composition of
the population is somewhat as follows:

COMPOSITION OF THE POPULATION, 1890

Colored	7,500,000
White of native extraction	30,000,000
White of foreign extraction	25,000,000

The principal elements of the latter are:

German	6,800,000
Irish	6,500,000
British	4,000,000
Canadians	1,600,000
Swedes and Norwegians	1,000,000
Hungarians	500,000
Italians	500,000
Total	20,900,000

The remainder of the 25,000,000 is distributed among various nationalities in small numbers. The white element of native extraction is apparently in the minority to-day in this country, being exceeded in number by the sum of the foreign element and the colored. British blood, however, is still largely in the ascendant; for by adding to the native element the 4,000,000 of British and 6,500,000 of Irish, we get 40,500,000, about two-thirds of the entire population, and three-fourths of the entire white population of the country.

POTENTIAL VOTERS

The number of potential voters—that is, males above the age of twenty-one—was, in 1890, 16,940,311; in 1880 the number was 12,830,349. The increase during the ten years intervening was at the rate of 32.03 per cent., which was far in excess of that of population; as in the case of the militia, this was doubtless due to the excessive immigration of the decade, which consisted in large proportion of adult males. The potential voters formed, in 1890, 27.05 per cent. of the population. In 1880 the same class constituted 25.58 per cent., showing a notable increase in the proportion.

Of the potential voting strength of the nation, 12,591,852, or 74.33 per cent., were native born, and 4,348,459, or 25.67 per cent., were foreign born. The corresponding figures regarding

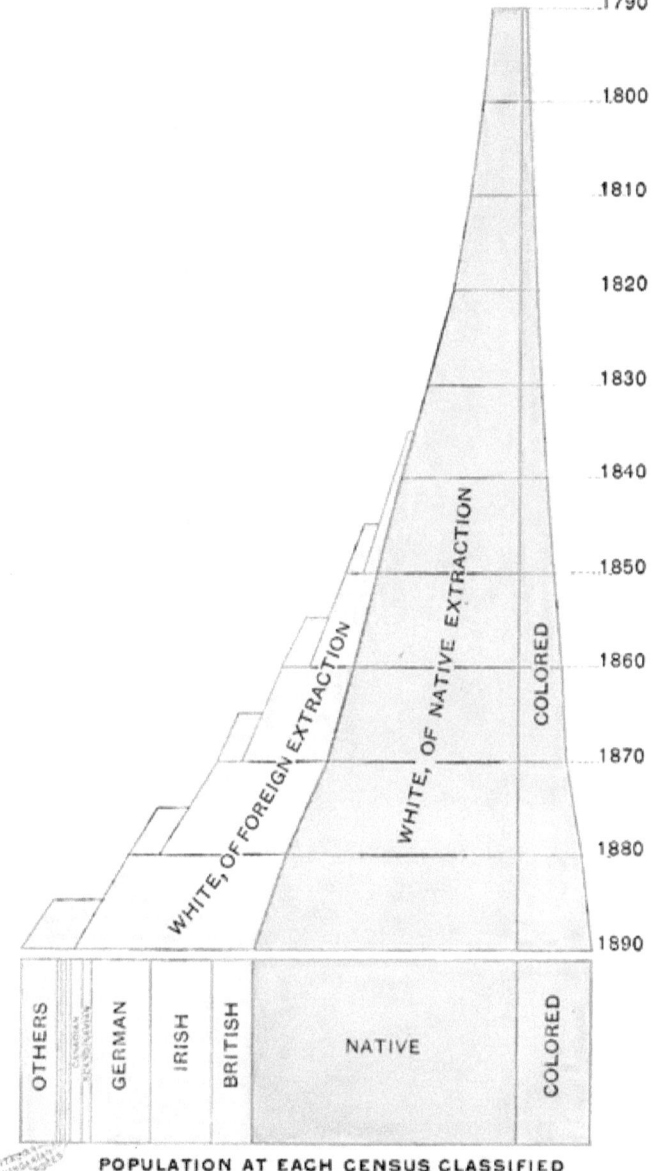

the total population, are 85.23 native born and 14.77 foreign born. This brings out forcibly the great disproportion which the voting strength of the foreign element bears to the total of that element.

Of the total number, 10,957,496, or 64.68 per cent., were native whites, and 1,740,455, or only 10.27 per cent., were colored. The native whites of native parents, or, as nearly as may be, the whites of native extraction, constitute but 52 per cent. of the voting strength of the nation, nearly one-half of the possible voters being either foreign born, native born of foreign parents, or colored. Like the corresponding element of the total population, the strength of the native element is in the south, while in the northwest it is in many states outnumbered, and in a few states greatly outnumbered, by the element of foreign extraction. Thus, in North Dakota the white voters of native extraction form but 21.20 per cent., of the total possible voters. In Minnesota the corresponding proportion is 23.06 per cent.; in Wisconsin, 22.24 per cent. In each of these cases more than three-fourths of the voting strength of the state is of foreign extraction. The following table shows the proportion of the potential voting strength contained in each division of the United States, contrasted with the corresponding proportion of the total population:

PROPORTION OF POTENTIAL VOTERS AND OF TOTAL POPULATION

	Percentage of Voters	Percentage of Population
Northeast division	29.85	27.39
Southeast division	11.89	14.44
North Central division	36.62	35.74
South Central division	14.83	17.52
Western division	6.81	4.84

As in the case of the potential militia, it will be seen that in the northern and western groups of states, the potential voting strength is disproportionately large as compared with the total population, while the reverse is true as to the southern groups.

ALIENS

The number of adult males of foreign birth in 1890 was 4,348,459. Of this number 2,546,037, or 58.55 per cent., have been naturalized, and 236,069, or 5.43 per cent., have taken out first papers. Thus it appears that nearly two-thirds of the possible voters among our foreign born, have either acquired citizenship or have taken the preliminary steps toward that end; 1,160,214, or 26.68 per cent., are returned as aliens; while the remainder, constituting 9.34 per cent., furnish no information regarding citizenship.

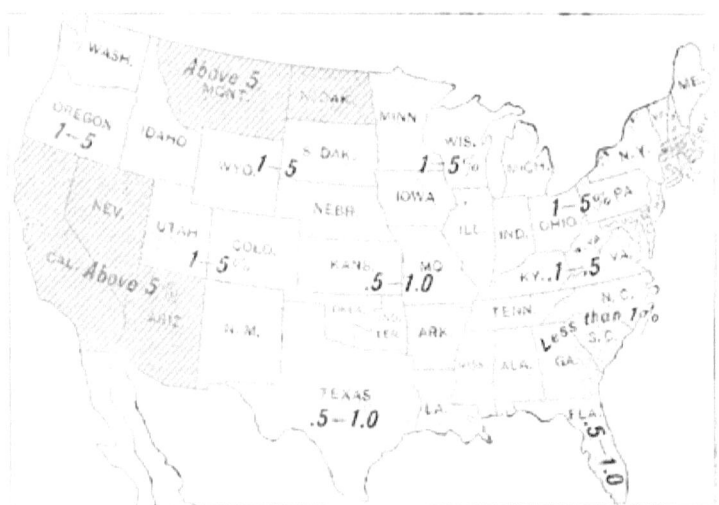

PROPORTION OF ALIENS TO TOTAL POPULATION IN 1890

The distribution of the aliens is a matter of much interest. It is illustrated on the above map. Since the foreign born element is of slight importance in the Southern states, the question of its citizenship is of still less interest and may therefore be dropped from discussion; it is in the Northern and Western states only that the foreign element is of importance. In the North Atlantic division more than a third of the foreign born males of voting age—to be exact, 34.43 per cent.—are aliens; in Maine the proportion is no less than 44.51 per cent.; in New Hampshire, 50.05 per cent.; in Rhode Island, 49.78 per cent. This large proportion in the New England states is probably due in great measure to the irruption of the French-Canadians, most of whom have come over the border as an alien people with no intention of forming a part of our body politic. The proportion of aliens in the North Central division is, on the other hand, comparatively small, being but 18.78 per cent. The largest proportion among these states is in North Dakota, where it is 26.53 per cent.; while in Minnesota it is 16.85 per cent., and in Wisconsin 15.49 per cent. These, it will be remembered, are the three states in which the foreign born element and the element of foreign extraction are greatest.

The proportion of aliens in the western division is 32.09 per cent. It is greatest in Arizona, where it is 48.17 per cent., and least in Colorado, where it is but 23.89 per cent. In Utah, where the element of foreign extraction constitutes two-thirds of the population, the proportion of the foreign born males of voting age who are aliens is but 25.51 per cent.

ILLITERACY

For the statistics of illiteracy we are dependent upon the census, and unfortunately, these are among the last statistics to be compiled from the schedules. Thus, while most of the other matter has been digested and is before the public, the statistics of illiteracy for 1890 are not yet available, and we are thrown back upon those for 1880. With these figures, coupled with our information concerning the movement of population and of social conditions, it is possible to form a very close estimate of the condition and distribution of illiteracy at the present time.

We know that in the ten years that have elapsed the school system of the Southern states has been greatly improved, both for whites and blacks, and that the enrollment and attendance have increased; hence it may safely be inferred that throughout the south the proportion of illiteracy, both of white and colored, has been reduced, and probably to a considerable extent. In the north, on the other hand, we cannot expect to find any favorable change. The schools of the north have improved, but the enrollment and attendance have diminished, and consequently we may look for an increase in the proportion of illiterates in this part of the country. It is scarcely necessary to explain that this condition of things in the north is due to the unprecedented immigration of the last decade, which has brought not only large numbers of foreigners, but foreigners of a lower class in all respects than ever before. It is probable that the net result of all these factors upon the illiteracy of the country, will show but trifling change as a whole.

With this preface let us see what the statistics of the tenth census had to show regarding the illiteracy of the population. The census asks two questions on this subject: "Can he read?" and "Can he write?" Either of these is a sufficient test of elementary education, and so it will be unnecessary to give the answers to both. Let us therefore consider only the second of these interrogatories: "Can he write?"

In 1880 75 per cent. of the population were of the age of ten years and upward. Taking the country at large, including all sections, all races and all nativities, 17 per cent., or very nearly one-sixth, of those of the age of ten and over were unable to write. Of the whites, only 9.4 per cent. were unable to write; and dividing the number into those of native and of foreign birth, the proportions of those unable to write were respectively 8.7 and 12 per cent. Of the colored element, not less than 70 per cent. were unable to fashion letters. As regards sex, there appears to have been slightly more illiteracy among females than among males, particularly with the colored race.

The geographical distribution of illiteracy differs widely in different parts of the country, especially when the results are analyzed by race and nativity. The maps on Plates 17 and 18 show the geographical distribution of illiteracy among the total population, the native whites, the colored, and the foreign born. In the south generally, not only among the colored people but among the whites also, the proportion of illiteracy was high,

THE BUILDING OF A NATION
PLATE 17

PROPORTION OF PERSONS WHO CANNOT WRITE, TO POPULATION, TEN YEARS OF AGE OR OVER IN 1880

PROPORTION OF NATIVE WHITES WHO CANNOT WRITE, TO ALL NATIVE WHITES OF TEN YEARS OF AGE OR OVER IN 1880

PLATE 18

PROPORTION OF COLORED PERSONS WHO CANNOT WRITE, TO ALL COLORED TEN YEARS OF AGE OR OVER IN 1880

PROPORTION OF FOREIGN BORN WHO CANNOT WRITE, TO ALL FOREIGN BORN TEN YEARS OF AGE OR OVER IN 1880

doubtless owing in great part to the absence of public schools in that section except during the fifteen years preceding the tenth census. In the South Atlantic and South Central states, taken as a whole, the proportion of those unable to write was 40 per cent.; of colored it was 75 per cent., and of whites 20.8 per cent.

In the North Atlantic and Northern Central states there was but little illiteracy among the native born, the proportion to the inhabitants of ten years of age and over being but 4 per cent.; while among the foreign born it was more than three times as great, being 12½ per cent. Thus, the illiterate element of the north in 1880 was the foreign born element, as it doubtless is at present.

Illiteracy is not, however, uniformly distributed among the foreign born, being much greater at the east than at the west. In the North Central states the proportions of illiteracy among the native whites, and among the foreign born, were respectively 4.9 and 8.8 per cent., while in the northeastern states the like proportions were 2.8 and 15.4 per cent., respectively.

In New England the proportions were still more sharply contrasted. Of the native whites, only 1.3 per cent. were unable to write, while of the foreign born no less than 21.4 per cent. were deficient in this regard. It is probable that the greater proportion of ignorance among the foreign born of the eastern than of the western states, was due partly to the difference in the nativities represented in these two sections of the country. In the northeastern states there were many French-Canadians, who are not only ignorant, but refuse to avail themselves of the facilities for education afforded by the public schools. In these states are found also the great majority of the Irish immigrants, who are measurably in a similar condition. Moreover, the poor and less enterprising of the immigrants, those who are content to remain where they are dropped upon our shores, or who, lacking the means to reach the interior, remained in the seaboard cities, have thus increased the proportion of illiterates of the eastern states.

9

EDUCATION

Public Schools.—Even as long ago as colonial times, the New England colonies recognized the need of education as an essential to good citizenship, and provided the means of acquiring it at public cost. The system of public schools which originated in New England, was carried by her sons wherever they migrated. Thus the system grew up with the Northern Central and Western states. In the Southern states, on the other hand, the public school system, now universal, is of comparatively recent introduction. Before the civil war, there were few public schools in the south, the system having been developed in those states since that struggle.

The public schools are supported mainly by direct taxation, which in many states is laid for that express purpose. Moreover, in most of the states there are school funds, derived from various sources, the income from which is thus applied. One prominent source of these funds consists of the public lands donated by the general government to the states in aid of education. In each of the states in which public lands existed, the United States has thus given the sixteenth, and in most of them also the thirty-sixth section of each township for this purpose, and from the sale of these lands large funds have been created.

Besides the public school system, now in full operation in every state and territory, certain religious organizations, particularly the Lutheran and Catholic churches, maintain separate schools, and, furthermore, there are large numbers of private schools, which, strange as it may appear, are well supported.

The public school system embraces, in all cities, high schools which carry forward the education of the young to the point of fitting them to enter colleges and professional schools.

Throughout the south separate schools are maintained for the white and colored races.

Enrollment.—The total number of children enrolled in schools, in 1890, was 14,219,571. The total number of children of school age, which is arbitrarily assumed at from five to seventeen years inclusive, was 18,543,200, or nearly 30 per cent. of the population. The school enrollment was 75 per cent. of the children of school age. The attendance at school was about two-thirds of the enrollment. Therefore it appears that about one-half of the total number of children of school age attended school.

Of the total number of children enrolled in all schools, 12,728,-417, or about nine-tenths of the whole, were enrolled in the public schools; 753,972 were enrolled in private schools, and 737,182 in parochial schools.

The upper map on Plate 19, facing page 132, shows the proportion, by states, which the enrollment in schools of all kinds bears to the number of children of school age. It shows that the highest proportion of enrollment is at the north, and the lowest at the south, as was to have been expected. In Kansas, Iowa, Maine, and Vermont more than nine-tenths of all children of school age are enrolled in the schools. The banner state in this regard is Kansas, which enrolls not less than 94 per cent. of her children, while Maine and Iowa each enroll 93 per cent.

The converse of this picture is seen at the south. Arkansas enrolls but 58 per cent. of her children, and South Carolina but 52 per cent., while of all the states Louisiana stands at the foot, with but 40 per cent. Strangely enough the purely rural state of Mississippi, with an immense colored population, enrolls not less than 79 per cent. of her children, or nearly double the proportion of the adjoining state of Louisiana.

Expenditure.—In the public schools the total number of teachers, in 1890, was 363,935; of these a little more than one-third were males, and a little less than two-thirds females. The total expenditure on account of the public schools was $140,277,-484, being at the average rate of $17 for each pupil in average attendance. The lower map on Plate 19, facing page 132, shows the average amount expended per pupil enrolled, in different parts of the country.

The amount thus expended in the several states ranged from about $2 in Alabama to $25 in Colorado. Throughout the south generally the amount expended was small, the highest expenditure in any state being $7 per capita, in Texas.

Of all the Northern states Maine expends the least per pupil enrolled, the amount being only $7. In the upper Mississippi valley and in the lake states the amount ranges from $10 to $14. Generally speaking, the rate of expenditure in the western states is very high, exceeding $20 per capita in Montana, Wyoming, Colorado, Nevada, and California. The only eastern state in which the rate exceeded $20, was Massachusetts.

A comparison of the statistics of enrollment in the public schools of the country in 1890, with similar figures for 1880, is highly suggestive of the ill effects of immigration upon the community. While in the ten years between 1880 and 1890 the whole number of children enrolled in the public schools of the country, as a whole, increased more rapidly than the population, it appears, when these figures are analyzed, that this increase has been effected almost entirely in the Southern states; while in the northern states east of the Great Plains, with the single exception of Rhode Island, the increase of enrollment has not been as great as that of population. In every northern state east of the plains, with this one exception, fewer children are now enrolled in the public schools, in proportion to the population, than ten years ago. This situation is developed by the first map on Plate 19. Considering the advanced position of the northern states in matters relating to the education of the young, this result can be attributed to no other cause than the swarm of foreign ignorance let loose upon us.

The following is a summary statement of the colleges and professional schools throughout the country, and the attendance thereat:

COLLEGES AND PROFESSIONAL SCHOOLS, AND ATTENDANCE

	Institutions.	Students.
Colleges	415	118,581
Colleges for women	179	24,851
Theological schools	145	7,053
Law schools	54	4,518
Medical schools	117	15,484

THE BUILDING OF A NATION

PLATE 19

PROPORTION OF ENROLLMENT IN ALL SCHOOLS, TO CHILDREN OF SCHOOL AGE IN 1890

EXPENDITURE IN DOLLARS, PER CAPITA, OF CHILDREN ENROLLED IN PUBLIC SCHOOLS IN 1890

OCCUPATIONS

For our conceptions of the occupations of the people we are dependent, as in the case of illiteracy, upon the statistics of the tenth census, which portrayed the situation as it existed in 1880. It is modified by certain considerations of which we are able to take cognizance, such as the character and extent of the immigration, and the known course of development in certain branches of industry.

Let us first look at the situation as it existed in 1880. The census takes account only of those occupations which can be classified as gainful; i. e., those at which men and women labor for a pecuniary reward. The occupations of housewives, of children attending school, etc., do not come into this category.

In 1880, out of a population of 50,000,000, 17,400,000 persons were engaged in gainful occupations. This was 34.8 per cent. of the whole number; in other words, a little more than one-third of the entire population were breadwinners. Classifying these breadwinners by sex, it will be seen that about 85 per cent. were males and 15 per cent. females.

The census separates occupations into four great general classes, according to the character of the industries:

First, Those which relate to agriculture, including farmers, planters, cattle raisers, nurserymen, farm laborers, etc.

Second, Professional and Personal Services, which includes all persons performing personal services of whatever grade or degree, from the highest professional character down to that of domestic servants and bootblacks. Were the two classes, professional and personal, separated one from another, the classes would have a definite meaning.

Third, Trade and Transportation. Here again are two classes which should be distinguished. Merchants and dealers, with their clerks, salesmen, etc., can be easily separated from the employés of the agencies of transportation, such as railroads, water craft, etc.

Fourth, Manufactures and Mining. This is a sufficiently distinctive group, although it includes not only skilled workmen but unskilled laborers.

This classification tells very little concerning the number of breadwinners in the various stations of life, since each group includes persons in all stations, from the highest to the lowest. It is a classification based upon product rather than upon occupation.

The following little table shows the proportion which each one of these classes bears to the total number of breadwinners:

DISTRIBUTION OF BREADWINNERS BY CLASSES

    Agriculture................................44 per cent.
    Professional and personal services.... ....24 "   "
    Trade and transportation............ ....10 "
    Manufactures..... ....22 "

The proportion of persons engaged in agriculture is constantly diminishing, while that of the other three classes is as constantly increasing, and it is probable that within a generation the proportion of those engaged in manufactures and mining will become the ruling class. The following table shows by states, and groups of states, the proportion which those engaged in gainful occupations bear to the total population, and the proportion which the number of workers in each of these four classes bear to the total number of workers in each state. The maps on Plate 20 show the distribution of those engaged in agriculture, and in manufacturing and mining, expressed in terms of the proportions which their numbers bear to the total number of wage-earners.

PROPORTION OF THE NUMBER OF PERSONS IN THE UNITED STATES ENGAGED IN EACH CLASS OF OCCUPATIONS

STATES AND TERRITORIES	Proportion of those engaged in Gainful Occupations to Total Population	Proportion of those engaged in Agriculture to all persons occupied	Proportion of those engaged in Professional and Personal Services to all persons occupied	Proportion of those engaged in Trade and Transportation to all persons occupied	Proportion of those engaged in Manufactures, Mechanical and Mining Industries to all persons occupied
The United States	35	44	24	10	22
Alabama	39	77	15	3	5
Arizona.............	55	15	37	15	33
Arkansas............	32	83	9	4	4
California...........	44	21	32	15	32
Colorado............	52	13	25	15	47

THE BUILDING OF A NATION

PLATE 20

PROPORTION OF PERSONS ENGAGED IN AGRICULTURE TO ALL WAGE EARNERS IN 1880

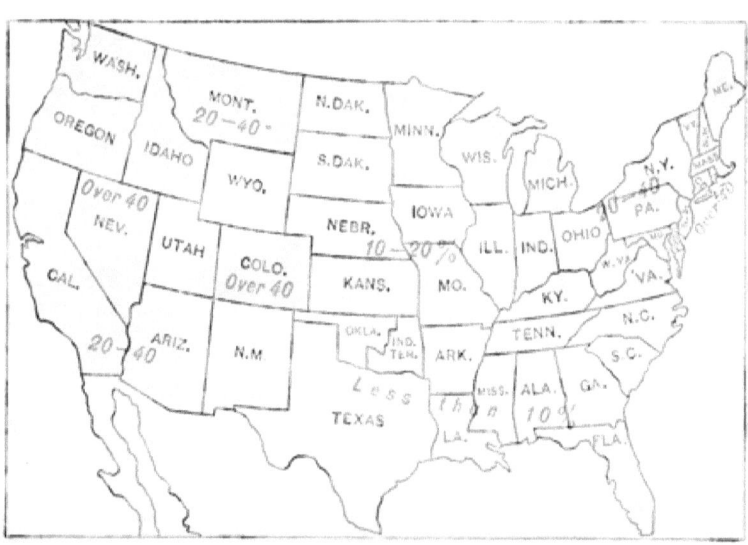

PROPORTION OF PERSONS ENGAGED IN MANUFACTURING AND MINING TO ALL WAGE EARNERS IN 1880

PROPORTION OF THE NUMBER OF PERSONS IN THE UNITED STATES ENGAGED IN EACH CLASS OF OCCUPATIONS—*Continued*

States and Territories.	Proportion of those engaged in Gainful Occupations to Total Population.	Proportion of those engaged in Agriculture to all persons occupied.	Proportion of those engaged in Professional and Personal Services to all persons occupied.	Proportion of those engaged in Trade and Transportation to all persons occupied.	Proportion of those engaged in Manufactures, Mechanical and Mining Industries to all persons occupied.
Connecticut	39	18	21	12	49
Dakota	43	49	24	11	16
Delaware	37	33	32	9	26
District of Columbia	38	2	60	15	23
Florida	34	64	20	7	9
Georgia	39	72	17	4	7
Idaho	48	25	25	9	41
Illinois	32	44	23	13	20
Indiana	32	52	22	9	17
Iowa	33	57	20	10	13
Kansas	32	64	17	8	11
Kentucky	32	62	20	6	12
Louisiana	39	57	27	8	8
Maine	36	35	20	13	32
Maryland	35	28	31	15	26
Massachusetts	40	9	24	16	51
Michigan	35	42	25	10	23
Minnesota	33	52	23	10	15
Mississippi	37	82	12	3	3
Missouri	32	51	22	11	16
Montana	57	20	31	13	36
Nebraska	34	59	19	10	12
Nevada	52	13	32	14	41
New Hampshire	41	31	20	8	41
New Jersey	35	15	28	17	40
New Mexico	34	35	47	8	10
New York	37	20	29	18	33
North Carolina	34	75	15	3	7
Ohio	31	40	25	10	25
Oregon	39	40	25	9	26
Pennsylvania	34	21	31	12	36
Rhode Island	42	9	21	13	57
South Carolina	39	75	16	4	5
Tennessee	29	66	21	5	8
Texas	33	69	19	7	5
Utah	28	36	28	10	26
Vermont	36	47	24	7	22
Virginia	33	51	30	6	13
Washington	40	42	22	12	24
West Virginia	28	61	18	6	15
Wisconsin	32	47	25	9	21
Wyoming	43	19	45	17	19

Taking the country over, the average proportion of those engaged in gainful occupations to the total population, as stated above, in 1880, was 34.8 per cent. In all the North Atlantic states, with the exception of Pennsylvania, this proportion was exceeded; and in southern New England it was greatly exceeded, being in Rhode Island not less than 42 per cent., in New Hampshire 41 per cent., and in Massachusetts 40 per cent. The excessive proportion of persons engaged in gainful occupations in these states is doubtless due in the main to the great extension of the factory system, employing female labor, as is further shown by the statistics of occupations distributed by sex. In the North Central states the proportion of persons engaged in gainful occupations was below the average in nearly every case, being exceeded only in the then territory of Dakota. The Southern states showed great diversity in this respect. The Virginias, North Carolina, Kentucky, Tennessee, Arkansas, Texas, and Florida had less than the average proportion of persons with occupations, while in the other states the average was exceeded. The excess in the cotton states is probably due to the fact that the colored population, men, women, and children, work in the fields. In the Western states, with the exception of Idaho and New Mexico, the proportion of persons with occupations ranged very high in 1880, for the reason that they were then in an unsettled social condition, the proportion of adult males being great.

The distribution of the classes of occupations over the country, accords with the relative prevalence of the different industries suggested by these occupations. Of all persons in the country reported as having gainful occupations, 44 per cent. were engaged in agriculture. In all the states lying south of the Potomac and Ohio rivers, and west to the western boundary of Texas, those engaged in agriculture constituted more than half of all those having occupations. This was true also among the Northern Central states of Indiana, Minnesota, Iowa, Missouri, Kansas, and Nebraska, which are the agricultural states *par excellence* of the Northern Central section. In some of the Southern states, mainly those of the cotton belt, the proportion ranged very high. Thus in Arkansas 83 per cent. of the persons occupied were engaged in agriculture; in Mississippi, 82 per cent.; in Alabama, 77 per cent.; in the Carolinas, 75 per cent.; and in Georgia, 72 per cent. The other extreme was reached in New England, where in Massachusetts and Rhode Island but 9 per cent. were engaged in agriculture; in New Jersey, 15 per cent.; in Connecticut, 18 per cent.; in New York, 20 per cent.; and in Pennsylvania, 21 per cent. In the far west the proportion engaged in agriculture is generally low, owing mainly to the prevalence of mining. Thus in Colorado and Nevada but 13 per cent. were engaged in agriculture; in Arizona, 15 per cent.; in Wyoming, 19 per cent.; in Montana, 20 per cent.; and in California, 21 per cent.

The obverse of this picture is presented by the statistics of those engaged in manufacturing, mechanical, and mining occupations. In this class of occupations the Southern states are very feebly represented; in Mississippi but 3 per cent. were so engaged, and in Arkansas but 4 per cent.; in South Carolina, Alabama, and Texas, but 5 per cent.; in North Carolina and Georgia, only 7 per cent. On the other hand, in Massachusetts and Rhode Island more than half the population were engaged in this class of avocations, and very nearly half in Connecticut. In New Hampshire 41 per cent. were so engaged; in New Jersey, 40 per cent.; and in Pennsylvania, 36 per cent. Passing westward, we find that Ohio had gained rapidly as a manufacturing state, one-fourth of the population being occupied in these avocations. Indiana was less advanced, having but 17 per cent., and was exceeded on the north by Michigan with 23 per cent., and on the west by Illinois with 20 per cent. The states of the plains had smaller proportions: Kansas, 11 per cent.; Nebraska, 12 per cent.; and Dakota, 16 per cent. In the states and territories of the far west, in which mining was prominent in 1880, the proportion engaged in this class of avocations was high. Colorado showing 47 per cent., Nevada and Idaho each 41 per cent., and Montana 36 per cent. At that time the average of the entire country showed 22 per cent. engaged in this group of occupations.

The following table gives, for the whole United States, the proportion which the breadwinners of each principal nationality bore, in 1880, to the total number of that nationality living in the country:

PROPORTION OF BREADWINNERS OF EACH NATIONALITY

United States	32 per cent.
Ireland	53 " "
Germany	53 " "
Great Britain	51 " "
Norway and Sweden	54 " "
Canada	49 " "

From this it appears that the proportion of breadwinners among the foreign born was far greater than among the native born. This prominent fact is due to several causes. In the first place, the immigration consists in large proportion of adult males, a fact which in itself is sufficient to account for this difference. Moreover, the greater part of the immigration comes from countries in which women as well as men play a considerable part as breadwinners, especially among the lower classes from which the immigration is largely drawn.

The following table shows the proportion in which the breadwinners of different nationalities are distributed among the great groups of occupations above described:

DISTRIBUTION OF BREADWINNERS BY OCCUPATIONS

	Agriculture	Professional and Personal	Trade and Transportation	Manufactures and Mining
United States	50	22	10	18
Ireland	14	43	14	29
Germany	28	21	15	36
Great Britain	22	17	12	49
Norway and Sweden	45	25	8	22
Canada	21	26	9	44

This table brings out in strong relief certain facts regarding the occupations of different nationalities. The farming class is mostly recruited from the native born, one-half of these being engaged in that group of occupations. No other nationality approaches it in this regard, excepting Norwegians and Swedes, of whom 45 per cent. pursue agricultural callings. Next are the Germans with 28 per cent., and least of all the Irish with only 14 per cent. In personal and professional services the Irish come first, 43 per cent. being engaged in this great mixed group of occupations, while our native citizens stand very low, and the natives of Great Britain lowest of all. In manufactures and mining the natives stand lowest, only 18 per cent. of their number being engaged in this group of avocations, while the British stand at the head with fully one-half their number, followed by the Canadians with 44 per cent.

Let us now examine into the distribution of the native and foreign elements that compose our mixed body politic, with reference to certain selected occupations which are indicative of stations in life. In the following table these selected occupations are arranged in order, from the highest to the lowest, and the figures opposite them express by percentages the proportion which the number of wage-earners in each occupation bears to the total number of wage-earners among the native born, and the foreign born:

RATIO OF NATIVE AND FOREIGN BORN WAGE EARNERS TO TOTAL POPULATION, BY CLASSES

	Native Born	Foreign Born
Clergymen, physicians, lawyers	1.5	0.7
Teachers	1.5	0.4
Farmers	26.0	17.6
Traders	2.5	4.0
Clerks, accountants, and salesmen	2.7	1.9
Iron and steel workers	0.5	1.2
Miners	0.8	3.6
Textile operatives	1.3	3.7
Domestic servants	5.9	7.3
Farm laborers	22.0	4.6
Laborers	9.6	14.9

From this table it is at once apparent that, as a rule, the native born occupy stations higher in life than the foreign born. Thus the proportion of clergymen, physicians, and lawyers among the native born is double that among the foreign born; of teachers, it is nearly four times as great; of farmers, it is 50 per cent. greater; of traders, it is, however, considerably less. Of clerks, accountants, and salesmen the proportion is greater, while of skilled workers it is less than one-half; of miners, less than one-fourth; and of textile operatives, a little more than one-third. The proportion of native born domestic servants and of laborers is much smaller; while of farm laborers it is, on the other hand, many times as great, owing to the indisposition of the foreign born to engage in agricultural pursuits, a matter that has been treated more fully elsewhere.

Occupations of Immigrants.—All of the foregoing figures and conclusions relate to the status of the population as it existed in 1880. Since that time we have the statistics of immigration during the decade, an immigration which numbered 5,250,000. These immigrants have been classified by the Bureau of Statistics according to occupations, and the results supplement those of the census of 1880 and indicate very clearly what we may expect to learn when the statistics of occupations from the eleventh census become available. Of the total number of immigrants, 2,246,000, or about 43 per cent., were wage-earners. This proportion is somewhat less than that of the foreign element in the country in 1880. The immigrants having no occupations probably consisted almost entirely of women and children under fifteen years of age. These two classes comprise just about one-half of the total number of immigrants. Of those reported as having gainful occupations, the following proportions are found, 3 per cent. being unknown:

OCCUPATIONS OF IMMIGRANTS CLASSIFIED

Professional occupations	1 per cent.
Traders and dealers	3 " "
Farmers	14 " "
Household servants	9 " "
Skilled labor	20 " "
Unskilled labor	50 " "

So far as this classification conforms to that in the last table, derived from the tenth census, it shows a great increase in the lower classes of occupations, especially in that of unskilled labor. The proportion of traders and dealers, and of farmers, has diminished, while that of household servants and of common laborers has greatly increased.

The Bureau of Statistics has published a classification of occupations of immigrants from 1820 to 1890, and it will be instructive to analyze the tables—especially since 1840, when immigration began on a considerable scale to determine whether, as is commonly asserted, the quality of the immigration, as indicated by occupations, has deteriorated in recent years. The following table shows by decades the proportion which the number of immigrants, in each of four characteristic classes, bears to the total number of immigrants:

RATIO OF IMMIGRANTS ENGAGED IN CERTAIN CLASSES OF LABOR TO TOTAL IMMIGRANTS

	Professional	Skilled	Farmers	Laborers
1840–50	0.4	1.0	11.6	15.8
1850–60	0.3	0.9	15.9	20.8
1860–70	0.6	1.3	9.5	22.9
1870–80	0.8	1.2	9.2	17.9
1880–90	0.5	1.0	7.0	25.4

From this table it appears that the professional class, though always very small, increased up to 1880, but that in the last decade it has diminished decidedly; that skilled labor increased somewhat up to 1870, and since then has been diminishing; that since 1860 the farming class have diminished steadily and rapidly, and now constitute less than half the proportion they did between 1850 and 1860; that the class of unskilled laborers increased up to 1870, diminished between 1870 and 1880, and in the last decade has increased very greatly and constituted a much larger proportion of the total immigration than ever before, exceeding one-fourth of the whole number of immigrants.

On the whole, this table certainly indicates, so far as occupations go, a decided deterioration in quality, especially during the last ten years, and fully substantiates the popular idea.

Changes in Occupations.—Owing to the rapid substitution of machinery for human labor and skill in manufacturing, a radical change has taken place during the last quarter of a century in the character of the occupations of the manufacturing classes. Within the recollection of most persons now living, things were made by skilled workmen—blacksmiths, wheelwrights, cabinet makers, tailors, etc. At present, however, the skilled trades are but feebly represented, and will soon be obsolete. In their place has sprung up a vast army of machine tenders, whose function is simply to feed the machines and see that they do their work properly. The same machine, under the same superintendence, may make a great variety of articles.

Thus the occupations of labor, instead of becoming more complex, as is commonly supposed, are in fact becoming greatly simplified. Labor, instead of being differentiated, is becoming homogeneous.

Science, in its application to the industrial arts, is constantly bearing fruit in the form of new machines to supplant human skill and manual labor. Yet the demand for labor is greater than ever, if we may judge by a comparison of the past and present rates of wages. This would be a paradox were the demand for manufactured articles to remain constant; but with the introduction of machinery comes a cheapening of the product, and with the cheapening of the product comes in turn an increased demand, as the community rises to a higher scale of comfort and luxury, and thus the demand keeps pace with the supply.

Wages.—The condition of the laboring classes in the United States is greatly superior to that in any European country. It is well known that wages are higher; but the fact that the purchasing power of their wages is greater, though equally true, is perhaps not so generally accepted. In other words, the wages in terms of food and clothing are higher. The Bureau of Labor finds that wages in Massachusetts are higher than in Great Britain in the proportion of 170 to 100, while commodities are also higher in the proportion of 117 to 100. To sum up, it appears that wages, expressed in commodities, are about 40 per cent. higher in Massachusetts than in Great Britain.

The American workingman is better fed, clothed, and housed, and enjoys more luxuries, than his European brother. Why? The protectionists attribute it to the tariff. If so, why are not the working classes of Germany, Russia, Austria, Italy, and Spain, all of them protected countries, equally prosperous? Is it not due rather to the fact that this is a new country, in which development is going on rapidly; in which, speaking broadly, there is an abundance of work, and comparatively few to do it? In short, is not the demand for labor crowding upon the supply?

The high price and scarcity of labor have greatly stimulated invention. It is a common saying, that, thanks to machinery, a man of to-day can produce as much as a hundred men of the last century, and the saying is in great part true. We have devised machines for making almost everything, and they can do almost everything except think.

TRADES UNIONS

In recent years, the laboring classes have formed organizations, or trades unions. These are much more complete and powerful among the various classes of skilled labor than among the unskilled classes, which are as yet but feebly organized. Most of the skilled trades are represented in the American Federation of Labor, which is said to include a membership of about 650,000, thus representing not far from one per cent. of the population, and ten per cent. of the laboring classes. The principal trade organizations included in the Federation, are as follows:

ELEMENTS OF THE AMERICAN FEDERATION OF LABOR

Carpenters and Joiners	63,000
Brotherhood of Locomotive Firemen	24,000
Brotherhood of Locomotive Engineers	30,500
Brotherhood of Railway Trainmen	24,000
Iron Molders' Union	36,000
Amalgamated Association of Iron and Steel Workers	45,000
International Typographical Union	29,000
Journeymen Tailors' Union	18,500

Whatever may be the avowed purposes of trades unions, their principal object is to control rates of wages in their own interest. In this matter they have shown the want of foresight and breadth of view which was to have been expected from the classes making up their membership. The controlling element in these organizations is of foreign birth or immediate foreign extraction. Their plan of operations is direct and simple; it is to obtain, in detail, every concession that it is possible to wring from the employers, using every weapon at hand, legal or illegal, such as blackmail, boycott, or violence. By such a policy they have scored many seeming successes, but at the cost of alienating to a large extent the sympathies of the community, and of discouraging industry in many localities, thereby reducing the demand for labor therein. The struggle between employers and employés has already become so bitter, that a large and rapidly increasing proportion of the former refuse to employ members of labor organizations.

This narrow, short-sighted policy of the labor organizations is certain to injure the laborer in the long run. Any hostile attitude toward employers is as injurious to the interests of the laborers as would be a similar attitude on the part of employers toward employés.

There are, however, many things which these organizations can undertake that would be of permanent good to their class, and that would injure no one. Indeed, there are measures which, if carried out, would better their condition permanently and rationally; prominent among them is the restriction of immigration. The worst enemy of the American laboring man is the European laboring man. If immigration is to go on unchecked, labor before many decades will become as abundant here, in proportion to the demand, as in Europe; and when that time arrives, all the trades unions in America will be unable to keep its price above the European standard.

INVENTION

The high price of labor in this country has induced an activity of invention unparalleled in other times and in other lands. From the cotton-gin to the telephone, the list of American inventions is almost identical with that of the world.

The steamboat and the locomotive have revolutionized traffic and reduced the earth to a fraction of its former dimensions. Not only has the railway increased the rate of travel ten times, but it has also vastly increased the comforts of travel, chief among which are sleeping-cars. The safety of travelers is provided for, not only by the character of the railway employés, but by scores of devices, such as the Westinghouse air brake and the block system of running trains.

By means of refrigerator cars perishable goods are transported to great distances, and the fruits of Florida and California reach New York as fresh as when plucked. Rapid transit in cities has been brought about by street cars, which, drawn at first by horses or mules, are now driven by cables or by an electric current. Elevators carry us up and down our high buildings, reducing them practically to one story. As to the communication of messages, the telegraph, and later the telephone, have simply annihilated space.

These are a few of the things that Americans have done in the way of expediting, cheapening, and rendering more comfortable, the great business of transportation.

It is not so easy to go into details concerning manufactures, because of the great multiplicity of inventions for cheapening and bettering the product. Almost everything is made by machinery; and though many of the machines may have originated in foreign lands, there are none of them in their present form but show, in modifications and adaptations, the fine inventive genius of the American. Thus the printing-press, although a German invention, has been brought to its present high state of excellence mainly through American ingenuity. So with the countless machines used in metal working, in boot and shoe making, and in spinning and weaving.

In the applications of electricity the Americans have always occupied the leading place. Besides the telegraph, the telephone, and the electric street car, already mentioned, they have introduced and developed electric lighting and the transmission of power by wire for all sorts of domestic and light manufacturing purposes.

Even the farmer's condition has been vastly improved by invention. In place of the spade and hoe we have to-day gang plows and harrows driven by horse or steam power. The flail has given way to the steam thresher, and the scythe and sickle to the mowing-machine, the reaper and binder. "In the sweat of thy face shalt thou eat bread," was not written of this day or generation.

RELIGION

In the United States absolute religious freedom prevails. There is no restriction upon belief, although in certain cases, notably that of the Mormons, restrictions have been placed upon actions growing out of such belief. As a result of this freedom, coupled with the great variety of peoples assembled here from all parts of the globe, the number of religious denominations, with their petty subdivisions, is almost bewildering. There are hundreds of species and varieties of religious belief, each represented by some form of organization.

The total number of clergymen, preachers, etc., in 1890, as returned by the eleventh census, was 108,879; of church edifices, 142,378. The value of church property was $680,000,000, and the number of communicants 20,661,016. This number constitutes more than one-third of the population of the country, and half of that part of the population which exceeds ten years of age. The principal denominations, and the number of communicants in each, are shown in the following table:

MEMBERSHIP OF PRINCIPAL RELIGIOUS DENOMINATIONS

Catholic	6,257,871
Methodist	4,589,284
Baptist	3,762,729
Presbyterian	1,278,332
Lutheran	1,231,072
Christian	744,723
Episcopal	540,509
Congregational	512,771
Reformed	309,458
United Brethren	225,158
German Evangelical Synod	187,432
Latter Day Saints	166,125
Evangelical Association	133,313
Jews	130,496
Friends	107,208
Dunkards	73,795
Unitarian	67,749
Adventist	60,491
Universalist	49,194
Mennonite	41,541

From the foregoing table it appears that the Catholics and Methodists together outnumber all other denominations, constituting more than one-half of the total church membership of the country; that the Catholics, Methodists, and Baptists jointly represent more than two-thirds of the church membership; while these, with the Presbyterians and Lutherans, comprise no less than seventeen-twentieths, leaving only three-twentieths of the entire church population to be distributed among other denominations.

Catholics.—It will be seen that the Catholics form the most numerous religious body; but it must be understood that this denomination counts in its membership all members of a family of which either or both the heads are connected with the church, while in the other denominations this practice does not prevail. A moment's reflection will show that this method of counting must swell greatly the apparent number of Catholics, and that in order to make their membership comparable with that of the other denominations, it should be reduced nearly or quite one-half, since of the inhabitants of the United States, and presumably of the Catholic element, approximately one-half are under age.

The Catholic population is derived from several sources, and is widely dispersed over the country, as will be seen by the map on Plate 21, facing page 148. It is present in strong force throughout the northeastern states, where it is composed mainly of Irish immigrants and their descendants, and of French Canadian immigrants. It forms a considerable part of the population of the states bordering the Great Lakes, where it is mainly composed of French Canadians. A notable proportion is found in Maryland and the District of Columbia, made up mainly of the descendants of the original settlers; also in Louisiana, of the descendants of the French and Spanish founders of that state. The Catholic is almost the sole religion represented in New Mexico, and is prominent in Arizona, southern California, and southern Texas, where its adherents are of Mexican blood.

Methodists.—Next to the Catholic the Methodist denomination is the strongest numerically upon the face of the returns, and is probably the strongest of all in fact. It is widely represented, at least one per cent. of the population of every state and territory, Utah and Nevada excepted, being Methodists, as is shown by the map on Plate 21. Its greatest strength is in the southern states—the colored element of these states belonging, with few exceptions, either to the Baptist or the Methodist denomination; and it reaches its maximum in South Carolina, where not less than twenty-two per cent. of the entire population are Methodists.

Baptists.—The Baptist denomination is almost as widely dispersed as the Methodist, as illustrated on Plate 22, although in the far west it is but feebly represented. Like the Methodist body it is strongest, both numerically and proportionally, in the southern states, especially among the colored element, and is proportionally weak at the north. In the Carolinas and Georgia twenty per cent. of the population are Baptists; in Virginia, nineteen per cent.; and in Alabama and Mississippi, seventeen per cent.

Presbyterians.—The Presbyterians are found in their greatest strength in New Jersey, Pennsylvania, and Ohio, and thence westward through the prairie states as far as Kansas. Notable proportions occupy the states lying north of these, such as New York and Michigan, and those lying immediately south, as the Virginias, Kentucky, Tennessee, and the Carolinas. In proportion to their total numbers they are a wide-spread denomination, as is shown on Plate 22. In New England, however, there are practically none, the New England Presbyterians being Congregationalists.

Lutherans.—The Lutherans are a German denomination, whose extent and density appear to be in direct ratio to those of the German element of the population. This is shown on Plate 23. They are found from Pennsylvania and New York, westward to the rocky mountain region, occupying the northern states of the Mississippi valley and the Lake states, and appear in the greatest proportion in Wisconsin, Minnesota, and the Dakotas, where the German population is most fully established.

Christians.—The Christians are a large denomination, numbering nearly three-quarters of a million. Members of this denomination are found in nearly every state in the Union, but

THE BUILDING OF A NATION
PLATE 21

PROPORTION OF CATHOLICS TO TOTAL POPULATION IN 1890

PROPORTION OF METHODISTS TO TOTAL POPULATION IN 1890

THE BUILDING OF A NATION

PLATE 22

PROPORTION OF BAPTISTS TO TOTAL POPULATION IN 1890

PROPORTION OF PRESBYTERIANS TO TOTAL POPULATION IN 1890

THE BUILDING OF A NATION
PLATE 23

PROPORTION OF LUTHERANS TO TOTAL POPULATION IN 1890

PROPORTION OF CHRISTIANS TO TOTAL POPULATION IN 1890

THE BUILDING OF A NATION
PLATE 24

PROPORTION OF EPISCOPALIANS TO TOTAL POPULATION IN 1890

PROPORTION OF CONGREGATIONALISTS TO TOTAL POPULATION IN 1890

its principal strength is in the states of the upper Mississippi valley—in Ohio, Indiana, Illinois, Missouri, Kentucky, Tennessee, and Kansas—while to the eastward they are found in considerable numbers in Virginia and North Carolina and to the southwest as far as Texas. The distribution of this denomination is shown on Plate 23, facing page 148.

Episcopalians.—The Episcopalians are found almost entirely in the northeastern states, and in the greatest numbers in Rhode Island, Connecticut, New York, and New Jersey. They extend in a notable ratio as far south as Maryland and even Virginia, but the denomination has not spread westward or farther southward in any appreciable proportion. Their distribution is shown on Plate 24, facing page 148.

Congregationalists.—The Congregationalists (see Plate 24, facing page 148) are practically confined to the New England states, in which they form proportionally a very important body, but are quite inconsiderable in other parts of the country.

Other Denominations.—The foregoing are the principal denominations. Of the legion of others, none have a membership reaching half a million, and few of them present any features of distribution of special interest, with the possible exception of the Church of Jesus Christ of Latter Day Saints, popularly known as the Mormons. These peculiar people, numbering 166,000, are found almost entirely in Utah and the states and territories immediately adjacent; 118,000, or two-thirds of all the Mormons, are found in Utah; and in neighboring parts of Idaho, Wyoming, Colorado, Arizona, and Nevada are 25,000 more. The few remaining are scattered widely over the east. It will doubtless be a matter of surprise to many to learn that over 5,000 members of this community are still to be found in the state of Iowa, and 3,000 in Missouri.

Distribution of Communicants. Finally, the distribution of church membership as a whole is brought together upon the diagram on page 150, and upon the map constituting Plate 25, facing page 150. Of all the states and territories the greatest proportion of church membership to population is found in New Mexico, where, as above stated, the people are almost entirely Catholics; 65 per cent. of the 69 per cent. which church members bear to population being of that denomination. Next in order is Utah, where 61 per cent. of the people are church members, nearly all of them being Mormons. Then follows Arizona, where the high proportion of 47 per cent. is produced mainly by the Catholics of Mexican blood. Next comes South Carolina

PROPORTION OF CHURCH MEMBERS TO AGGREGATE POPULATION IN 1890

with 45 per cent., mainly Methodists and Baptists. Other southern states have a high percentage of church membership; as 42 per cent. in North Carolina, and 36 in Alabama, Florida, and Louisiana. But the proportions in these states are, on the whole, exceeded in southern New England, where the proportion

THE BUILDING OF A NATION—PLATE 25

PROPORTION OF CHURCH MEMBERS TO TOTAL POPULATION IN 1890

is 43 per cent. in Rhode Island, 42 per cent. in Massachusetts, and 41 per cent. in Connecticut. These large proportions are due chiefly, as already stated, to the presence of great numbers of Irish and French-Canadian Catholics. In the upper Mississippi valley the proportion of church membership to population is about the same as in the country at large; that is, about 33 per cent. At the west, with the exception of the territories, the proportion is low, reaching only 14 per cent. in Nevada, 17 per cent. in Washington, and 18 per cent. in Nebraska. The extremely low proportion given for Oklahoma, 7 per cent., may be regarded as merely a temporary condition of things, produced by the influx of lawless elements to that newly opened land.

MORTALITY

Continuous records of mortality have been kept only in the states of Massachusetts, Rhode Island, New Jersey, of late years in Alabama, and in some of the larger cities. It is for these states and cities alone that we have complete and reliable statistics of the total number of deaths, and of the diseases to which they were respectively due.

Census Statistics.—The statistics of the eleventh census were secured partly by an extensive correspondence with physicians, and partly from the schedules of the enumerators. Circular letters were sent to all the physicians of the country whose addresses could be obtained, asking for records of all deaths occurring in their practice. These inquiries were quite generally answered, but of course the replies did not by any means include all deaths occurring during the year. The failures in this regard were due to several reasons:

First, The lack of a complete list of physicians;

Second, The failure of a certain proportion of those called upon, to answer;

Third, The failure of memory in the case of many who did answer; and,

Fourth, The fact that a considerable proportion died unattended by physicians.

The enumerators' returns were also deficient, owing mainly to defects of memory on the part of those answering the questions in the schedules, and, perhaps, in certain individual cases to the carelessness of the enumerators themselves.

The returns from these two sources were, of course, to a large extent, duplications one of another. The first work, and a very important one, was to eliminate these duplications. When this had been done, and the returns footed, they were compared with the record of the states and cities which had kept careful records of mortality, and the extent of the deficiencies and their character examined.

These registration states and cities indicate that the annual death rate of the United States is about eighteen deaths per thousand inhabitants. The census returns show an apparent death rate of fourteen per thousand, proving that, on the whole, the omissions amounted to not far from four deaths per thousand.

But the extent of these omissions is by no means uniform in different parts of the country; neither is it the same at different ages nor for the different races and nativities; nor even for different classes of diseases. In the densely settled northeastern states the census returns are much more nearly complete than among the scattered rural population of the south. The returns are more complete as to mature persons than as to children, especially children less than one year of age. It is also true that the returns are much more complete for the native whites than for the foreign born, and these in turn than for the colored population. As to the foreign born, the returns are doubtless more complete in the case of nationalities known to be higher in the scale of civilization than in the lower. Thus, among the Germans, Irish, and Scandinavians, the returns are more satisfactory than among the Poles, Hungarians, and Bohemians.

As regards the inequality in the returns of mortality from different diseases, it is found that the returns for the diseases prevalent among children are less complete than those prevalent among grown persons.

Having thus qualified the mortality statistics, they are given for what they are worth. The total number of deaths reported

THE BUILDING OF A NATION

PLATE 26

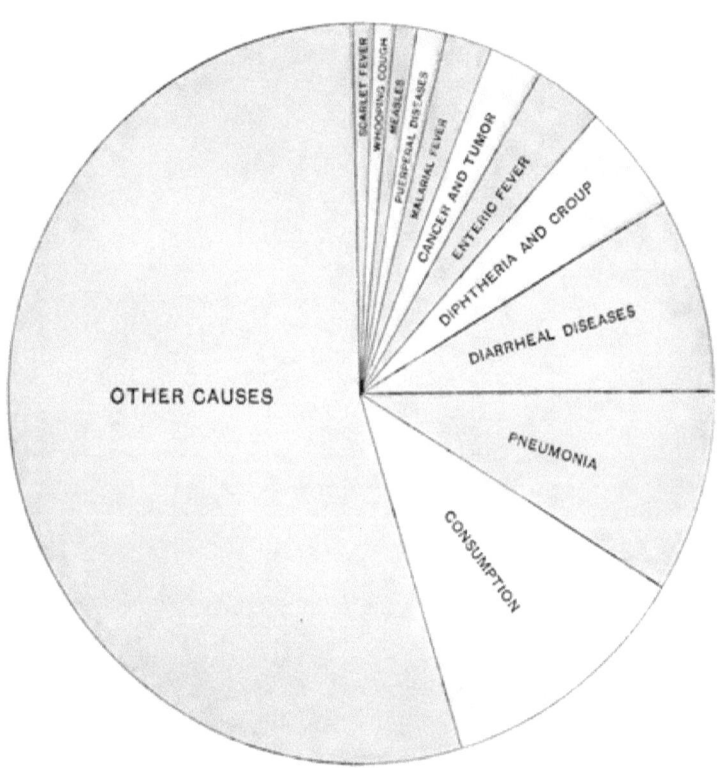

PROPORTION WHICH THE NUMBER OF DEATHS FROM CERTAIN
DISEASES BORE TO ALL DEATHS IN THE
UNITED STATES, IN 1890

by the census in the year 1890 was 872,944, showing a death rate for that year of fourteen per thousand. The number of deaths of native whites was 596,055, a death rate for that class of thirteen per thousand. The number of deaths of foreign whites was 140,075, showing a death rate of fifteen per thousand; and the number of deaths reported among the colored was 114,313, also a death rate of fifteen per thousand.

The mortality statistics of the registration states of Massachusetts, Rhode Island, and New Jersey, show that the death rate of the foreign born is slightly greater than that of the native whites.

Again, in the registration state of Alabama, and in the cities of Baltimore, Washington, St. Louis, Louisville, and New Orleans, where a considerable proportion of the population is colored, the statistics show that the mortality of the colored element is very nearly double that of the whites, ranging in these cities from thirty-two to thirty-eight per thousand, while that of the whites ranges from seventeen to twenty-two per thousand; thus demonstrating the fact that the mortality returns for the colored element, as compared with those for the white, are greatly understated.

Causes of Death.—The following table gives the number of deaths from several leading causes, with the proportion which each bears to the total number of deaths. The diagram on Plate 26, facing page 152, presents the same facts in a graphic manner.

RATIO OF DEATHS FROM CERTAIN DISEASES TO TOTAL MORTALITY

Causes of Death	Percentage of Total Deaths
Scarlet fever	0.7
Measles	1.1
Whooping cough	1.0
Diphtheria and croup	4.8
Enteric fever	3.1
Malarial fever	2.1
Diarrheal diseases	8.5
Cancer and tumor	2.4
Consumption	11.6
Pneumonia	8.8
Puerperal diseases	1.3

Thus it appears that the principal cause of death is consumption, which has produced 11.6 per cent. of all deaths. Next follows pneumonia with 8.8 per cent., and diarrheal diseases with 8.5 per cent.

Mortality in Registration Cities.—The following table gives the statistics of mortality in most of the registration cities of the country, which comprise the twenty-five largest cities. This is illustrated also in the diagram on page 155. The table shows the death rate of the total population, of the native and foreign born white, and, in the case of five southern cities where the proportion of colored is considerable, the death rate of the colored.

MORTALITY IN REGISTRATION CITIES

	Total	Native White	Foreign	Colored
New York	29	32	23	....
Chicago	21	19	26	....
Philadelphia	23	26	14	....
Brooklyn	26	22	23	....
St. Louis	19	17	21	35
Boston	23	26	22	....
Baltimore	25	22	23	37
San Francisco	23	26	20	....
Cincinnati	22	21	25	....
Cleveland	22	26	15	....
Buffalo	20	21	17	....
New Orleans	29	22	38	36
Pittsburg	22	23	19	....
Washington	26	18	28	38
Detroit	20	24	14	....
Milwaukee	20	21	16	....
Newark	29	31	24	....
Minneapolis	15	17	10	....
Jersey City	28	29	24	....
Louisville	22	18	25	32
Omaha	10	10	7	....
Rochester	17	15	18	....
St. Paul	17	21	10	....
Kansas City	19	16	16	...
Providence	22	23	19	...

The small death rate of the foreign born in many of these registration cities, is probably due to the fact that there are in this element no young children, among whom the death rate is exceptionally large.

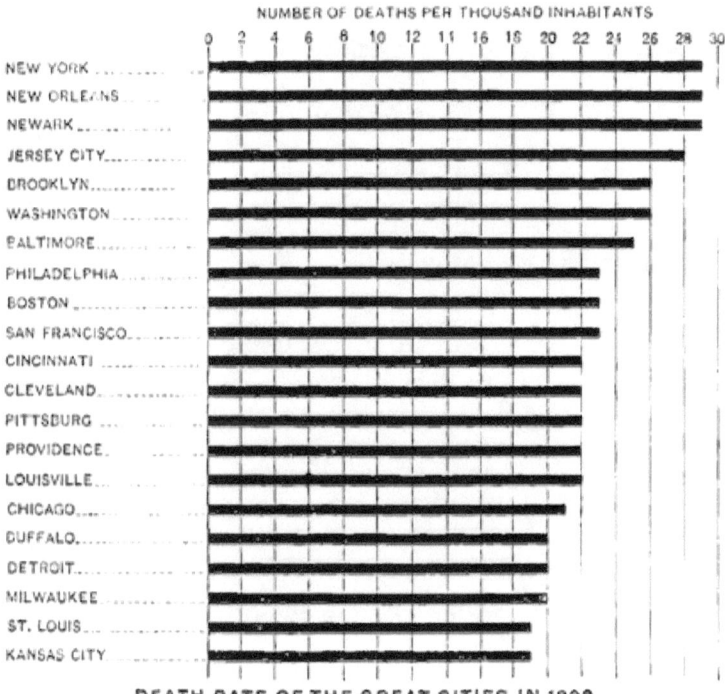

DEATH RATE OF THE GREAT CITIES IN 1890

Death Rates of Countries. The following table, and the diagram on page 156, give the death rate per thousand in this country, in comparison with that in most of the European nations:

DEATH RATES PER THOUSAND IN VARIOUS COUNTRIES

United States	18
Denmark	19
England and Wales	19.5
Scotland	19.7
Netherlands	20.5
Portugal	20.5
Belgium	20.6
Switzerland	20.9
France	22.8
German Empire	24.1
Italy	26.1
Austria	29.1
Spain	29.7
Hungary	33.9

From this showing it would appear that the Americans live longer than the citizens of any European country.

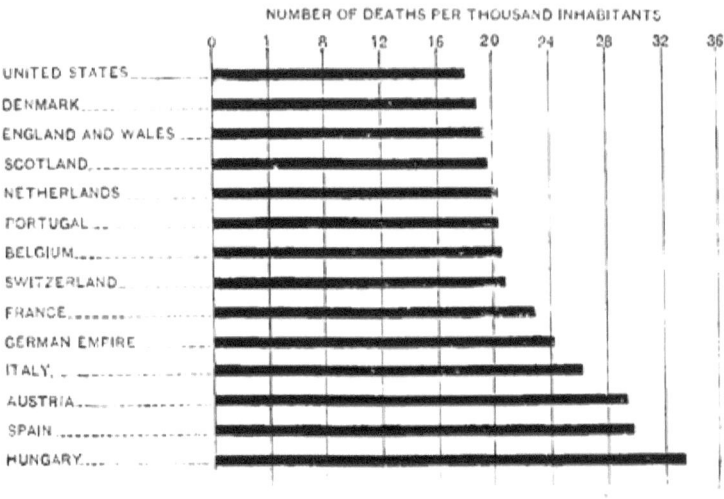

DEATH RATES OF VARIOUS COUNTRIES IN 1890

CRIME

In 1890 there were in the United States, under conviction for crime, 82,329 persons, or 13 in every 10,000 of the inhabitants. Of these 18 per cent. were in juvenile reformatories, 24 per cent. in county jails, and 55 per cent. in penitentiaries. Only 8 per cent. were females, the remainder, 92 per cent., being males. Of the whole number, 7,386, or 9 per cent., were under sentence for homicide.

The following table shows the distribution of the total number of prisoners by race and nativity, this distribution being expressed in terms of the proportion between the total number of prisoners and the number in each class. Together with it is placed, for contrast, the like proportion between the total population and the total number of persons of each class in the population:

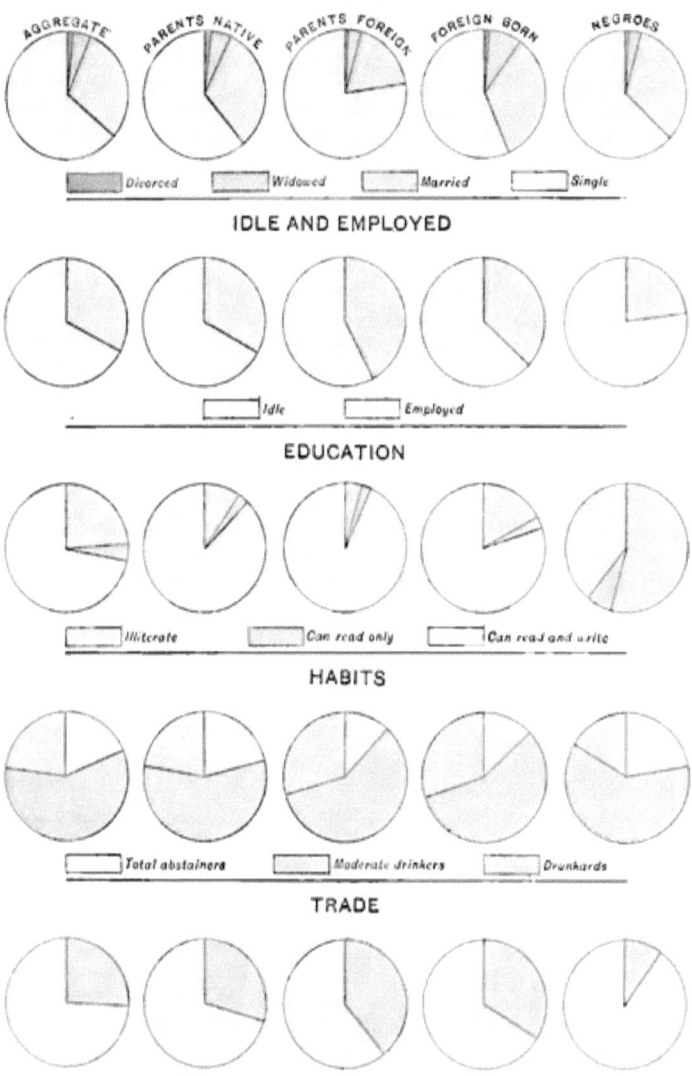

THE PRISONERS OF THE UNITED STATES IN 1890

RACE AND NATIVITY OF PRISONERS AND OF POPULATION

	Proportion of all Prisoners	Proportion of all Population
White native of native parents	26	55
White native of foreign parents	19	18
Foreign born	19	15
Colored	30	12
Unknown	6	

The relations of the number of prisoners to the various elements of the population, is expressed in different form in the following table:

NUMBER OF PRISONERS OF EACH CLASS IN 10,000 INHABITANTS

Total	13
White natives of native parents	6
White natives of foreign parents	13
Foreign born	17
Colored	32

These figures show that the proportion of criminals among whites of native extraction is very small; that the proportion of criminals of native birth, but of foreign parentage, is more than twice as great as among those of native extraction; that the proportion of criminals of foreign birth is nearly three times as great as among those of native extraction, and much greater than that of native birth but foreign extraction. It shows, furthermore, that the proportion of colored criminals is far greater than that of any other element, being more than double the proportion of the whites, and more than five times that of the whites of native extraction. It is the colored and foreign elements that burden our courts and fill our jails. Could they but be eliminated from our population, the millennium would be near.

In the diagram on Plate 27, facing page 156, are illustrated other facts concerning the social condition of the prisoners. It will be noted that the majority of prisoners were unmarried, that the proportion of the widowed and divorced was very small, and that two-thirds of them were employed when the crimes were committed. In the matter of education, it appears, taking the whole group together, that about one-fourth were illiterate; of the native born the proportion was very much less, while of the foreign born about one-fifth were unable to read or write; of the colored element, considerably more than one-half were illiterates.

Regarding the use of intoxicating liquors, it will be seen that more than one-half of each element were moderate drinkers, and that but a comparatively small proportion were drunkards. Three-fourths of all prisoners had no trade; the proportion is less in the case of the whites, particularly those of foreign extraction. In the case of the colored element, probably nine-tenths were without any well-defined means of earning a livelihood.

PAUPERISM

The amount of pauperism is a function of two elements: first, the poverty of the masses; and, second, the provision for its relief. The more elaborate and complete this provision, the greater the amount of pauperism.

In the United States the abundance of work and its ample remuneration keep down the numbers of the destitute; while, on the other hand, no such provisions exist here for the support of those who are willing to accept support, as are found in most European countries. It is true that almshouses are maintained by most of the New England towns and by many of the counties elsewhere, and that there are many charitable organizations of one sort or another; but altogether the provision for the support of the needy is in no way comparable with that of older countries.

Our available statistics relate only to indoor paupers; i. e., those supported in almshouses. No figures are given for those receiving casual aid or outdoor relief.

In 1890 the number of paupers in almshouses was 73,045, or 12 in every 10,000 of the population. The number of males was slightly in excess of females, a fact for which it is difficult to account. The following table shows the distribution of paupers by race and nativity, this proportion being expressed in terms of the number in 10,000 of each element of the population:

DISTRIBUTION OF PAUPERS BY RACE AND NATIVITY

Total... 12
White.. 12
White natives of native parentage....................... 9
White natives of foreign parentage...................... 9
Foreign born.. 30
Colored.. 9

Thus it appears that the proportion of all these elements is equal, with the exception of the foreign born, which is more than three times as great, a fact that speaks volumes in favor of the restriction of immigration.

CONJUGAL CONDITION

The last census furnishes, for the first time, the statistics of the single, married, widowed, and divorced. These are classified by sex, race, general nativity and nativity of parents, and by age.

Of the total population 59.29 per cent. were single, 35.66 per cent. married, 4.74 per cent. widowed, and 0.19 per cent. divorced.

Analyzing the figures by sex, it is seen that of males 62.20 per cent. were single, while of females there were only 56.24 per cent. single. The proportions of married were: males, 34.94 per cent., and females 36.41 per cent., the latter being slightly the greater. Of widowed the proportion of males was but 2.54 per cent., while of females it was not less than 7.05 per cent., showing that a much greater proportion of widowers remarry than of widows. Of the divorced, the proportion of males was 0.15 per cent., and of females 0.24 per cent., showing that divorced men remarry more freely than divorced women.

The classification by race and nativity develops many interesting features. This is, in a measure, a broad classification by station in life, and the facts brought out by it throw light upon the conjugal condition of different social classes.

Native whites of native parentage, when taken as a whole,

form the highest social class of the community, as measured by education, occupations, and freedom from pauperism and crime. The native born of foreign parentage occupy, as a whole, the second place, while the foreign born and the colored form the lowest class.

The native whites of native parentage, and the colored, have the normal proportions of children and mature persons. The native whites of foreign parentage, and the foreign born, on the other hand, contain abnormal proportions of these classes. Among the first the proportion of children is very large; or, to put it in another way, the proportion of mature persons is very small, because the parents are of foreign birth. With the foreign born the reverse is the case; the proportion of children is very small, because the immigration is mainly of mature persons. These facts affect greatly the proportions of single, married, widowed, and divorced. Of the native whites of native parentage, 59.76 per cent. were single, 35.41 per cent. were married, 4.46 per cent. were widowed, and 0.21 per cent. were divorced. Among the native whites of foreign parentage the corresponding proportions were 76.79 per cent., 21.48 per cent., 1.63 per cent., and 0.10 per cent., respectively; while among the foreign born they were 32.75 per cent., 57.95 per cent., 8.91 per cent., and 0.20 per cent., respectively.

The classification of the population by sex and groups of ages also develops many features of interest. For example, of the males under 15 years of age, the proportion of married is inappreciable, while of females about one in ten thousand were married. Between the ages of 15 and 20, one-half of one per cent. of the males and one per cent. of the females were married. At ages above 20 the proportion of married increased rapidly. Between 20 and 25, nearly one-fifth of the males and nearly one-half of the females were married, while for the next five years the proportions had increased to nearly one-half of the former and nearly three-fourths of the latter. Between 30 and 35, three-fourths of the males and four-fifths of the females were married. At ages between 35 and 45, the proportion of married of the sexes was nearly equal, about four-fifths of them being married. From this point the proportion of married females diminished, owing to the increase of widows, while that of married males went on increasing, and reached its maximum at between 45 and 55 years. At ages over 65, only a little more than one-third of the females were found to be married, while the proportion of widows exceeded it. At these ages the proportion of married men was seventy per cent. The proportion of widows exceeded that of widowers at all ages.

The native whites of native parentage married younger and in greater proportion than the native whites of foreign parentage or the foreign born. Furthermore, there was among them a smaller proportion of widowed, owing, probably, to the smaller death rate. The colored married earlier and in greater proportion than the whites, and the proportion of widowed was greater among them; owing, again, to the greater death rate.

What has been stated above shows that marriage among the higher classes of society is not less universal than among the lower, but rather the reverse, and thus disposes of another popular tradition.

Further proof of this is afforded by a study of the geographical distribution of the married. Among the native whites of native parentage, the greatest proportion of married is found in the oldest and most thickly settled section of the country, viz., the northeastern states, and the smallest proportion at the south.

Divorce.—Among the aggregate population the proportion of divorced to married people was 0.54 per cent.; in other words, there was found one divorced person to 186 married persons. The proportions differed with different classes, as follows: Native white of native parentage, 1 to 164; native white of foreign parentage, 1 to 200; foreign born, 1 to 294; and colored, 1 to 152.

The proportion among the total population ranges widely in different parts of the country, being least in the southeastern states, where it was but 1 to 322; next in the northeastern states, where it was 1 to 263. Next in order were the south central states, where the proportion was 1 to 182; then the north central states, with 1 to 150; and, finally, the western states, where it reached not less than 1 to 88. Of course a part of this difference in geographical distribution is due to the migration of divorced persons, but another part must be due to a difference in the laws regulating divorce in different states.

A comparison of divorce statistics of the great cities with those of the country at large shows that, on the whole, there were fewer divorces in cities than in the country, in proportion to married people.

AGRICULTURE

For statistics of agriculture we are dependent primarily upon the census. Through its agency we are enabled to obtain every tenth year a reasonably faithful picture of the condition of this great industry.

Basing its work upon the census reports, the statistical office of the Department of Agriculture furnishes estimates each year of the state of the leading crops. Naturally enough, these estimates are much more reliable in the early years of the decade than in the later ones.

The statistics of the last census were for the crops of the year 1889. The tabulation of the results has been completed for certain leading crops only, such as the cereals, cotton, wool, tobacco, and sugar, and the general statistics of agriculture, the principal among which are those relating to areas, numbers, and values of farms, the extent of improved land, and total value of agricultural products. These figures are sufficient for a clear presentation of the condition and growth of this industry.

Relative Importance of Agriculture.—Considering the number of persons employed and supported, agriculture is still, as it has always been, the leading industry of the United States. In 1880 forty-four per cent. of all the inhabitants engaged in gainful occupations were devoted to agriculture, and probably at the present time the proportion, while less, has not greatly diminished. Certainly two-fifths of all those engaged in gainful occupations are concerned in the cultivation of the soil, and a corresponding proportion of the total population is supported by their labor.

But if the value of product, instead of persons occupied, be considered, a different proportion will be found. The value of all agricultural products in 1880 was $2,213,000,000. In 1890 it had increased to $2,460,000,000, being at the rate of only a little more than eleven per cent., a rate very much less than the rate of increase of population.

As stated elsewhere, the estimated net value of manufactures in 1890 was a trifle over $4,000,000,000, being no less than thirty-three per cent. greater than the product of agriculture. Ten years before, the net product of manufactures was $1,973,000,000, being slightly less than that of agriculture. If these estimates are correct, manufactures have, during the past decade, passed agriculture in importance, as measured by value of product. For a graphic comparison of the proportions of the leading industries in 1890, see diagram, Plate 28.

General Statistics. In 1880 the number of farms was, in round numbers, 4,000,000. In 1890 it was 4,565,000, having increased during the decade at the rate of fourteen per cent. This, which is also much less than the rate of increase of population, indicates that the accessions to our numbers during the past decade have been, in the main, additions to the ranks of other avocations.

The value of farms in 1880, including all improvements, was, in round numbers, $10,200,000,000. In 1890 this item had grown to $13,276,000,000, showing a rate of increase of thirty per cent., an increase greater than that of the number of farms, thus showing a decided advance in the average value of farms.

Farming tools and machinery had a value in 1880 of a trifle over $400,000,000. The same item had a value in 1890 of $494,000,000, or nearly twenty-four per cent. greater.

Hence the capital invested in agriculture in 1890 was not less than $13,770,000,000; and this capital produced a return in that year, of $2,460,000,000, or less than eighteen per cent. upon the capital.

Since 1850, when agricultural statistics were obtained for the first time, the average size of farms has been diminishing, having decreased from 203 acres in 1850, to 134 in 1880. During the last decade the average size has slightly increased, being in 1890 137 acres.

In 1880 the extent of cultivated or "improved" land, as the census designated it, was 285,000,000 acres. Ten years later this had increased to 358,000,000 acres, or about 560,000 square miles.

RELATIVE VALUE OF THE INDUSTRIES OF
THE UNITED STATES, IN 1890

THE BUILDING OF A NATION

PLATE 29

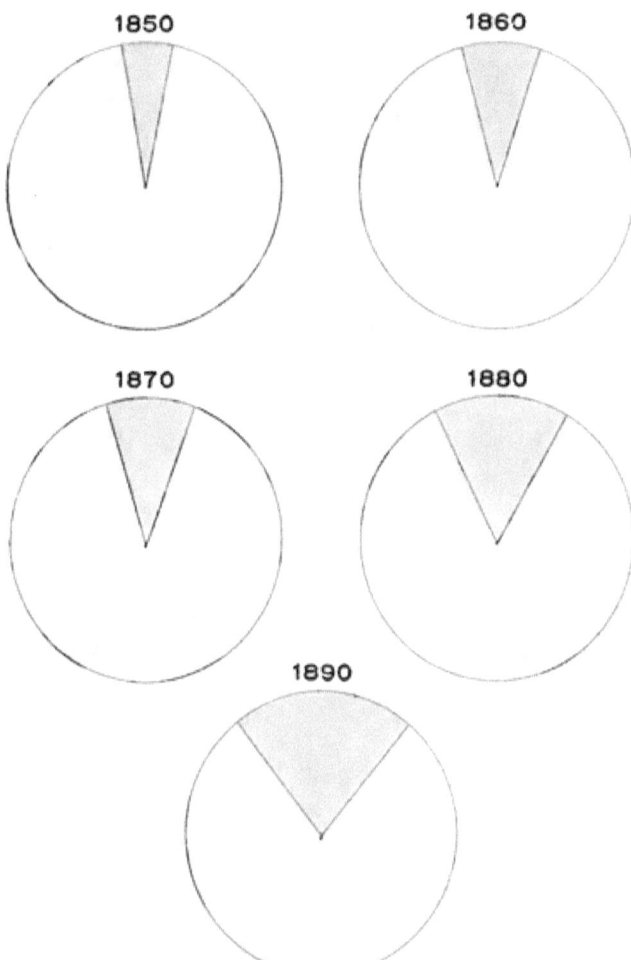

The areas of the circles represent the area of the country;
the red portions the cultivated land, and the
blue portions the uncultivated land.

**PROPORTION OF CULTIVATED LAND TO TOTAL AREA
OF THE COUNTRY**

In other words, in 1890 a trifle more than one-fifth of the total area of the country, excluding Alaska, was under cultivation.

The following table and diagram, together with the diagram on Plate 29, facing page 164, summarizes the statistics upon these subjects for the past forty years:

VALUE, NUMBER, AND SIZE OF FARMS, AND VALUE OF PRODUCTS, BY DECADES

	1850	1860	1870	1880	1890
Value of farms, implements and machinery (millions of dollars)	3,424	6,891	7,700	10,604	13,770
Number of farms	1,449,073	2,044,077	2,659,985	4,008,907	4,564,641
Average size of farms (acres)	203	199	153	134	137
Cultivated land (millions of acres)	113	163	189	285	358
Value of products (millions of dollars)				2,213	2,460

VALUE OF FARMS, IMPLEMENTS AND MACHINERY (Billions of dollars, 1850–1890)

NUMBER OF FARMS (Millions, 1850–1890)

AVERAGE SIZE OF FARMS, 1850 TO 1890 (Acres)

Improved Land.—The proportion between the cultivated land and the total area of each state, follows quite closely the density of population of the states, except in the case of those most densely populated. It is affected, however, quite appreciably by the topography of the state; the level prairie states, such as Illinois and Iowa, having a higher proportion than the adjacent more broken ones.

This proportion is shown by the map on Plate 30. In the states and territories of the Rocky mountain region, with the exception of those of the Pacific coast and Colorado, scarcely one acre in a hundred is cultivated. In Oregon, Washington, Colorado, Florida, and North and South Dakota, less than one acre in twenty of the total area is improved. In the southern states the proportion ranges from twelve per cent. in Texas to sixty-one per cent. in Delaware, the proportion increasing northward and eastward. The maximum of land under cultivation is reached in the prairie region. In Illinois and Iowa nearly three-fourths of the total area is cultivated, in Ohio more than two-thirds, and in Indiana three-fifths. In the North Atlantic states about two-fifths of the land is under cultivation, although in Maine this proportion drops to less than one-sixth of the area.

Tobacco.—Tobacco is produced to a greater or less extent in forty-two states and territories; in most of them, however, only in small quantity for local consumption. In seventeen states only is it produced in commercial quantity. A large proportion of the supply, nearly one-half the crop of the entire country, comes from Kentucky. This state, with Virginia, Ohio, North Carolina, Tennessee, and Pennsylvania, produced in 1889 over 400,000,000 pounds, out of a total production of 488,225,896 pounds, or not less than eighty-two per cent. In proportion to its area Connecticut also is a heavy producer of tobacco, its production in 1889 reaching nearly 9,000,000 pounds; while that of Wisconsin, although the state lies very far north and has a correspondingly severe climate, reached more than 19,000,000 pounds. The relative importance of the various states in the production of tobacco is shown by the map on the next page.

THE BUILDING OF A NATION—PLATE 30

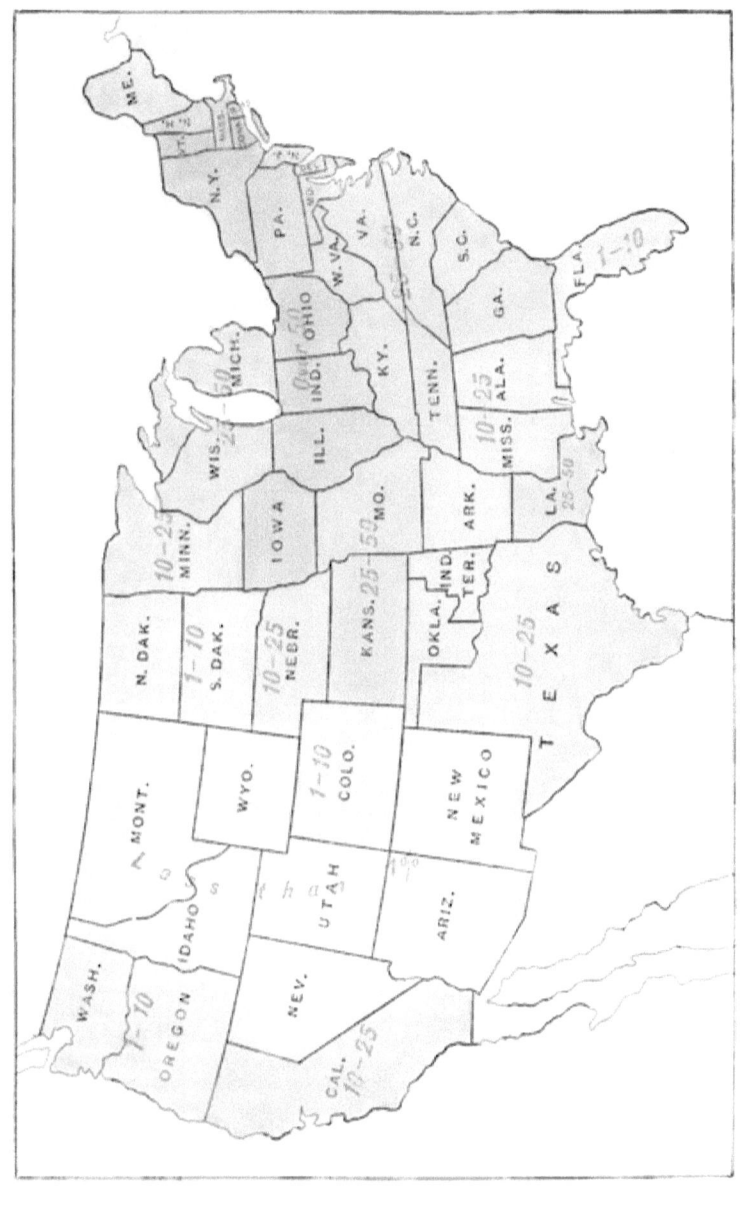

PROPORTION OF CULTIVATED LAND TO TOTAL AREA IN 1890

YIELD OF TOBACCO, IN POUNDS, PER SQUARE MILE OF TOTAL AREA IN 1889

Wheat.—This is the most important of the cereal crops; important not only to the United States, but to the world at large, inasmuch as the United States forms the principal source of wheat supply for those countries that are unable to supply themselves.

The wheat crop of the United States in the year 1889 was 468,000,000 bushels; in 1890, 399,000,000 bushels; in 1891, 612,000,000 bushels; and in 1892, 519,000,000 bushels. The year 1891 was an exceedingly prosperous one for the northern farmers; not only were their cereal crops enormous, but the price was high, owing to a shortage of the crops in Europe. This great yield was produced mainly in the northern states of the Mississippi valley. New England has long since ceased the attempt to supply herself with wheat. The cotton states depend upon their northern neighbors for their supply, but the northern central states produce enough for themselves and have to spare for the rest of the world.

The greatest diversity exists in the yield of wheat per acre; a diversity attributable mainly to the degree of care used in cultivation. Thus the small supply raised in the northeastern states shows a heavy yield per acre, ranging from fifteen to nineteen bushels. In the older of the northern central states, where the farms are subdivided into small holdings, the yield is almost equally large, ranging from fourteen to sixteen bushels; while in the Dakotas, where land is cheap and wholesale methods prevail, and where the aim is to get the greatest possible yield with the least amount of labor, without regard to area, the yield per acre is small, being but nine bushels in North Dakota and but seven in South Dakota. In that part of the west where the land requires irrigation, and where for this reason the holdings are comparatively small and cultivation closer, the yield is large, running as high as twenty-two bushels per acre in Nevada and Colorado, and twenty-four in Montana. The other extreme is found in certain of the cotton states, the average yield in South Carolina, Georgia, and Alabama being but five bushels per acre. The production of wheat per square mile and the yield per acre, are illustrated by the maps on Plate 31.

The United States is by far the largest wheat producing country of the globe. In 1891 it produced 612,000,000 bushels, while India produced only 235,000,000 bushels, France 231,000,000 bushels, Russia 186,000,000 bushels, Hungary 119,000,000 bushels, and Italy 102,000,000 bushels.

Corn.—Indian corn is cultivated to an enormous extent in the United States, and its cultivation is very widespread. From Florida and Texas to Minnesota, and from Maine to California, fields of maize greet the eye on every hand. The production of the country in 1889 exceeded two thousand million bushels—2,124,798,728, to be exact. This was an unusually heavy crop. In 1890 it fell to 1,490,000,000 bushels; in 1891 it rose to 2,060,000,000, and it fell again in 1892 to 1,628,000,000 bushels. While cultivation of corn is thus widespread, it is of the greatest importance in those states which occupy a middle position in point of latitude—that is, in New Jersey and Maryland, and westward through Kansas and Nebraska to the Pacific coast—and is of the least consequence in the states of the extreme north and of the extreme south. In the latter states it is supplanted to a considerable extent by cotton, and, on the other hand, the climate of the extreme northern states

THE BUILDING OF A NATION

PLATE 31

PRODUCTION OF WHEAT, IN BUSHELS, PER SQUARE MILE OF TOTAL AREA IN 1889

YIELD OF WHEAT PER ACRE, IN BUSHELS, IN 1889

PLATE 32

PRODUCTION, IN BUSHELS, OF INDIAN CORN PER SQUARE MILE
OF TOTAL AREA IN 1889

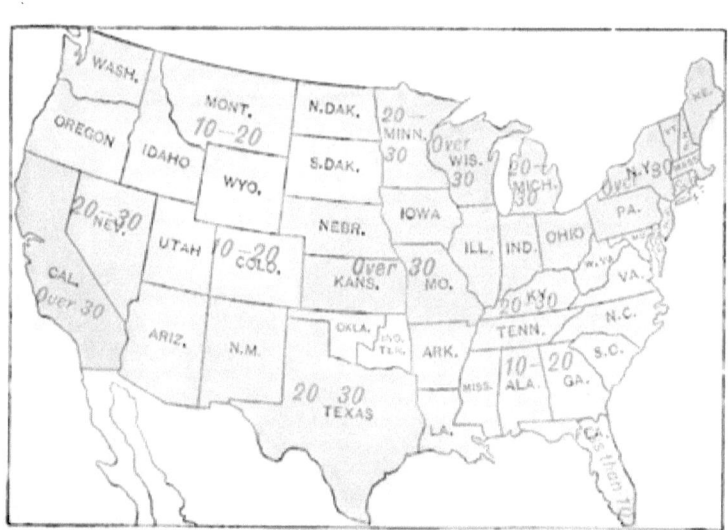

YIELD, IN BUSHELS, OF CORN PER ACRE IN 1889

PLATE 33

PRODUCTION, IN BUSHELS, OF OATS PER SQUARE MILE OF TOTAL AREA IN 1889

YIELD, IN BUSHELS, OF OATS PER ACRE IN 1889

THE BUILDING OF A NATION

PLATE 34

YIELD OF COTTON, IN BALES, PER SQUARE MILE OF TOTAL AREA
IN 1889

YIELD OF COTTON PER ACRE, IN TENTHS OF BALES, IN 1889

THE BUILDING OF A NATION

PLATE 35

NUMBER OF TONS OF HAY RAISED PER SQUARE MILE OF TOTAL AREA IN 1888

NUMBER OF BUSHELS OF POTATOES RAISED PER SQUARE MILE OF TOTAL AREA IN 1888

is too severe to permit its cultivation upon an extensive scale.

The yield of this crop per acre cultivated, is also greatest in the middle tier of states. It is large in New England and also in New York, on account of the thorough cultivation practiced there. At the south it is small, as a rule, mainly because of careless cultivation or exhausted soil.

The corn crop is used directly as food to a large extent, especially at the south; and it contributes indirectly to the food supply, to a still larger extent, by being fed to cattle and hogs.

The importance of this crop, and the yield per acre, are illustrated by the maps on Plate 32, facing page 168.

Oats.—The production of oats has increased greatly of late years, partly at the expense of wheat and the minor cereals, such as barley and rye. In 1889 the total product far exceeded that of wheat, amounting to 809,000,000 bushels. In 1890 it diminished greatly, being but 524,000,000 bushels. It increased in 1891 to 738,000,000 bushels, and dropped again to 661,000,000 bushels in 1892. Being a hardy crop, it is raised almost exclusively in the northern states, from New England to the plains, and to the greatest extent in the states bordering the Great Lakes and in the prairie states.

The same states show also the greatest yield per acre cultivated, ranging as high as thirty-nine bushels in Iowa. The yield is high in New England, and very low in the southern states. The importance of the crop and the yield per acre are shown by the maps on Plate 33, facing page 168.

The other cereals are of minor importance. The production of rye in 1889 was 428,421,413 bushels; of barley, 79,334,381 bushels; and of buckwheat, 12,107,785 bushels. These are all hardy crops, and are produced mainly in the northern part of the country.

Cotton.—The culture of cotton is confined to the region lying south of the Potomac, the Ohio and the Missouri rivers. Within this area the principal region of production, where the crop acquires its greatest prominence, is in the Carolinas, Georgia, Alabama, Mississippi, Louisiana, Texas, and Arkansas.

Cotton holds a very high rank among agricultural products,

in absolute money value and in relative importance to the other crops in the region where it is cultivated.

The crop of 1892 was the largest ever raised, reaching a total of not less than 9,038,707 bales; in 1891 it was 8,655,518 bales, and in 1890 7,313,726 bales, as appears from the estimates of the Department of Agriculture.

According to the census returns, the crop of 1889 consisted of 7,434,687 bales, which was somewhat below the average of preceding years. This product was distributed as follows among the contributing states, arranged in the order of production:

YIELD OF COTTON IN 1889, BY STATES

States	Bales	States	Bales
Texas	1,470,553	Tennessee	189,072
Georgia	1,191,919	Florida	57,928
Mississippi	1,154,406	Missouri	14,461
Alabama	915,414	Virginia	5,375
South Carolina	746,798	Kentucky	873
Arkansas	691,423	Oklahoma	425
Louisiana	659,583	Kansas	213
North Carolina	336,245		
			7,434,687

It will be seen that Texas, chiefly because of its enormous area, produces a larger amount of cotton than any other state. Next in rank are Georgia and Mississippi, in which, most emphatically, cotton is king. In the border states, Missouri, Virginia, Kentucky, etc., this crop is of very little importance. The entire value of the cotton crop of 1889 is estimated at $375,000,000.

The accompanying maps, on Plate 34, facing page 168, show, first, the relative importance of the cotton crop to the state, as indicated by the production in bales, compared with the area of the state in square miles; and, second, the production of cotton to the acre, expressed in fractions of a bale, which may perhaps be taken to indicate the relative fertility of the soil and the thoroughness of cultivation.

The latter subject was discussed by Professor Hilgard in his report of the tenth census, and he showed that in the eastern

THE BUILDING OF A NATION

PLATE 36

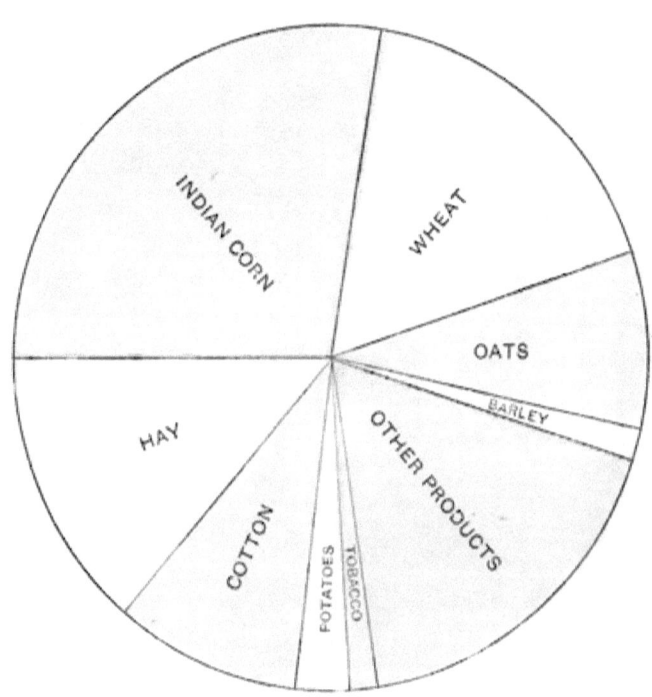

PROPORTIONAL VALUE OF THE PRINCIPAL
PRODUCTS OF AGRICULTURE IN 1889

and western cotton states the yield per acre cultivated was greater than in the middle states of that region. The reason he assigned was, that in the eastern states cultivation had been going on so long that it had become necessary to fertilize the fields, which had largely restored them to their original fertility. In the middle states of this region the process of depleting the soil had gone on to a considerable extent, but renewal by means of fertilizing had not yet commenced; while in the western states the soil was still, to a great extent, in its originally fertile condition, not having been impoverished by continuous cultivation.

Hay.—Among agricultural products hay is not generally credited with the high rank it deserves. It is one of the most valuable of all crops. In 1888 the product amounted to 47,000,000 tons, and was valued at $408,000,000. It is too bulky an article to bear long distance transportation, even when compressed; therefore it is chiefly consumed where grown, and is at last disposed of mainly in the form of beef, mutton, and pork. The bulk of the crop is raised in the North Atlantic and north central states, but little comparatively being produced at the south or west. The greatest quantity, in proportion to area, is raised in Connecticut and New York, followed closely by Iowa and Illinois. This distribution is brought out by the upper map on Plate 35, facing page 168, showing the number of tons raised per square mile of total area.

Potatoes.—The Irishman's staple is a cosmopolite, being cultivated in every state of the Union, but in the northern states much more extensively than at the south and west, as appears by the lower map on Plate 35, facing page 168. The production is greatest in the thickly settled states of the North Atlantic group, in several of which it exceeds five hundred bushels per square mile of area. In 1888 the total product of this vegetable was 202,000,000 bushels, valued at $81,000,000.

The diagram on Plate 36, facing page 170, shows the relative importance of a number of the principal crops in 1889.

Live Stock on Farms and Ranches. The total number of farm animals in 1892 was 169,100,000, and their value was $2,464,000,000. The number and the value of each class are set forth in the following table:

NUMBER AND VALUE OF FARM ANIMALS IN 1892

	Number	Value
Horses	15,500,000	$1,008,000,000
Mules	2,300,000	175,000,000
Cows	16,400,000	351,000,000
Other cattle	37,600,000	570,000,000
Sheep	44,900,000	116,000,000
Swine	52,400,000	241,000,000
	169,100,000	$2,461,000,000

Thus it appears that each farm possesses, on an average, about three and one-half horses or mules, eleven head of cattle, nine sheep, and ten and one-half swine; or, altogether, thirty-four head of live stock, valued at about five hundred dollars.

Distribution of Live Stock.—The maps on Plates 37 and 38 illustrate the distribution of horses and mules, cattle (including milch cows), sheep, and swine, on farms and ranches, expressed in the number of each class per square mile of area. This distribution follows in a broad way that of the rural population, with certain distinctive features. Horses and mules are most abundant in the northern states, and diminish southward, while at the west they are comparatively few in number. They are most abundant in proportion to area, in the prairie states, ranging from twenty-three per square mile in Illinois and Iowa, to twenty in Indiana.

Cattle are distributed in much the same way, as a rule, but the proportion is greater at the west, relatively, than in the case of horses, the number being swollen by the immense herds on the western ranges, as in the case of Texas, where there are thirty cattle to the square mile. The maximum is reached in Iowa, with over seventy to the square mile.

The distribution of sheep shows several marked differences from that of cattle. The densest sheep population is found in Ohio, where there are one hundred and nine to a square mile, nearly three times as many as in any other state; while at the south the number dwindles to six, five, and two to a square mile. In certain western states the great herds bring up the

PLATE 37

NUMBER OF HORSES AND MULES PER SQUARE MILE IN 1892

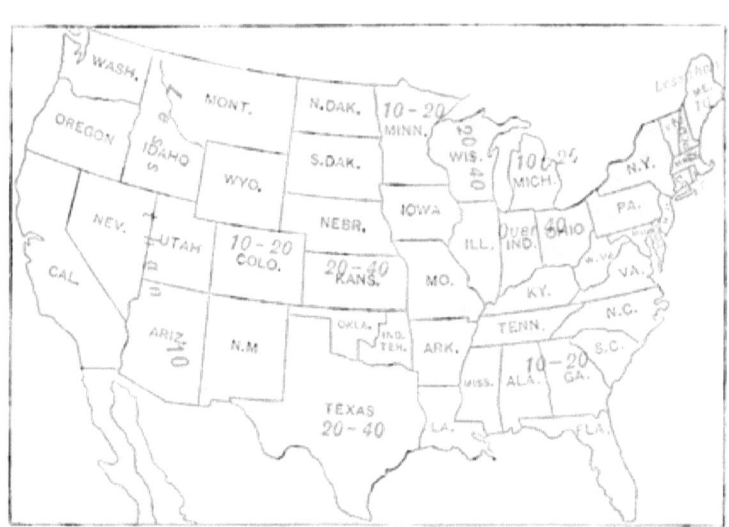

NUMBER OF CATTLE PER SQUARE MILE IN 1892

THE BUILDING OF A NATION

PLATE 38

NUMBER OF SHEEP PER SQUARE MILE IN 1892

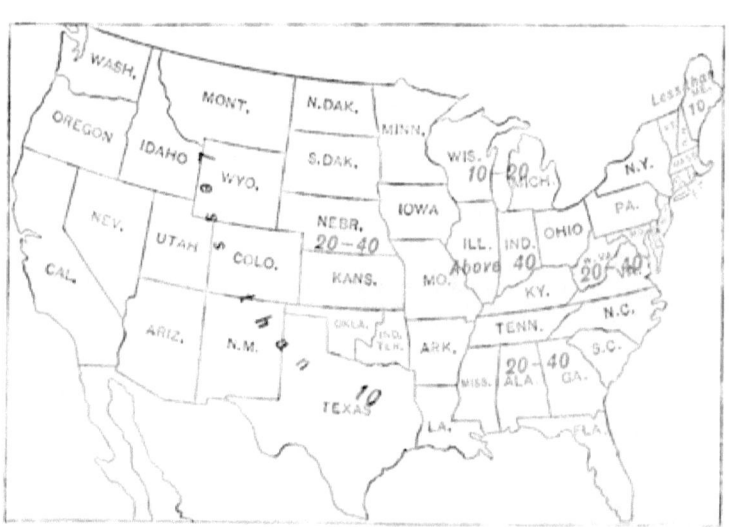

NUMBER OF HOGS PER SQUARE MILE IN 1892

density to quite large figures, in spite of the sparse population. Thus in California there are twenty-six, in Oregon twenty-five, in New Mexico and Utah twenty-four, and in Texas nineteen, to a square mile.

In the raising of pork New England and the west scarcely figure at all. The northern states of the Mississippi valley are the most densely populated with hogs. Iowa has one hundred and twenty-seven to a square mile, Illinois eighty-five, Indiana seventy, and Ohio sixty-nine. Thence southward the number decreases, the razor-backs of Mississippi, Georgia, and Alabama numbering twenty-eight to the square mile.

Irrigation.—In the states and territories of the Cordilleran region, with the exception of western Washington and Oregon and northwestern California, the rainfall is generally insufficient for the needs of agriculture, and throughout this region irrigation is commonly practiced. This area, in which the farmer is dependent mainly upon the streams for a water supply, comprises about one and one-fourth million square miles, or two-fifths of the area of the United States, excluding Alaska. The possible water supply from this source, supposing it to be entirely utilized and with the utmost economy, cannot, it is estimated, supply more than one-tenth of the land, only a small part of that which, aside from the question of water supply, is arable.

In this region irrigation, although practiced for many years, is still in its infancy. Only one-half of one per cent. of the area is under irrigation. With few exceptions, no attempts have yet been made to store the waters of the spring floods. Wasteful systems of irrigation have grown up, due to the want of broad, intelligent plans at the outset; and an enormous waste of water goes on, owing to badly devised forms of contract between the water companies and the farmers. The usual agreement is to supply water for the irrigation of a certain number of acres, not to supply a certain amount of water, to be applied by the farmer to as many or as few acres as he may judge best. A contract calling for a given quantity of water would infallibly lead to great economy in its use, and to an increase in its duty. This "duty," by which is understood the number of acres irrigated by a flow throughout the season of one cubic foot of water per second, ranges widely at the west, from thirty or forty up to one thousand acres, depending upon the crop, the soil, the rainfall, and the experience and economy of the irrigator. The duty has been commonly assumed at one hundred acres, as an average; but as irrigation has developed, the duty has risen, and it seems probable that an average of two hundred acres will soon be reached.

The following table shows the area irrigated in each state and territory, with the proportion which it bears to the total area of the state. From this it appears that Colorado leads, with one and one-third per cent., and that California is second, with one per cent.

IRRIGATED AREA AND TOTAL AREA COMPARED

	Area Irrigated	
	Acres	Per cent of total area of State
Arizona	65,821	0.09
California	1,004,233	1.01
Colorado	890,735	1.34
Idaho	217,005	0.49
Montana	350,582	0.38
Nevada	224,403	0.32
New Mexico	91,745	0.12
Oregon	177,944	0.29
Utah	263,473	0.50
Washington	48,799	0.23
Wyoming	229,676	0.37
Total	3,564,116	0.50

The average first cost of irrigation works is $8.15 per acre. To this must be added the cost of bringing the land under cultivation, which is placed at $12.12. The average yearly expense of maintaining the works is $1.07 per acre.

The average value of irrigated lands is $83.28 per acre, and the value of the product in 1889 was $14.89 per acre.

Thus it appears that, since the land costs practically nothing, the business of constructing irrigation works and placing land under irrigation is, on the whole, a very profitable one. Moreover, it is argued that these western lands, though requiring irrigation, are more profitable for the farmer than eastern lands which are blessed with an ample rainfall. The cost of preparing the latter for the plow is enhanced not only by the necessity of clearing the forest from them, but also by that of fertilizing them, a necessity from which the western farmer is relieved, since the irrigation water constantly supplies fertilizing material.

Artesian wells are used as sources of water supply for irrigation in certain parts of the west, especially for valuable crops, such as those of vineyards and market gardens. Altogether there are nearly four thousand such wells in use, irrigating fifty-two thousand acres, an average of about thirteen acres per well. This method is expensive, its cost averaging nearly twenty dollars per acre, and owing partly to the expense and partly to the necessarily limited supply of underground water, it cannot become an important source of supply.

MANUFACTURES

Although it is well known that the United States is far ahead of other countries in respect of the agricultural industry, and that its mineral product greatly exceeds that of any other, it is not so generally known that this is also the leading manufacturing nation of the globe. The impression prevails that our manufacturing industries, as compared with those of the mother country, are in an infantile stage and require careful nursing to enable them to retain the breath of life; therefore, it will doubtless surprise the majority of people to know that as a manufacturing nation the United States is far in the lead. According to Mulhall, its manufactures exceed those of the mother country in the proportion of seven to four, and are increasing at a rate which, if maintained for a quarter of a century, will make the United States as important a source of supply for manufactured articles as it is now of agricultural products.

General Statistics.—Manufactures have had a very rapid development. The first statistics of this branch of industry were obtained in 1850, when it was found that the capital invested was slightly more than half a billion of dollars. In 1890, forty years later, the invested capital exceeded six billions. Wages had increased from two hundred and thirty-seven millions to two billions of dollars. The material used increased from five hundred and fifty-five millions to nearly five billions of dollars, the gross value of the product from a trifle over a billion to nearly nine and four-tenths billions, and the net value of the product from four hundred and sixty-four millions to four and four-tenths billions. The figures for each census are given in the following table, expressed in millions of dollars, and in thousands of hands employed.

STATISTICS OF MANUFACTURES FROM 1850 TO 1890, BY DECADES

Year	Capital	Hands	Wages	Material	Gross Product	Net Product
1850	533	957	237	555	1,019	464
1860	1,010	1,311	379	1,031	1,886	855
1870*	1,692	2,055	500	2,000	3,384	1,384
1880	2,780	2,739	948	3,397	5,370	1,973
1890	6,180	4,665	2,000	5,000	9,400	4,400

* The figures for 1870 have been reduced to gold.

The figures for 1890 are only approximate, being deduced from statistics covering about one-half of the entire capital, wages, material, and product. It is improbable, however, that the final statistics will materially change the results, or the conclusions derived from them.

The rapid development of manufacturing industries is in obedience to economic laws already alluded to. The country is rapidly filling up, especially in the northeastern states, and as the population becomes more and more dense, it passes the point at which it can be sustained by the cultivation of the soil. Other forms of industry, especially those requiring the aggregation of people, become necessary; and hence we find that all through this part of the country the people are leaving the plow for the shop. They are making things instead of raising things. In the northeastern states agriculture has made little progress during the past quarter of a century, while manufactures have made enormous strides. Moreover, the field of manufactures is increasing year by year. The frontier of the manufacturing industry is spreading westward and southward. In the ten years just passed, the south has made enormous strides in manufactures. The bulk of the increase in the cotton manufacturing industry has taken place in the southern states where the cotton is raised. The manufacture of iron and steel is also increasing in that section with wonderful rapidity. Another Pennsylvania is growing up in the mountains south of Mason and Dixon's line, and in the iron industry will soon rival if not surpass that great state.

The preceding table, which gives a summary of the principal items relating to manufactures for the past forty years, is full of information concerning this great industry. A few deductions from it will prove of interest. Coupled with the enormous extension of manufacturing industries has been a rapid concentration of them. The number of establishments has not increased as rapidly, by any means, as the manufacturing capital, for the average capital of each factory has grown from $4,000 in 1850 to about $15,000 in 1890, as appears from the following table:

AVERAGE CAPITAL INVESTED IN EACH ESTABLISHMENT

1850	$4,000
1860	7,300
1870	6,800
1880	11,000
1890	15,000

The average yearly wages of employés have also increased almost continuously since 1850, the average in 1890 being $429 as contrasted with $247 forty years earlier. These facts are set forth in the following table:

AVERAGE WAGES PER HAND EMPLOYED

1850	$247
1860	290
1870	243
1880	346
1890	429

The proportion of the net product of manufactures received by employés in the form of wages, has ranged from thirty-six to fifty-one per cent.; it was but little less in 1890 than in 1850, despite the immense increase in capital and the introduction of machinery. Indeed, while the capital was nearly twelve times as large in 1890 as in 1850, the number of hands was less than five times as great. The proportions of the net product which came to capital and to labor, are set forth in the following table:

PROPORTIONS OF NET PRODUCT SHARED BY EMPLOYÉS AND BY CAPITAL

	Employés	Capital
1850	51	49
1860	44	56
1870	36	64
1880	48	52
1890	45	55

A comparison of the net product with the amount of capital invested, has produced the table below: it shows that the proportion between capital and product has steadily diminished since 1850, from eighty per cent. down to seventy-one per cent. In the same table is a column showing the proportion which the net product, minus wages, bears to capital; from which it appears that this proportion, while it has not greatly changed, has slightly diminished during the forty years under consideration.

RATIO OF NET PRODUCT TO CAPITAL

	Proportion of Net Product to Capital	Proportion of Net Product, Minus Wages, to Capital
1850	87	43
1860	85	47
1870	82	52
1880	71	37
1890	71	39

The diagram on page 180 shows the products of manufactures, expressed in millions of dollars, of the leading cities of the country in 1890. It will be seen that New York, our greatest commercial city, is also incomparably our greatest manufacturing city; that Chicago is second, leading Philadelphia. Then there follows a great gap, Brooklyn having less than half the manufactures of Philadelphia; Milwaukee stands very high, and Washington very low, in proportion to their population.

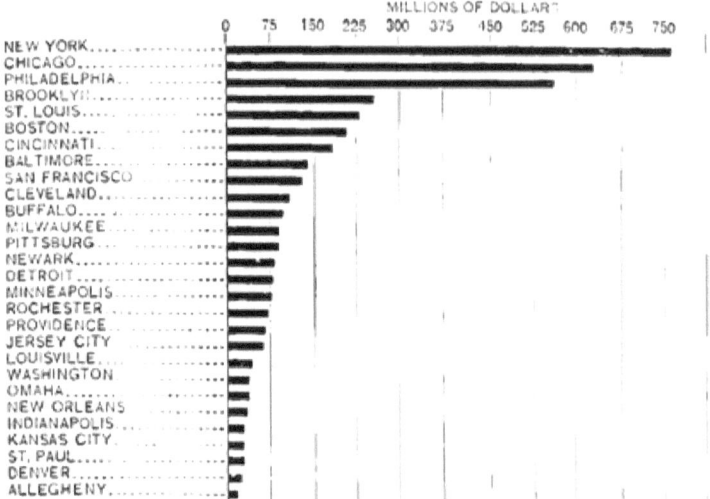

PRODUCTS OF MANUFACTURES IN LEADING CITIES IN 1890

Iron and Steel Manufactures.—Of all the branches of manufactures this has claimed and received the fullest protection which can be afforded by a protective tariff. There has never been a moment, from the time when the first iron furnace was established to the present, when this industry was not in danger of being overwhelmed and swallowed up by the rapacity of the iron men of Great Britain. Such, at least, is the popular idea. Since we are engaged in idol breaking, let us see how much truth there is in it. How far inferior to the mother country are we in the production and manufacture of iron and steel? Twenty years ago, in 1872, she produced nearly three times as much iron, while our production of steel bore no appreciable proportion to hers. In 1890-1-2 we produced twelve per cent. more iron than Great Britain; while in the production of steel we passed her in 1886, and now produce twenty-five per cent. more than she does. Thus it would seem that she is rather in need of protection against our overgrown industries.

The accompanying diagram rehearses the history of the iron and steel production of this country for the past twenty years. The increase since 1872, in the production of pig-iron, was from

2,500,000 tons to nearly 10,000,000, and of steel from 160,000 tons to 5,000,000. The production of both iron and steel has been greater during the year 1892 than in any previous one, and this in spite of the low price of these metals.

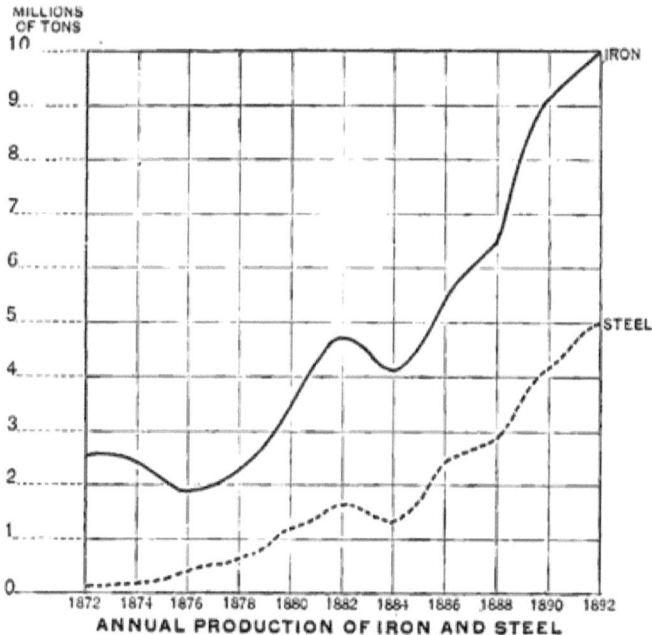
ANNUAL PRODUCTION OF IRON AND STEEL

The manufacture of steel by the Bessemer process began in 1867, and has increased with the greatest rapidity, until in the past year the production amounted to nearly 4,500,000 tons, being by far the greater part of all steel produced in that year.

The rails used in laying our first railways were of iron, and it is within the time of the present generation that steel rails were first employed. Their use has increased to such an extent, however, that they have almost entirely supplanted iron rails, and the manufacture of steel rails for both steam and street railways has become an enormous industry. In 1892 nearly 1,500,000 tons of steel rails were manufactured, while the manufacture of iron rails has almost entirely disappeared.

A similar change has taken place in the matter of nails. The maximum production of cut nails has probably been reached and passed, while the manufacture of wire nails is increasing with great rapidity, and they will doubtless virtually supplant cut nails in the near future.

On June 30, 1890, there were in the United States 562 blast furnaces; of these, 224 were in the state of Pennsylvania. At the same date there were 158 steel works, half of which were in Pennsylvania.

Cotton Industry.—The cotton industry is one of the largest in the country. It is widely dispersed, cotton manufactures being found in most of the states; but its principal seat is in New England, where 63 per cent. of the cotton manufacturing of the country is carried on. Next in importance are the southern states, with 23 per cent., or nearly one-fourth. The number of factories in 1880 was 756; ten years later it had increased to 904; about one-half of this increase was in the southern states, where the industry has developed with great rapidity. In 1880 the capital invested in cotton manufacturing was $208,000,000, and in 1890 it was $354,000,000, having increased 70 per cent., or at a much more rapid rate than the number of establishments, thus illustrating the greater centralization of the industry. Another expression of this fact is seen in the average capital per factory, which in 1880 was $275,000, and had increased in 1890 to $392,000. The number of hands employed in 1880 was 174,659, and in 1890 the number was 221,585, an increase of 27 per cent. During the same period wages had advanced 57 per cent.,—i. e., from $42,000,000 to $66,000,000—showing a notable increase in the average pay of the employés. The materials used had a value in 1880 of $102,000,000, and in 1890 of $155,000,000, an increase of 51 per cent.; and the product rose in the same time from $192,000,000 to $268,000,000, which was at the rate of 40 per cent.

Wool Industry.—The wool industry is strongly established. Its factories are located almost entirely in New England, New York, New Jersey, and Pennsylvania. In 1890 they numbered 2,503, as against 2,689 in 1880, a marked diminution in number. On the other hand, the capital invested in 1890 was $297,000,000, as against $159,000,000 ten years earlier. Thus, while the factories have been reduced in number, the amount of capital has been almost doubled, a striking illustration of the tendency toward aggregation in this as well as other industries. The number of hands employed increased from 166,557 in 1880, to 221,087 in 1890; the wages, from $47,000,000 to $77,000,000, showing not only a large increase in total wages paid, but an increase in the wages paid per hand. Between 1880 and 1890, the gross product of the wool manufacturing industry increased from $267,000,000 to $338,000,000, a gain of 27 per cent.; while the net product, by which is meant the gross product less the cost of the raw material, was scarcely increased at all, notwithstanding the above-mentioned increase of 62 per cent. in the total amount of wages paid.

Silk Industry.—Until recently the manufacture of silk was one of the Republic's babies. It had been carefully nursed and coddled, and for a long time seemed likely to die of anæmia. Recently, however, it has taken a new lease of life, and now appears able to stand alone. During the past ten years the industry has doubled. In 1890 its establishments numbered 472, with a capital of $51,000,000. It employed over 50,000 hands, and paid them wages to the extent of $19,700,000; and the product of the factories was valued at $87,000,000.

Books, Periodicals, and Newspapers.—"Of making many books there is no end." If this was true when first written, how much more true is it to-day, and of America! Our market for literature is the best in the world, and the supply is equal to the demand. The number of books published here is not greatly in excess of the number published in Great Britain, the total in 1891 being 4,665, exclusive of cheap editions, as against 4,429 in the mother country. The excess is seen rather in the enormous amount of periodical literature. In 1891 19,373 periodicals of all classes were published in the United States and Canada; of these 837 were Canadian, leaving 18,536 for the United States.

The following table shows the grouping of the whole number, as to the period of publication, and also the average and total circulation of each group:

NUMBER AND CIRCULATION OF PERIODICALS, BY CLASSES

	Number	Circulation Total	Average
Weekly	14,000	26,638,250	1,903
Monthly	2,625	11,734,750	4,470
Daily	1,591	6,885,000	4,300
Semi-monthly	327	1,487,500	4,549
Semi-weekly	238	434,250	1,824
Quarterly	180	451,750	2,509
Bi-weekly	90	210,250	2,336
Bi-monthly	76	166,250	2,188
Tri-weekly	46	48,400	1,051
Total	19,373	48,856,500	

Thus it will be seen that the total circulation of all periodicals, per issue, is three-fourths of the number of the total population of the United States.

Spirits, Wines, and Malt Liquors.—It has been said that, in the olden time, no southerner was thought to be a gentleman who did not get drunk at least once a week. It is perhaps safe to conclude that matters were much the same at the north in colonial days, judging from the quantity of New England rum that was consumed at house-raisings and kindred gatherings. There has been a great improvement in this regard within the century; but a vast amount of liquor of one sort or another is still produced and disposed of.

The following table shows the product of spirituous and malt liquors in the year 1891 alone:

SPIRITUOUS AND MALT LIQUORS PRODUCED IN 1891

Whisky	44,316,804 gallons.
Alcohol	12,260,821 "
Rum	1,784,342 "
Wines	24,306,905 "
Fruit brandy	1,223,775 "
Beer	30,021,079 barrels.

It will be noted that the product for this single year aggregated more than a gallon of spirits and nearly half a barrel of beer for every man, woman, and child in the nation. It is gratifying to observe, however, that the use of malt liquors is increasing rapidly among all classes, and that these, together with light wines, are gradually displacing the great American beverage.

MINERAL RESOURCES

BENEATH the surface of our country lies hidden wealth of almost incalculable value. The mineral deposits are enormous and of the most varied character. Nearly every mineral and metal valuable in the arts, is mined within our limits.

The value of the total mineral product of the United States in the year 1891, as appears from the statistics collected by the United States Geological Survey, footed up the enormous total of $668,524,537; of this a little less than one-half consisted of metals, and a little more than one-half of non-metallic substances. The following tables show the principal items of mineral production, expressed in quantities and values, and the diagram illustrates their relative values.

As will be seen, the value of coal, anthracite and bituminous, is greater than that of all other non-metallic substances together.

QUANTITY AND VALUE OF NON-METALLIC PRODUCTS IN 1891

	Quantity	Value
Bituminous coal	105,294,724 long tons.	$117,106,483
Pennsylvania anthracite	45,296,992 long tons.	73,943,795
Building stone		47,294,746
Petroleum	54,291,980 barrels.	32,575,188
Lime	60,000,000 barrels.	35,000,000
Natural gas		18,000,000
Cement	8,222,792 barrels.	6,680,951
Salt	9,987,945 barrels.	1,716,121
Phosphate rock	587,988 long tons.	3,651,150
Mineral waters	18,392,732 gallons sold.	2,906,259

QUANTITY AND VALUE OF METALLIC PRODUCTS IN 1891

	Quantity	Value
Pig iron, value at Philadelphia	8,279,870 long tons.	$128,347,985
Silver, coining value	58,300,000 Troy ounces.	75,416,565
Gold, coining value	1,604,840 Troy ounces.	33,175,000
Copper, value at New York City	295,810,076 pounds.	38,455,300
Lead, value at New York City	202,406 short tons.	17,000,322
Zinc, value at New York City	80,337 short tons.	8,033,700
Quicksilver, value at San Francisco.	22,904 flasks.	1,036,386

MILLIONS OF DOLLARS

COAL	
PIG IRON	
SILVER	
BUILDING STONE	
LIME	
GOLD	
PETROLEUM	
COPPER	
NATURAL GAS	
LEAD	
ZINC	
CEMENT	
SALT	
LIMESTONE	
PHOSPHATE ROCK	
MINERAL WATERS	
ZINC WHITE	
QUICKSILVER	

VALUE OF PRINCIPAL MINERAL PRODUCTS IN 1889

Coal. Of all our mineral products, coal is probably the most widely distributed. It occurs in three-fourths of the states and territories, and is mined in thirty, or three-fifths of them. The total product of coal for 1891 was 150,528,713 long tons; of this 45,236,992 tons were Pennsylvania anthracite, the remainder consisting almost entirely of bituminous coal.

Of the world's coal product, amounting to a little over half a billion short tons, that of the United States was almost precisely one-third. Great Britain is the only country that exceeded the United States in the coal output of 1891, her total being 185,-479,126 short tons.

Nearly all the anthracite coal of the country is produced from a limited region in the eastern part of Pennsylvania. A trifling amount is mined in Rhode Island and Colorado, and a little is produced from two or three other limited fields.

The deposits in Pennsylvania have been worked continuously since 1820. The demands upon them and the output have increased year by year, until, as already stated, this small area produced in 1891 the vast quantity of 45,236,992 long tons. Their product since 1820 has reached the enormous total of 853,000,000 tons.

Bituminous coal exists in all varieties, from what may be denominated semi-anthracite, through all grades of softness to lignite. The deposits in the eastern part of the country and in the Mississippi valley are of the carboniferous age, and as a rule the coal is harder than that in the Rocky mountain region, which is of the tertiary or cretaceous age, and in many localities grades into lignite. The following table shows the production of bituminous coal in the various states for the year 1891:

COAL PRODUCT OF THE SEVERAL STATES IN 1891

STATES	Total Amount Produced (Short Tons)	STATES	Total Amount Produced (Short Tons)
Alabama	1,759,784	New Mexico	462,328
Arkansas	542,359	North Carolina	20,355
California	93,301	North Dakota	30,000
Colorado	3,512,632	Ohio	12,868,683
Georgia	171,000	Oregon	51,826
Illinois	15,660,698	Pennsylvania	42,788,490
Indiana	2,975,474	Rhode Island	500
Indian Territory	1,091,632	Tennessee	2,413,678
Iowa	3,825,195	Texas	172,100
Kansas	2,716,705	Utah	371,045
Kentucky	2,916,069	Virginia	736,399
Maryland	3,820,239	Washington	1,056,249
Michigan	80,307	West Virginia	9,220,665
Missouri	2,674,606	Wyoming	2,327,841
Montana	511,861		
Nebraska	1,500	Total	117,901,238

Of the total product, more than one-third comes from the single state of Pennsylvania, and about one-half from the two states of Pennsylvania and Illinois. Eight states—namely, Alabama, Colorado, Illinois, Iowa, Maryland, Ohio, Pennsylvania, and West Virginia—produce four-fifths of the entire bituminous coal output.

Iron.—Iron ore, like coal, is very widely distributed. There are few states or territories in which it does not occur, and in 1890 it was mined commercially in twenty-eight of them. Again, as in the case of coal, its profitable mining depends upon the existence of facilities for reaching the market. The production of pig iron in 1891 was 8,279,870 tons, a reduction of nearly 1,000,000 tons below the product of the preceding year; this reduction was due to the low price of iron, which had thrown many furnaces out of blast.

The principal ores of iron are the sesquioxide and the hydrated sesquioxide. The former, commonly known as red hematite, constitutes the principal ore mined in the Marquette district of Michigan, which supplies fully two-fifths of the entire product of the country. Next to Michigan in the production of iron is Alabama, which has but recently passed Pennsylvania, while both states together yield but little more than half the amount produced by Michigan alone. The ores of Alabama are principally red hematite and limonite. Those of Pennsylvania are mostly magnetite, a variety of hematite, and limonite. New York holds the fourth place, with its large deposits of magnetite; it is closely followed by Minnesota and Wisconsin with their immense deposits of red hematite, which have recently been discovered and opened. These six states jointly produced more than four-fifths of the entire output.

In 1889 the production of iron ore in the United States was one-fourth of the entire product of the globe. It was exceeded only by Great Britain, and in 1890 the United States took the lead over that country, producing 9,202,703 long tons of pig iron, as against 7,904,214 tons by Great Britain. Of the world's production of pig iron, in that year, 26,973,113 tons, the output of the United States exceeded one-third.

In 1882 the production of pig iron by Great Britain was

nearly double that of the United States; but in 1890, only eight years later, the latter passed the former in production, as above stated. The following table shows the production of pig iron in this country and Great Britain in every tenth year since 1820:

PRODUCTION OF PIG IRON IN THE UNITED STATES AND GREAT BRITAIN, BY DECADES

Year	United States	Great Britain
	Tons	Tons
1820	22,400	400,000
1830	181,800	677,417
1840	324,334	1,396,400
1850	632,526	2,500,000
1860	919,770	3,826,752
1870	1,865,000	5,963,515
1880	4,295,414	7,749,233
1890	9,202,703	7,904,214

Steel.—The production of steel of all kinds in the year 1890 was 4,790,319 short tons, nearly all of it being Bessemer steel. In the manufacture of steel Pennsylvania stands far in advance among the states.

In the world's production of steel the United States leads all other countries; its product is much greater than that of its greatest competitor, Great Britain, and nearly double that of Germany. Of the entire production of the world in 1890, that of this country constituted 34.9 per cent., or more than one-third.

For generations Great Britain had produced this, the metal of metals, for the entire world. No greater or more significant industrial victory has been achieved by our country, than that of wresting from her brow the iron crown.

Gold.—Since the days of '49, when gold was discovered in the placers of the Sierra Nevada, the United States has been the principal source of its supply to the world. As the early placers were exhausted, others were discovered. When the supply from this form of deposits diminished, new forms of deposit were discovered in other places, and thus the supply has been maintained.

Starting with a yield of $40,000,000 in 1849, the yearly product has risen and fallen, the maximum being $65,000,000 in 1853, and the minimum $30,000,000 in 1883. The production in 1890 was $32,845,000. Of this amount two-fifths was from California, which still maintains its position as the Golden State; over $4,000,000 came from Colorado, where gold is mined in connection with silver; more than $3,000,000 from Montana, and an almost equal amount from the Black Hills of South Dakota.

To the world's production of gold in 1890, the United States contributed 28 per cent., and leading competitors in the production of this precious metal, are Australia, which in 1890 produced $30,000,000, and Russia, which produced $21,000,000.

Silver.—Prior to 1860 the production of silver in the United States was trifling. The discovery in 1861 of the Comstock lode in Nevada, was the first of a series of discoveries that have placed our country far at the front as the leading producer of this metal. As in the case of gold, silver is now mined in every state and territory of the Cordilleran region. The product has increased steadily from the time of the first discoveries, reaching in 1890 a total value of $70,485,714.

For a long time Nevada was the leading state in the production of silver; but the decline of the Comstock and Eureka mines, together with the discoveries at Leadville, Colorado, and Butte, Montana, have placed the latter states far ahead of her in this regard. Colorado led in silver production in 1890, her output for that year being valued at over $24,000,000; Montana followed with a production of more than $20,000,000; while Nevada had dropped to $5,750,000, being exceeded by Utah with over $10,000,000. From the states of Colorado and Montana, and Utah Territory, is derived nearly four-fifths of the entire silver product of the nation.

To the world's production of silver in 1890, the United States contributed more than two-fifths. Our leading competitor is Mexico, whose product in that year was $50,000,000.

Copper.—The United States commenced to produce copper about the year 1845, the first source of supply being the native copper deposits at Keweenaw Point in northern Michigan. The production from these deposits increased gradually, and for a long time they were practically the only source of native supply. Within a few years deposits of great commercial importance have been discovered in Montana and Arizona, and those in Montana have been developed to such an extent that in 1890 their yield was in excess of that in northern Michigan. The total production of the country in 1890 was 115,669 long tons—twice that of Spain and Portugal, more than four times that of Chile, and more than two-fifths of the production of the whole world.

To illustrate the enormous wealth of the Lake Superior deposits, it may be said that in 1876 nine-tenths of all the copper in the United States was produced in this district, and that in 1890 the yield of this district was greater than that of the whole country eight years earlier. For a long time one mine in this district, the Calumet and Hecla, produced more than all the rest of the district; and, indeed, until very recently it has controlled the copper market of the world. In 1876 the Calumet and Hecla mine contributed one-half of all the copper output of the country. Again, in 1890 the product of this mine was one-fourth that of the entire country, and one-tenth of the product of the world. It has proved a veritable bonanza to its owners.

Lead.—This country began to produce lead about 1825, and the production has increased up to the present time. In 1890 it was 161,754 short tons. Lead was first mined in the district comprising parts of southwestern Wisconsin, northwestern Illinois, and northeastern Iowa, a district which is still producing, although on a very limited scale. Later, deposits were discovered in southwestern Missouri and southeastern Kansas, where they are associated with zinc. These mines, especially those in Missouri, are still yielding lead in large quantities.

More recently lead has been mined in the western states and territories in connection with silver; their product has increased greatly, and now far exceeds that from the more eastern states. Thus, of the total product of lead in 1890, that from Colorado, mainly from the Leadville district, reached 70,888 tons, or nearly one-half the product of the country; Idaho produced 23,172 tons; Utah, 16,675 tons; and Montana, 10,183 tons. These four states and territories collectively contribute more than three-fourths of the lead product of the entire country. Nearly all of that from the more eastern states was produced in Missouri, whose yield was 29,258 tons.

Zinc.—The early production of zinc in this country was from deposits in northern New Jersey; at one time they yielded largely, but the production has fallen off greatly in recent years. The supply now comes mainly from northwestern Illinois, southeastern Kansas, and southwestern Missouri, where it is mined in connection with lead. The total product in 1890 was 63,683 short tons, distributed as follows:

SOURCES OF THE PRODUCTION OF ZINC IN 1890

Illinois	26,243
Kansas	15,199
Missouri	13,127
All other sources	9,114
	63,683

Quicksilver.—California is practically the only source of quicksilver in the United States. Several mines, mainly in the Coast ranges, have contributed to the supply. In recent years the production has been carefully adjusted to the demand, and it is said that the mines now are beginning to show signs of exhaustion. Of these deposits, the one known as New Almaden is by far the largest, and has a controlling influence upon production.

Petroleum.—Nearly all the petroleum of the world is produced in this country. The only other source of supply of any importance is southern Russia, and its competition is scarcely felt in the world's market. Within the United States petroleum is widely distributed, but the supply comes almost entirely from a comparatively limited area in western Pennsylvania, southwestern New York, and Ohio. Indeed, of the total production in 1890, 45,822,672 barrels, not less than 44,582,864 barrels were produced in these three states.

The production and distribution of petroleum are controlled by the Standard Oil Company. It is transported from the wells to the markets in our large cities by means of pipe lines. The economies in its production and transportation have been carried to such an extent that the price, which in 1865 was $6.59 per barrel, has been reduced, until in 1886 the average price was but eighty-six cents per barrel.

Natural Gas.—Within the past few years a new source of light and heat has been discovered in the form of natural gas, which has rapidly come into extensive use, not only for domestic but for manufacturing purposes. Its occurrence coincides quite closely with that of petroleum, and within its range of occurrence it has displaced coal to a great extent. In 1890 the consumption of natural gas is estimated to have been 552,150,000,000 cubic feet, displacing 9,774,417 tons of coal.

Salt.—Salt is produced by evaporating the waters of salt springs. The supply comes almost entirely from the lower peninsula of Michigan and from western New York. The production from all sources, in 1890, was 8,776,994 barrels.

TRANSPORTATION

WITH its great extent and variety of climate the United States possesses capabilities for producing almost everything required for the sustenance and comfort of man, and these capabilities are being rapidly improved. The distribution throughout the country of its varied products has developed a domestic commerce that is almost fabulous in amount, and the means of transportation are upon a corresponding scale.

Wagon Roads.—First in order of mention are the wagon roads. Of their extent only an approximate estimate can be made. Throughout the densely settled parts of the northeastern states they average in length two and one-half miles to each square mile, while upon the great western plateau, as a rule, the roads are few and far between. It is probable that, taking the country over, there is nearly a mile of road to each square mile of area; this would make a total of three million miles of wagon roads, including all that through courtesy can be so designated.

Taken as a whole, the wagon roads of the United States are poorly built; to speak more correctly, they are not built at all. Little attention has been paid to the selection of easy grades or direct routes, but they have generally been laid out to suit the convenience of the farms through which they run. The construction of roads, as a rule, is limited to grading and leveling, and practically none of them have been paved in any way, at least beyond the outskirts of the cities. In the northern states the roads are commonly kept in good repair, as regards grading and leveling, and in dry weather, as a rule, they are tolerably good for travel.

In the southern states, on the other hand, the roads as a class are very bad. The aim appears to be to work them as little as possible, consistent with mere passability. A large proportion, indeed one might almost say a majority, are almost impassable for wheeled vehicles. In very recent years a strong movement has arisen in behalf of better roads, and it is to be hoped that this movement will result in a general and marked improvement of their quality.

RAILWAYS

The railway system of the United States, considering the stage of settlement, is the most complete of all the countries of the earth. It supplements to a great extent the system of wagon roads, and not only excuses but explains their poor average quality. In few parts of the country are extended highways required. Transportation by wagon road is everywhere toward the railway, and, therefore, highways between points at a distance from one another are but little needed. In no respect, perhaps, have the Americans shown their good sense and foresight more forcibly than in the rapid extension of railway transportation.

Extent.— At the end of the calendar year 1891 there were in the United States not less than 171,048 miles of railway, an average of one linear mile to 17.5 square miles of area, excluding Alaska. This proportion of linear miles to area differs widely in different states; it is greatest in Massachusetts, where there is a mile of railway to each 3.73 square miles; and least in Nevada, where there is but one mile of railway to 121 square miles of area. This enormous railway system, which has cost nearly ten thousand millions of dollars, and which transports each year many billions of passengers and many billion tons of freight, has grown up entirely within a little over sixty years. The diagram on page 197 shows its trifling beginnings, and its rate of growth each year, from 1830 to the present time.

The railway system of the United States is perhaps one of the finest examples to be found of the nice adaptation of means to ends, so characteristic of Americans. In the densely settled parts of the country, where railway traffic is heavy, the construction and equipment are of the best in all respects. The

RAILWAY MILEAGE OF THE UNITED STATES, 1830 TO 1890

Pennsylvania, the New York Central, and other roads of the northeastern states, are, in everything that contributes to the safety and comfort of travel, and in the capacity and facilities for transporting freight, unequaled upon the globe.

But upon the frontier, where the present demands of traffic

RAILWAY MILEAGE OF THE WORLD FOR 1890, BY COUNTRIES

are slight, railways are built and equipped in the cheapest manner possible. A poor railroad is, however, vastly better than none, and under such traffic conditions it would be folly to build an expensive one. Thus the traveler finds the quality of the roadbed, equipment, and train service, closely associated with the density of population.

The above diagram shows the railway mileage of the principal

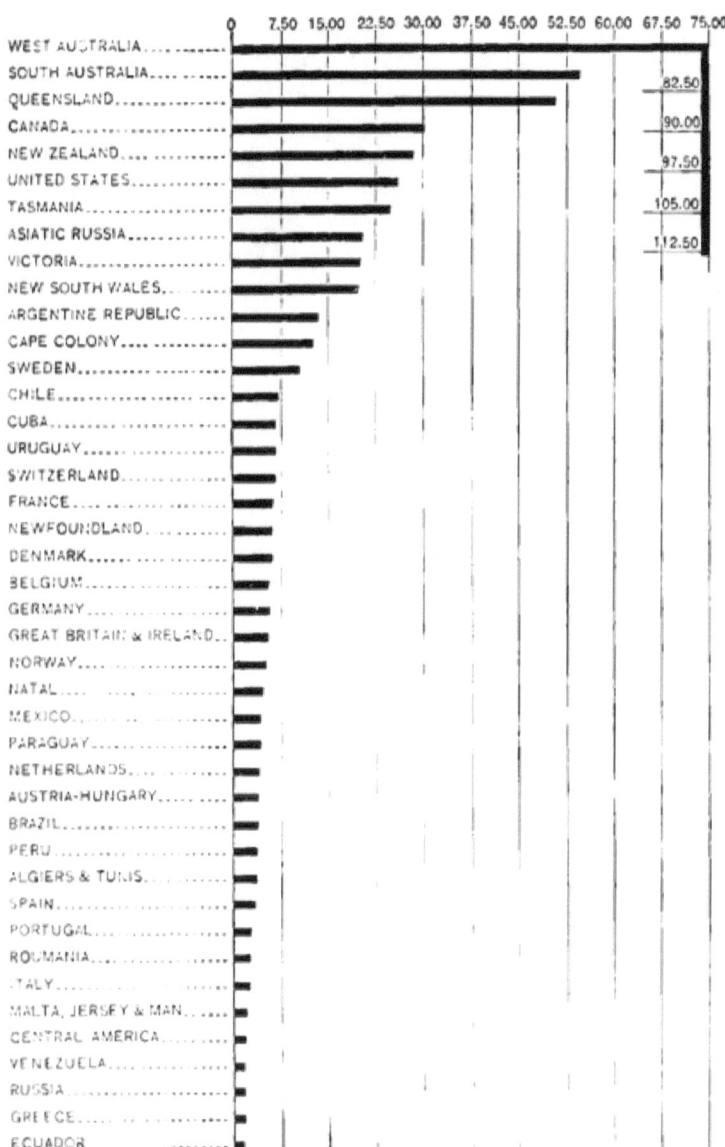

MILES OF RAILWAY PER 10,000 INHABITANTS, BY COUNTRIES, IN 1890

countries of the globe, and that on page 199 the mileage of each country in proportion to population.

The railway mileage of the United States is to-day much greater than that of the whole of Europe, and is rapidly gaining on that of the rest of the globe. Instead of showing any signs of being completed, it is extending more rapidly than ever. Almost as many miles have been built in the past ten years, as were in operation at the beginning of that decade. In a single year, 1887, nearly as many miles were built as the entire number of miles in operation throughout England and Wales.

GENERAL STATISTICS

The following statistics, taken from the report of the Interstate Commerce Commission, show the volume of business and other interesting facts for the year ending June 30, 1890:

RAILWAY CAPITAL, OPERATING EXPENSES, EARNINGS, ETC.

Miles of railway	163,597
Capital and funded debt, assumed to be the cost of construction	$9,871,378,389
Cost of construction per mile	60,340
Gross earnings	1,051,877,632
Operating expenses	692,093,971
Income from operations	359,783,661
Other income	126,767,064
Total income	468,550,725
All deductions from income	384,792,138
Net income	101,758,587
Dividends declared	89,688,204
Surplus	12,070,383

The cost of construction as here given is almost equally divided between capital stock and funded debt. Dividends, as will be noted, amount to only about two per cent. on the capital stock, showing that railways *per se* are not, as a whole, profitable property. But, as will be shown hereafter, they are frequently built as means to ends rather than for direct profit.

Traffic Statistics.—To what extent does the railway

system serve the public? What is the volume of its traffic? These queries are answered by the following figures:

RAILWAY TRAFFIC FOR THE YEAR ENDING JUNE 30, 1890

Number of passengers carried	492,430,865
Number of passengers carried one mile	11,847,785,617
Average journey per passenger (miles)	24.06
Number of tons of freight carried	636,541,617
Number of tons of freight carried one mile	76,207,047,298
Average carry of each ton of freight (miles)	119.72

From the above figures concerning the passenger movement on railways, an idea may be obtained of the extreme mobility of the population. It appears, supposing each person in the United States to have traveled an equal amount during the year, that the distance traveled by each was one hundred and ninety miles. The extent of the freight movement, the internal commerce by rail, may be summarized by the statement that for each inhabitant over ten tons of freight are moved annually to a distance of about one hundred and twenty miles.

Of the total earnings of all the railways, 29.41 per cent. are derived from passenger travel and 68.23 per cent. from freight traffic.

Organization.—This great system is held under 1,797 different corporate bodies, but it is operated almost entirely by but 747 of them, the property of the remainder being either leased or operated under other forms of contract.

Consolidation.—The tendency of railway property is toward consolidation. Although built originally as short lines with numerous owners, connecting lines have been merged, until now the greater part of this enormous system is in few hands. Indeed, consolidation has gone so far that forty companies are to-day operating no less than 77,872 miles of railway, or 47.51 per cent. of the whole. Again, seventy-five companies operate 102,305 miles, or 65.41 per cent. of the entire mileage of the country; that is, one-tenth of the operating companies of the United States control nearly two-thirds of the entire system. If we consider the extent of traffic, the proportion is still greater, for the gross revenue of these seventy-five companies is no less than 80.51 per cent. of the entire gross revenue of the system. These roads do 83.56 of all the railway passenger traffic, and carry 85.38 per cent. of all the freight.

The process of consolidation is going on as rapidly as ever, and it is hard to say whether it will stop short of the formation of one vast system for the United States. It is easy to decry the tendency and to describe the dangers attendant upon the formation of such enormous corporations. To the traveling public, however, and the traveling public constitute the people, it is unnecessary to point out the great advantages incident to consolidation—the increased rapidity, safety, and comfort of traveling, and the reduction in rates.

It is said that consolidation between railways serves to eliminate competition. This may be true as regards the competition of other railways, but the people supply an element of competition which is not generally considered. Railway travel is measurably a luxury, and with high rates people refrain from indulging in it unnecessarily, and traffic is thereby reduced. The prices of many commodities cannot bear high freight rates, and when they exceed a certain amount, a reduction in freight traffic is seriously felt. In these ways the public acts as a competitor of the railroads, to a large extent unconsciously as far as the public is concerned, but the railway manager feels it to the utmost and bows before it.

Cost of Transportation.— By means of this consolidation which we are so fond of decrying, the cost of transporting freight and passengers by rail has been reduced to an amount that seems almost trifling. During the year under consideration, that ending June 30, 1890, the average cost to the railway of transporting a passenger one mile was but 1.917 cents, while the revenue to the road of such transportation was 2.167 cents. As to freight, the average expense to the railway attendant upon moving a ton of freight one mile was .604 of a cent, and the receipts of the road for such service were .941 of a cent. In other words, to move a ton of freight from Chicago to New York, the distance being about a thousand miles, cost in the neighborhood of $6; to carry a barrel of flour the same distance, cost 60 cents. On this basis the entire yearly food supply for a family of five persons can be transported a thousand miles for the sum of $9.

Rolling Stock.—For the same year, ending June 30, 1890, there were in service 29,928 locomotives, 25,511 passenger cars, and 913,580 freight cars. These, with special cars of various kinds, made a total service of 1,164,188 cars. These figures may be compared with the length of railway lines, as follows: The number of locomotives to each hundred miles of line was 19; of passenger cars, 17; of freight cars, 548; and of total cars, 774. As to the service afforded by this equipment, the number of passengers carried per locomotive was 58,735; and the passenger mileage carried per locomotive, 1,413,142. Similarly, the number of tons of freight was 49,433, and the freight mileage per locomotive, 4,721,627.

The addition of the train brake is probably the most important among the modern improvements in connection with railway travel. Practically all passenger trains are now equipped with it, mainly with the Westinghouse air brake, and more than one-half of the freight engines are thus equipped. Automatic couplers have been adopted almost universally upon passenger cars; but as yet very few freight cars are equipped with them, and to this more than any other cause is to be attributed the large number of accidents among train employés.

Accidents.—Statistics for 1890 show that of a total of 749,300 employés of our railway system, 2,451 were killed and 22,396 injured during that year. It is unnecessary to add that these accidents occurred largely in the coupling and uncoupling of cars and in braking freight trains. The number of passengers killed during the same year was but 286, and but 2,425 were injured, a rate of mortality so trifling that one is tempted to join with Mark Twain in advocating railway travel as conducive to long life.

Objects of Construction.—There is one very suggestive item in the foregoing statistics; namely, the proportion that the dividends bear to the stock. This, as already stated, is about two per cent., showing that railway property on the whole, and in itself, is by no means profitable.

While many, perhaps most, railways have been built for the profits to be derived from their operation, a large proportion were constructed mainly as a means to an end, that end being the creation of an increase in values along the line of the road. It is partly with this object in view that railways have been extended so rapidly into unsettled regions, especially at the far west, and have thus paved the way to settlement. It goes without saying that most of these enterprises have not only lined the pockets of their projectors, but have increased the general wealth and well-being in thus developing the sections through which they run.

Many railways, however, are built for other purposes. Every system has its "territory," in which it seeks to maintain a sort of sovereignty. In self-defense against the encroachments of a rival, it is often forced to build and operate branches which it knows will not pay of themselves, at least for many years.

Again, many railways are built far into unsettled regions for the purpose of controlling the traffic which it is foreseen will be supplied when, through their agency, the country shall have become settled.

ENGINEERING WORK

Not only our railways, but the bridges, canals, dams, and all other like constructions, are characterized by a close adaptation of means to ends, of construction to special requirements and conditions.

Yet nothing is more common than to hear our engineering work decried by Europeans and by Europeanized Americans, on the score of lack of thoroughness in construction. Such criticisms do not take into account the peculiar conditions of our environment. They are rather the outgrowth of ignorance than of superior knowledge. Of all the peoples under the sun, the Americans have the keenest appreciation of the importance of adapting their structures to the necessities of the situation. Thus they build a Brooklyn and a St. Louis bridge to last for all time; and in the same breath, as it were, they build a wooden trestle over the Platte, in Wyoming, to last only until the traffic will warrant a more durable structure.

An American engineer knows what he is about when he builds the cheapest possible railway across the sparsely settled plains. The same engineer would build an entirely different sort of road in New York, and in building it would be guided by the same principles which obtained in the Dakotas; that is, of fitting means to ends.

As in railway and bridge construction, so it is in mining and irrigation works. No greater injury has been done to our mining interests than by the introduction of German engineers, with their peculiar ideas of thoroughly exploiting mines and erecting expensive reduction works, before taking out ore. Hundreds of valuable properties have been wrecked by such mismanagement, wrongly characterized as conservatism.

The same is true as to irrigation. Many an enterprise has been ruined by an engineering plan too elaborate and thorough for the prevailing financial conditions. The American engineer commonly understands and considers them, while the English or German engineer is too apt to look only at the engineering aspects of the case, and to shut his eyes to its financial side.

A generation ago the foreign-bred engineer was highly regarded, and much dependence was placed on him. To-day the American-bred engineers, the graduates of Boston, Yale, Columbia, Troy, Lehigh, and a score of other schools, have come to the front, and Americans realize that only through American training can be obtained a just appreciation of American needs in engineering matters.

We have built cheap railways on the frontier because we need railways there, and because thoroughly built ones would not pay interest on the investment. We have built cheap bridges for the same reason, and so on. This has not resulted from any inherent disposition to do cheap work, but because of our deliberate, thoughtful conclusion that it was the best thing to do under the prevailing conditions. That we can do the other thing is shown by numberless examples which throw in the shade any engineering works of foreign countries, not only for boldness of conception, but also for thoroughness of construction.

Among these are the great suspension bridges over the East River at New York, and over the Niagara at the Falls; the great steel arches which span the Mississippi at St. Louis, the score or more of steel and iron trusses which bridge the Father of Waters, and the jetties which have made a seaport of New Orleans. These illustrate one class of our engineering triumphs, and our railway system illustrates another.

We have built railways everywhere. A generation ago, when wishing to pay a tribute of praise to our railway engineers, we were accustomed to say that they could build a railway wherever a wagon-road could go. But the railway soon outgrew that saying. It outgrew the possibilities of a pack-road, and now there are few paths accessible to a mountain sheep which cannot be followed by a locomotive. If a mountain side, it scales it by loops, by switch-backs, or by a cog-rail; if it be a close cañon, the road is hung from the cañon walls; if every other device fails, with true American directness the engineer drives a tunnel through the obstacle and finds a route on the other side.

WATER TRANSPORTATION

The merchant fleet of the United States is of enormous dimensions, far beyond popular belief. Much has been written about the decadence of American shipping, and, so far as foreign trade is concerned, the amount has, indeed, diminished greatly. But this diminution in shipping engaged in foreign trade, has been far more than counterbalanced by the increase of that engaged in domestic traffic. The number of vessels engaged in both foreign and domestic trade, in the year 1890, was 25,540, and their tonnage was 7,633,676. Compare this with the merchant fleet of the United Kingdom, the queen of the seas. She had in the same year a tonnage of 7,915,336, which is only a trifle larger than that of our own fleet.

The shipping of the United States may be classified as follows:

CLASSIFICATION OF THE AMERICAN FLEET

CLASSES	TONS
Engaged in foreign trade	928,062
Coast-wise trade	2,385,879
Lake trade	926,355
River traffic	3,393,380

These vessels may be classified again as follows:

CLASSES	TONS
Steam vessels	1,820,386
Sailing vessels	1,795,443
Unrigged vessels	4,017,847

The fleet has a total value exceeding $215,000,000, and employs 106,436 men.

Vessels Engaged in Foreign Trade.—The tonnage of vessels engaged in foreign trade increased quite steadily up to the beginning of the late civil war, when it reached a total, in 1861, of 2,496,894 tons. The risks attendant upon this class of property during the war produced a rapid diminution, which has continued with scarcely a break until the present time. In 1890 the tonnage was almost precisely the same as in 1846, fifteen years before the beginning of the war.

But this is not the whole story. In 1820 the United States surpassed all other countries in foreign trade. Its ships were more frequently seen in foreign ports than those of any other nation. At that time commenced the decadence of its merchant marine relatively to that of other countries, and the civil war was but an episode that hastened the change. To understand the cause of this decadence it is necessary to go behind the facts as they appear on the surface. The real cause was not the civil war, although that doubtless aided it to some extent. Neither was it the tariff nor the onerous navigation laws, although they have had their influence in hastening what was inevitable under the prevailing conditions. Nor was it due to a change from sails to steam as a motive power, for the Americans are as competent to build steamers, and iron steamers at that, as are the people of any other nation.

The fact is simply that American capital finds better investments at home in the development of home industries, than in competing with the older countries upon the sea. The situation may be summed up as follows: So long as capital can earn ten per cent. upon the land, it is folly to expect it to invest in ships which can earn but five per cent. The question may be asked why it was that up to 1820 there was a rapid development of the maritime interests of the nation. To this comes the ready answer that, up to that time, the nation had been extremely slow in developing its internal resources. We had not realized in any degree the capabilities of the domain to which we had fallen heir.

In 1890 the total tonnage of vessels cleared from American for foreign ports, was 18,148,862. Of this but 4,066,757 tons were American; the remainder, 14,082,105, being represented by vessels sailing under foreign flags. Of the latter, vessels representing 5,687,053 tons sailed under the flag of the United Kingdom.

Coast and Internal Traffic.—The tonnage engaged in coast-wise traffic has increased steadily since our earliest history. That upon the Great Lakes, commencing at a comparatively recent date, has increased with the greatest rapidity, and amounts to very nearly as much as the entire foreign traffic of the country.

The river traffic, which has always heretofore been underestimated, is of enormous dimensions, the tonnage engaged in such traffic being greater than that upon the Atlantic, Gulf, and Pacific coasts. It is of a peculiar character; the freight is carried mainly in barges towed by steamers, the outfit resembling in its essential features a freight train drawn by a locomotive. These barges are of considerable capacity, and average nearly five hundred tons each.

The amount of freight moved by water in 1890, exclusive of that moved on canals, was 172,110,423 tons, classified as follows:

FREIGHT MOVED BY WATER IN 1890

Atlantic coast	77,597,626 tons.
Gulf of Mexico	2,864,956 "
Pacific coast	8,818,363 "
Great Lakes	53,424,432 "
Rivers	29,405,046 "
Total	172,110,423 "

This total is not great as compared with the railway traffic of the country, by which 636,541,617 tons were carried in the same year, the average distance carried by the two means of transportation being, perhaps, not greatly different.

COMMERCE

The commerce of the United States is of enormous magnitude; but by far the greater part of it is internal, consisting in an interchange of products between different sections. The country is broad. It extends from the northern temperate zone nearly to the tropics, and there is a corresponding difference in its products; the wheat, oats, and ice of the north being exchanged for the cotton, sugar, and tropic fruits of the south. East, west, north, and south, the railways, rivers, and canals are busied with the interchange of commodities.

The extent of this interchange may be understood from the statement made above, that no fewer than 76,207,047,298 tons of merchandise were transported one mile in the year 1890 by the railways alone. The average journey of each ton of freight was about 120 miles, and the number of tons carried that distance was 636,541,617. By vessels on rivers, and by coast-wise traffic, 172,110,423 tons were carried; and while the average distance transported is not known, in all probability it was not materially different from that of transmission by rail. Assuming them to be equal, it appears that the internal commerce of the United States in 1890, excepting that by canal, reached a total of over 800,000,000 of tons transported an average distance of 120 miles. This is truly a commerce of colossal proportions.

Foreign Commerce.—How does this compare in magnitude with our external commerce; i.e., that with foreign countries? Here we find it difficult to bring things to common terms. Our foreign commerce is given by the Bureau of Statistics in money value, not in terms of weight. But the statistics of entry and clearance from American for foreign ports, show that in the year 1892, vessels aggregating about 16,000,000 tons entered with cargoes, and that 19,000,000 tons cleared, a total of about 35,000,000 tons, which figures may fairly be assumed to represent approximately the volume of our foreign trade. It will be seen at once that our foreign trade is in volume but a bagatelle compared with the domestic trade, being in the proportion of 35 to 800, or about 1 to 24.

The volume does not, however, represent the value, since our exports to foreign countries have, on the average, a much higher value per ton than the commodities which we transport from one part of this country to another. These exports have a value of about one billion dollars annually. The annual product from our industries foots up at least ten billions in value, and of this we export only about one-tenth.

Therefore, whether we consider the volume or the value of our foreign trade, it is a matter of secondary importance as compared with our domestic trade.

This result may be attributed to two causes, but mainly to the second of them: first, our high tariff, which, by raising the scale of prices in this country, tends to make it unprofitable to sell abroad, where the prices are lower; second, the fact that with our great extent of country, our great variety of products, and the large population to be supplied, we have a home market sufficiently large and varied in its demands and its supplies, to render us almost independent of the rest of the world. There are few commodities, either of necessity or luxury, which we do not produce within our borders. A few products of the tropics we find it necessary to obtain from more southern latitudes. A few manufactured articles we still import from Europe. The latter we will soon supply in the requisite quantity and of the requisite quality. It will be of interest to note these articles of import from abroad, and to compare with them those given in exchange. The principal imports for the year 1891, in the order of importance, are as follows:

VALUE OF PRINCIPAL IMPORTS IN 1891, CLASSIFIED

ARTICLES	VALUE
Sugar, molasses, etc.	$108,458,621
Coffee	96,123,777
Iron and steel manufactures	53,544,372
Chemicals	47,317,031
Flax, hemp, jute, and manufactures	45,340,799
Woolen manufactures	41,060,080
Silk goods	37,880,143
Hides, furs, etc.	37,759,608
Cotton goods	29,712,624
Fruits and nuts	25,983,136
Wood and manufactures	19,888,186
Silk, raw, and cocoons	19,076,081
Wools	18,231,372
India-rubber and gutta-percha, crude	18,020,804
Tobacco and manufactures	16,763,141
Jewelry and precious stones	14,635,494
Leather and manufactures	12,683,363
Wines	10,007,060

The leading exports given in exchange the same year, are as follows:

VALUE OF PRINCIPAL EXPORTS IN 1891, CLASSIFIED

ARTICLES	VALUE
Cotton	$290,712,898
Provisions, comprising meat and dairy products	139,017,471
Wheat and wheat-flour	106,125,888
Mineral oils	52,026,734
Cattle	30,445,249
Iron and steel, and their manufactures	28,909,614
Wood, and its manufactures	26,270,010
Tobacco, and manufactures of	25,220,472
Maize	17,652,687
Cotton manufactures	13,604,857
Leather, and manufactures of	13,278,847
Copper, and manufactures of, including ore	11,875,490

These articles of import and export are illustrated in the diagrams on page 212.

Thus, with the exception of a few agricultural products which our climate does not permit us to produce, our imports consist

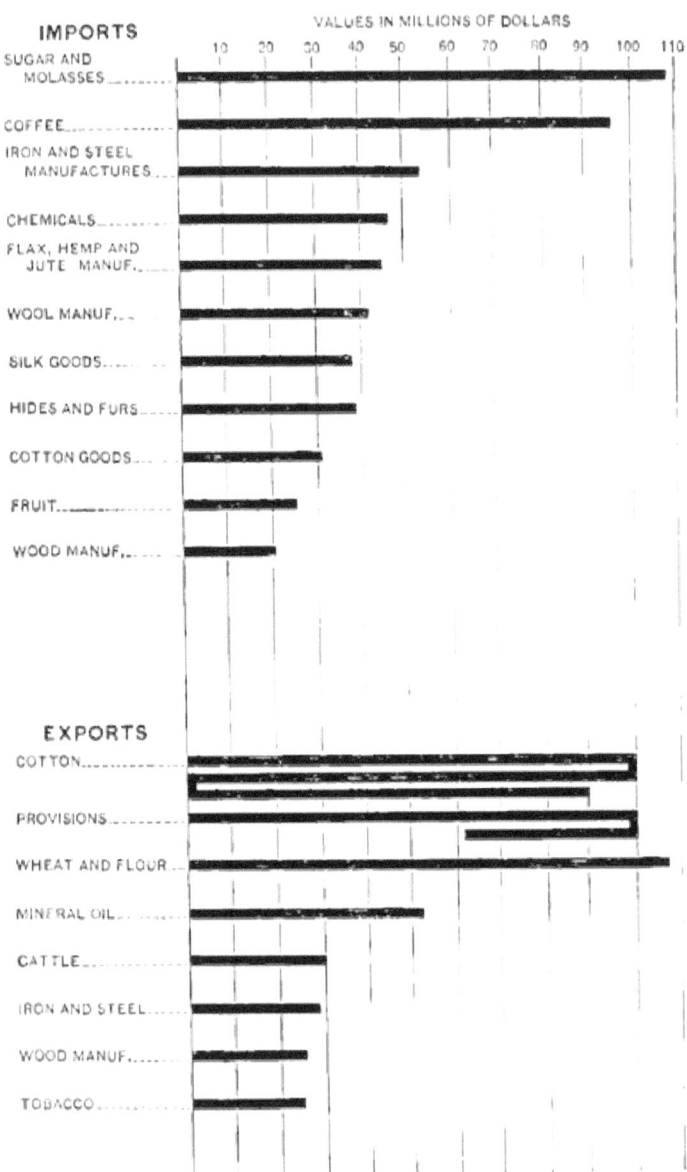

PRINCIPAL ARTICLES OF FOREIGN COMMERCE

of manufactured articles. Our exports, on the contrary, consist almost entirely of agricultural products. Our farms produce more than we require. Our factories are not yet equal to the supply of the home market, and this in the face of the fact that we are the leading manufacturing nation of the globe, as well as the first in agriculture.

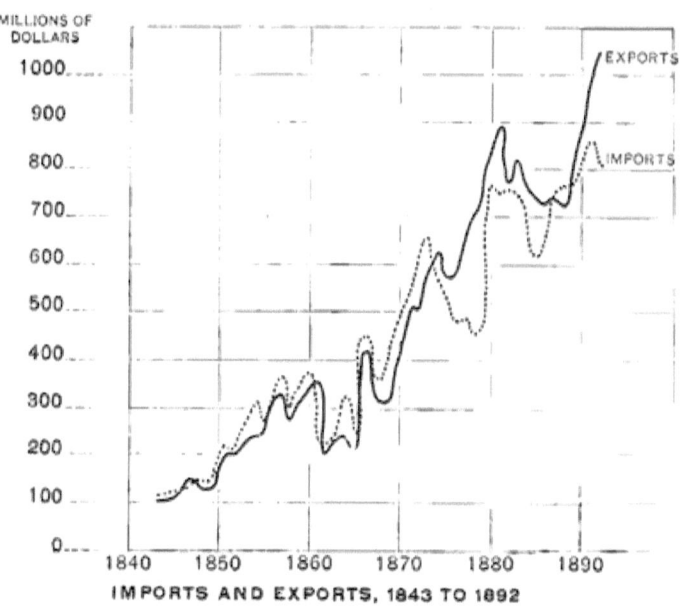

IMPORTS AND EXPORTS, 1843 TO 1892

The total value of our foreign trade in 1892 was $1,842,000,-000; of this $827,000,000 consisted of imports, and $1,015,-000,000 of exports. The balance of trade was in our favor, and has been so, with scarcely an exception, for twenty years. The above diagram shows the value of our imports and exports for the past half century. Our principal foreign trade is with Great Britain, with which country it amounted in 1892 to over $650,000,000; $494,000,000 being exports to, and but $156,000,000 imports from, that country. We send her mainly raw cotton, meat, and breadstuffs, and receive from her a great variety of manufactured articles.

Next in rank are Germany and France, with which countries we traded to the extent of $187,000,000 and $167,000,000, respectively. In the case of both these countries the balance of trade was against us, and the articles of exchange were quite similar to those in the case of Great Britain. To Brazil we sent but $14,000,000 worth of goods, and received from her not less than $119,000,000 worth, most of it being coffee. With Canada we had a limited exchange of commodities amounting to $78,000,000, exports and imports being almost equal in amount. To Cuba we sent but $18,000,000, while we received from that island $78,000,000, mainly sugar, molasses, and tobacco.

Of the entire products of our farms, mines, and factories, it is estimated that less than nine per cent. are exported. Of the agricultural products alone, this country spares for the sustenance of foreign lands fully one-fourth. Of the product of its mines, it sends abroad about one-fifth; while of its manufactured products, not over three per cent. go to foreign consumers.

About two-thirds of our cotton crop are annually exported, mainly to Great Britain. Of our wheat crop, about one-fifth goes abroad, and of corn only one-twentieth, the remainder finding consumers at home.

Shipbuilding.—The building of vessels, though by no means a prominent industry, is not a lost art among our people. In 1892 1,395 vessels, with a total tonnage of very nearly 200,000 tons, were built upon our shores. These were as follows:

NUMBER AND TONNAGE OF VESSELS BUILT IN 1892

	Number	Tonnage
Sailing vessels	846	83,217
Steam vessels	438	92,531
Canal boats	37	4,580
Barges	74	19,305
	1,395	199,633

It should be added that the tonnage constructed in 1892 was greater than for many years previous, which suggests a possible revival of this industry.

TELEGRAPH LINES

The telegraph lines are almost entirely in the hands of one corporation, the Western Union Telegraph Company, which has absorbed all competing companies, and holds almost as complete a monopoly of the telegraph business as does the general government that of the business of carrying the mails. In 1892 there were 189,576 miles of telegraph line in the United States, on which were strung 739,105 miles of wire. The railroad is everywhere accompanied by the telegraph, and the latter extends but little beyond the former. The number of offices maintained in 1890 was 20,700, and the number of messages sent during the year was in excess of 62,400,000, being nearly one message for every man, woman, and child in the country. The average charge per message was 31.6 cents. In this as in the postal service, the profits from the lines between the great cities are enormous; on the other hand, many thousands of miles of line and thousands of offices are maintained at a loss to the company. The receipts from the telegraph service, in 1890, reached an aggregate of $23,700,000, the expenses were $16,300,000, and the profits $7,400,000.

TELEPHONES

Among the agencies of transportation the telephone must be classed with the telegraph. Although of recent introduction, its use has spread and increased with wonderful rapidity. The entire service is practically in the hands of one concern, the American Bell Telephone Company, the other companies being of trifling importance. In 1892 the capital invested in the telephone interests, including both the parent company and its subsidiary companies, was $80,000,000, the great bulk of it probably representing franchises. The gross earnings of the parent company alone were $5,127,000, and its net dividends were $1,320,000. The number of instruments in use was 512,417; the number of miles of wire, 266,456; and the number of subscribers served, 216,017.

STREET RAILWAYS

The street railway is an American invention. Long before it occurred to the people of any other nation that the means of locomotion afforded by nature were deficient in the element of speed, we set about the work of supplying the deficiency. More than a generation ago the streets of our larger cities were intersected by lines of railway over which cars were drawn by horses or mules; and in 1891 we had, in all, 9,662 miles of street railway.

It is only within recent years that substitutes have been found for horse-power. The cable system was the first to materialize, and it has been applied widely and with economy on routes possessing a heavy traffic. Still more recently methods have been devised for using electricity; the one most highly developed, and at present the most economical, both as regards the transmission of power and economy of construction, is that known as the overhead trolley system. The underground trolley, which involves heavy expense in construction, is coming into use, and is likely to become the most practical system for crooked routes in the closely built parts of cities where trolley wires cannot safely be strung overhead. The storage battery system is still in the experimental stage, and no economical method of applying it to transportation has yet been devised.

The use of power for driving street cars means an increase of speed and a corresponding reduction in distance, if it be measured in terms of time.

The construction of electric roads, operated by the overhead trolley system, is going on with enormous rapidity. They are built and operated so cheaply that routes are made to pay even in the small towns. Moreover, it has been found commercially possible to operate roads between small places, and there is now a rapidly growing system of electric roads subsidiary to and connected with the steam railway systems of the country. In 1892 there were 385 electric roads in operation throughout the United States, having a capital of $155,000,000, and operating 3,980 miles of road.

These roads are built not only for the direct profits from their operation, but also for the purpose of bringing into the market and enhancing the value of suburban subdivisions of land. Indeed, they are so used to an astonishing extent—a fact that suggests the probable effect which this means of rapid transit may produce upon our cities. As has been pointed out in earlier pages, it is the fate of all countries, and of all parts of this country, to consist mainly of urban population. As our cities become larger they must either become more and more crowded, each person having fewer square feet in which to live and move and have his being, or they must spread outward. Heretofore, owing to the limitations of time, the tendency has been to accommodate the increase of population by crowding. The extreme of this crowding is seen in the tenement-house district of New York, while even well-to-do classes of that city have been forced to live in flats, the buildings spreading upward instead of outward.

The development of electric railways is changing all this and making it possible for the city to spread outward to many times its present area, without requiring the denizen of the suburb to devote more time to travel, morning and evening, than it formerly took for him to journey downtown from his flat, behind a pair of jaded car horses.

The city of the future will, thanks to electric roads, be spread out broadly over the land. Every dwelling will be a cottage with its plat of ground, and the tenement-house and the flat will gradually disappear with other relics of barbarism.

MAIL SERVICE

As in most civilized countries, the business of transporting and handling the mail matter is in the hands of the general government, and its volume is enormous. It is conducted with little regard to cost, the primary object being to best serve the public needs. Thus mail routes are maintained not only in the thickly settled parts of the country, where every convenience is afforded; but in the wildest and most remote sections, through the mountains of the south, and the deserts and mountains of the far west, where the service must of necessity be maintained at a loss, it is nevertheless conducted promptly and efficiently.

The receipts from the densely settled parts of the country, especially from the routes between the great cities, are greatly in excess of the expenditures, and go far toward meeting the deficit in the remote and sparsely settled regions. Still, it has been many years since the postal service paid its expenses. There is usually a deficit ranging from $2,000,000 to $6,000,000 annually. In 1892, 67,119 post-offices were maintained, by far the greater number being petty offices. The extent of post-routes was 447,591 miles. The expenses in that year were $76,000,000, and the receipts $71,000,000, showing a deficit of $5,000,000. The amount of mail handled was not less than 7,865,000,000 pieces; this was an average of 125 pieces for each man, woman, and child in the nation, a number far exceeding that in any other country, Great Britain not excepted.

FINANCE AND WEALTH

The total amount of circulating media used in the United States in the year 1891, was $1,175,000,000. This does not take account of the gold, silver, and paper money held in the United States Treasury, which, if added, would increase the sum total to $2,014,000,000. Of the money in circulation, $524,000,000 were in coin, consisting of $407,000,000 in gold, $59,000,000 in silver, and $58,000,000 in fractional silver. The balance was paper money, classified as follows:

MONEY IN CIRCULATION IN 1891

Gold certificates	$420,000,000
Silver certificates	307,000,000
Currency certificates	22,000,000
United States legal tender notes	40,000,000
National bank notes	162,000,000

The composition of our circulating media is illustrated in the diagram, Plate 39, facing page 220.

All attempts to force the silver dollar into actual circulation have failed, on account of its inconvenience as a circulating medium. Of 419,000,000 silver dollars coined, all except $60,000,000 lie in the Treasury, being represented in the circulation by silver certificates, which are used in preference to the coin itself. To a certain extent this is also true of gold, of which $438,000,000 lie in the Treasury, part of it being represented in the circulation by gold certificates. Indeed, gold, and silver also except as fractional currency, are seldom seen in the eastern and northern sections of the country. At the south, silver dollars are much more common; and throughout the far west, especially upon the Pacific coast, gold coin is in extensive use, supplanting paper money to a great extent.

The total coinage of the United States in 1890, was as follows:

COINAGE IN 1890, CLASSIFIED

Gold	$20,500,000
Silver	39,200,000
Minor silver	1,400,000
Total	$61,100,000

The coinage is executed mainly at the San Francisco mint, established in 1854, and that at Philadelphia (1793). There are two other mints, at New Orleans (1838) and Carson City, Nev. (1870). The so-called mint at Denver is used only as an assay office.

The total amount of gold coinage minted from 1793 to 1892 inclusive —just one hundred years—was $1,582,000,000, of silver coinage $657,000,000, and of minor coins $24,000,000.

NATIONAL BANKS

Most American citizens who have reached years of discretion can remember the old state banks and their circulating notes. They can recall how uncertain was the value of these notes, depending upon the ability of the bank to meet its obligations. They can remember the necessity for exchanging notes of one locality for those of another when traveling about the country, just as one is now obliged to exchange American for British money when crossing the ocean.

All these uncertainties, inconveniences, and losses were relieved by the institution of the national banking system in 1863. The circulation of the national banks is guaranteed by the general government, so that the individual character and standing of the bank is of no moment whatever to the person holding its notes. To obtain this security and thereby enable it to issue notes, each national bank is required to deposit with the United States Treasury an amount ten per cent. in excess of its circulation, of United States bonds, with which, in case of necessity, the government redeems its notes.

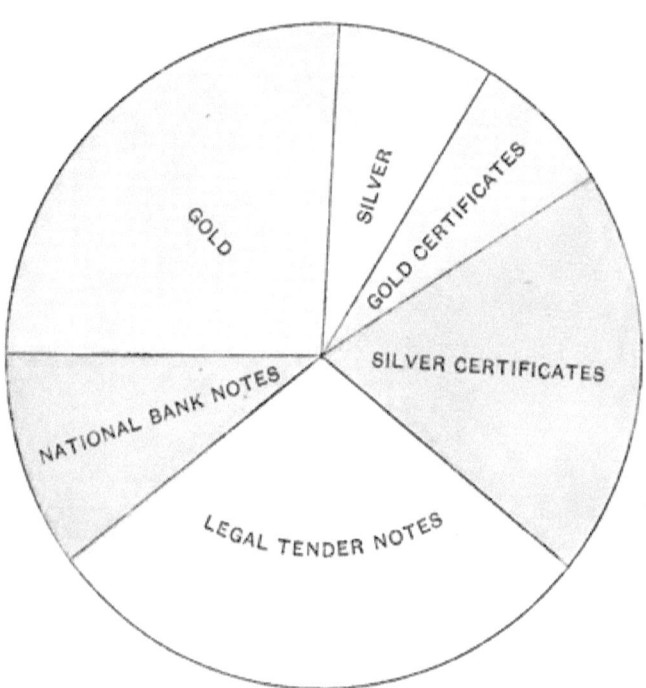

THE CIRCULATING MEDIA IN 1893

Upon the institution of the national banking system, the circulation of state banks disappeared at once, and the national system grew with unexampled rapidity. In 1891 the national banks numbered 3,677. They had a capital of $677,400,000, and resources amounting to $3,213,000,000.

SAVINGS BANKS

Savings banks are supported mainly by the poorer classes, those whose savings are limited in amount, and the measure of the success of such banks is a very good measure of the prosperity of those classes. In the year 1891 there were throughout the United States 1,011 of this class of banks. Their depositors numbered no less than 4,533,217, and the total amount of deposits was $1,623,000,000, an average of $358 to each depositor. The total assets of these banks were $1,855,000,000. In recent years the savings banks have increased greatly in number and in the amount of their deposits, showing, as far as they may be taken to indicate it, an exceedingly prosperous condition of the working classes.

The building associations, which, in certain large cities, such as Philadelphia, Baltimore, and Washington, have taken the place of savings banks, are in a correspondingly flourishing condition.

WEALTH

The wealth of a nation is a matter of estimate only. Certain of its elements are susceptible of being approximated more closely than others; but few of them can be given with greater certainty or accuracy than is expressed in the word "estimate."

Methods of Estimating. An illustration of the method used for determining the wealth of a nation, is given in the estimates of the wealth of the United States made in connection with the tenth census, in 1880; a description of it will enable the reader to form his own measure of the amount of dependence to be placed upon results of this character.

In the first place, the value of tangible objects only was included in the estimate, and only intrinsic values were admitted. No account whatever was taken of notes, bonds, and other promises to pay, whether public or private; since, whatever may be their value to the holder, they diminish the property of the maker in exactly the same degree, and therefore do not affect the wealth of the country as a whole.

First in importance among these tangible objects, is land and its improvements. The assessed value of this item was obtained from county and state authorities. As is well known, the assessed valuation is almost universally less than the true value, and that in varying proportions. In some cases the assessment is as low as twenty-five per cent. of the true value, while in others it approximates closely thereto. In order to obtain this relation of assessed to true value of real estate, an extensive correspondence was had with assessors, real estate dealers, officers of banks and building associations, and other classes of persons who have to do with buying and selling real estate and loaning money upon it. The information received from these sources was digested, state by state; and the net result, in the form of a proportion between assessed and true values, was applied to the assessed valuation of the state, thus approximating the true valuation.

The value of our railway system was assumed to be equal to the cost of construction and equipment, as reported by the railway companies, and similarly with the property of telegraph and telephone companies, and with shipping and canals. The value of live stock, farming tools, and farm machinery was accepted as returned upon the farm schedules of the census, as was also the value of mines.

A certain proportion of the annual product of agriculture, manufactures, and mines was assumed to be in the hands of dealers and shippers, and this was accepted as returned by the enumerators. The amount of specie was accepted as returned by the Treasury Department. The value of household furniture, clothing, and other personal belongings, which taken collectively is a large item, can be a matter of estimate only; it was estimated in different ways, and the results agreed sufficiently well to serve as some sort of verification of one another. The value of real estate exempt from taxation, was given in the reports of many of the state auditors, and its total amount in the country was estimated on the basis of that in the states where it was thus made known.

In this way the estimate published in the census report of 1880 was obtained. It showed that the wealth of the country at that time was approximately $43,642,000,000, or an average of $870 to each inhabitant.

Wealth in 1890.—Just now it is impossible to make a similar independent estimate of the wealth of the country in 1890, inasmuch as little of the necessary data is yet available. But assuming that the ratio of the total wealth to the assessed valuation of property, real and personal, remains the same as in 1880, the wealth of the country in 1890 was in the neighborhood of $62,000,000,000, or very nearly $1,000 per capita. In 1880 the United States was the wealthiest of all nations, and unquestionably the decade just passed has widened the gap between it and its closest competitor, Great Britain.

In earlier censuses different and inferior methods have been employed for making these estimates, and the results have been correspondingly less trustworthy. The usual custom has been to obtain the assessed valuation of all property, real and personal, and with it estimates of the relation between this assessed valuation and the true value, by applying which, figures for the latter were obtained. In most cases this has probably resulted in an underestimate of wealth, from two causes: One is the fact that a vast and increasing amount of personal property is never reported to the assessor. As a rule, the personal element of property is approximately equal in value to the real estate. In 1860, however, the assessed valuation of real estate was returned as about $7,000,000,000, and of personal property only $5,100,000,000, showing a probable shortage in the personal element, of between $1,000,000,000 and $2,000,000,000. In 1870 the assessed value of real estate was returned as $9,900,000,000, while that of personal property had apparently diminished to $4,300,000,000. The corresponding figures in 1880 were $13,000,000,000 and $3,900,000,000, respectively. Thus in twenty years the

assessed value of personal property had fallen from $5,100,-
000,000 to $3,900,000,000, an apparent diminution of $1,200,000,000,
and this in the face of an extraordinary increase in values
everywhere. Moreover, while the value of personal property is
nearly, if not quite, equal to that of real estate, in 1880 it was
apparently worth much less than one-third. The explanation
lies simply in the fact that a greater proportion of the personal
element had, on one pretext or another, escaped the assessor.

This formed one source of error in the method used prior to
1880 in determining the true valuation. The other lay in the
omission of a greater or less proportion of the property legally
exempt from taxation. In 1880 this was estimated at $2,000,-
000,000, or about one-twenty-second part of the entire wealth of
the nation, figures that serve to measure the possible extent of
this class of omissions. In 1870, however, strenuous efforts were
made to secure the data concerning this element, and it is probable that they were fairly successful.

In 1890 the wealth of the country was distributed very
unevenly. The northern and western states were far wealthier
in proportion to population than those of the south, since
wealth is massed in the great manufacturing states and within
their great cities.

Historical Résumé. — The following table shows the
total and per capita wealth of the United States at the date of
each census since 1850. This is illustrated also in the diagram
on page 225.

TOTAL AND PER CAPITA WEALTH, BY DECADES

Year	Total Wealth	Wealth per Capita
1850	$7,136,000,000	$308
1860	16,160,000,000	514
1870	30,069,000,000	780
1880	43,642,000,000	870
1890	62,600,000,000	1,000

The next table presents the rate of increase of wealth from
census to census:

RATE OF INCREASE OF WEALTH, BY DECADES

Decade	Rate of Increase
1850–60	126.5
1860–70	85.5
1870–80	45.0
1880–90	43.6

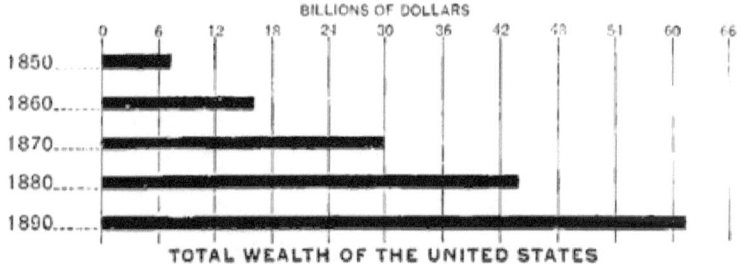

TOTAL WEALTH OF THE UNITED STATES

WEALTH PER CAPITA

In 1850 manufactures, trade, and commerce in this country were in an undeveloped stage. Most of the inhabitants were engaged in farming, and wealth was more uniformly distributed than at present. The people were more widely scattered, lines of communication were few and poor, and each family was much more independent of the rest of the community than at present. The farmer produced the food, and, to a large extent, the clothing and other necessaries for his family. There was much less interchange of commodities.

During the ten years between 1850 and 1860 there was an increase of wealth per capita over and above the increase of population, amounting to sixty-seven per cent. With the development of manufactures and trade, which was going on apace in the northern states, there was also a great increase in valuations, which accounted for a large part of this increased wealth of the country.

The decade between 1860 and 1870 witnessed several great changes. The first of these in importance was the civil war, and its effects upon wealth were confined mainly to the south. In that section of the country values were greatly depreciated. Vast quantities of property were destroyed, and the labor of practically the whole adult male element was taken away from production for a period of about four years. Moreover, the abolition of slavery destroyed, nominally at least, a vast body of wealth, which had a value, at the lowest estimate, of a billion and a quarter of dollars. The net result of all this was that the southern states, which had formerly held a high rank in respect of wealth in proportion to population, fell to the bottom of the scale.

The north, on the other hand, gained greatly in wealth, both during and after the war. Although between one and two millions of men were withdrawn from productive pursuits throughout the period of the war, still its prosecution stimulated and enlarged production in such a degree as to more than compensate for this loss. Moreover, the extension of all kinds of business during the war period wonderfully increased the value of real property. Indeed, the assessed valuation of the northern and western states was advanced during these ten years 56 per cent., while that of the former wealthy states of the south diminished 34 per cent. The true wealth of the northern and western states increased 159 per cent., while that of the south decreased over 18 per cent. In South Carolina, Georgia, Alabama, Mississippi, and Texas, the wealth of 1870 was less than half that of 1860. The net result to the nation, however, was a large increase of wealth in proportion to population, being at the rate of 52 per cent. per capita.

Between 1870 and 1880 there was great business depression and a shrinkage in values, extending quite generally throughout the country. This was caused probably by excessive production, which was stimulated by the war and continued after its close with increasing momentum, through the addition to the industrial army of the Republic of the vast military force released from service. For several years the country had been producing more than it needed to consume; deterred to a great extent from offering its wares in foreign markets by the high prices induced at home by its protective tariff, the natural result of an overstocked market followed. Prices fell, values shrank, and there were widespread commercial failures. Toward the close of the decade business revived and values rose again. Were it possible to make an estimate of our wealth in 1875, the result would doubtless show that the country was poorer than it had been five years before. In 1880, however, it had much more than recovered the lost ground; the wealth per capita had increased from $780 to $870, a gain of $90 per capita, or at the rate of 11½ per cent.

Between 1880 and 1890 there is little to record except an almost unbroken course of prosperity. There have been slight oscillations, but none of a general or serious character. We find that in 1890 the per capita wealth had increased from $870 to about $1,000, or at the rate of 15 per cent.

Thus close the four decades in the history of the wealth of the country. In these forty years our population has increased from 23,000,000 to 63,000,000, a gain of 171 per cent. Our wealth has increased from $7,136,000,000 to $62,600,000,000, being now nearly nine times as great as in 1850. It has increased from an average of $308 to $1,000 per capita, and the United States, from being one of the poorest of civilized nations, has become by far the richest of them all.

Assessed Valuation in 1890.—The map on Plate 40, facing page 228, shows the distribution of the assessed valuation of the country in 1890, among the states. While it measurably fails in presenting the relative true wealth of the several states, owing to the variable relation between the assessed and the true valuation, it serves to bring out the main features of the geographical distribution of wealth. The great preponderance of the northern states in wealth, and the comparative poverty of the south, are forcibly depicted.

Sources of Wealth.—Whence comes this vast increase of wealth, which, decade by decade, has been added to our capital? It is only in small part the product of our farms, factories, and mines. Nearly all of this product is consumed in the support of our people. We eat it or wear it. The part which we send to other countries is balanced by what we receive from them, and that also is consumed. As a matter of fact, the vast majority of the additions to our national capital consist in improvements upon land, in buildings, machinery, and railways, and in the appreciation of values, especially those of land.

In this country the last item is the one of greatest importance. The increase in the value of land has been enormous. To appreciate its extent, one has but to compare the former value of a city's site with its present value; for example, the worthless desert which constituted the site of Denver thirty years ago, with its value per square foot to-day. This is man's work. He alone has given to the land its value.

DISTRIBUTION OF WEALTH

The United States is worth to-day $62,600,000,000, an average, as already stated, of about $1,000 for every man, woman, and child. But how is our vast wealth distributed? Is the bulk of it owned by comparatively few, and are the great masses of people poor? Or is there some approach to uniformity in the distribution? Is the tendency toward concentration of wealth into few hands, or the reverse? These are questions of vital importance.

We know that the country contains many poor people and few millionaires, and we know that the number and wealth of the few are increasing. We know also, Henry George to the contrary notwithstanding, that the poor are not becoming poorer as the rich become richer; but that to a greater or less extent they share in the general prosperity. We know, too, that while all classes are becoming richer, those near the top of the scale are increasing in wealth faster than those near the bottom; so that the differences in pecuniary circumstances are becoming more pronounced.

An estimate of the distribution of wealth in the United States

THE BUILDING OF A NATION—PLATE 40

ASSESSED VALUATION PER CAPITA, IN HUNDREDS OF DOLLARS, 1890

has recently been made, which gives at least an approximate idea of the degree of inequality in the holdings of our people. It was obtained in the following manner: The wage-earners of the country, by which are to be understood all those engaged in occupations of whatever character for pecuniary reward, were grouped for convenience as business men—including bankers, manufacturers, merchants, etc.—professional men, clerks, farmers, skilled laborers, and unskilled laborers. The business group was classified as to wealth by the aid of the Bradstreet book of ratings. The professional group, a small one, was classified by estimate. The farmers were classified by the aid of the classification of farms, according to size, as given by the census; and the other groups, composed of men having small holdings, were classified by estimate.

The classification of these groups, expressed in percentages of the total number of wage earners, shows the following:

HOLDINGS OF THE DIFFERENT CLASSES OF WAGE EARNERS

	Business Class	Profes. Class	Farmers	Clerks and Skilled Lab.	Unskilled Labor.
Below $1,000	20.0	40	25	50	100
$1,000 to $10,000	50.0	50	73	50	...
$10,000 to $100,000	25.0	9	2	...	...
$100,000 to $1,000,000	4.8	1	...	...	...
Above $1,000,000	0.2	...	...	...	...
	100.0	100	100	100	100

The following table, which classifies all wage earners, was obtained by consolidating the columns of the preceding one:

HOLDINGS OF ALL WAGE EARNERS

	Proportion of Total No. Per cent.
Below $1,000	60.00
$1,000 to $10,000	37.24
$10,000 to $100,000	2.47
$100,000 to $1,000,000	0.28
Over $1,000,000	0.01

Thus it appears that ninety-five hundredths of the wage earners probably own less than $10,000 each, and 9,971 out of every 10,000 own less than $100,000 each. Only one wage earner in 10,000 is a millionaire.

So much for the distribution of the wage-earners; now glance at the distribution of wealth. The following table shows this, expressed in percentages of the total wealth of the country:

DISTRIBUTION OF WEALTH IN PERCENTAGES OF THE TOTAL

	Per cent.
Below $1,000	6
$1,000 to $10,000	37
$10,000 to $100,000	25
$100,000 to $1,000,000	27
Over $1,000,000	5

From this it appears that only 5 per cent. of the capital is owned by millionaires, and only 27 per cent. by the next most wealthy class. Nearly nine-tenths of the property of the country is held in sums ranging from $1,000 to $1,000,000.

Thus we find that one ten-thousandth of the wage earners possess one-twentieth of the property, and that twenty-eight hundredths of one per cent. of their number own 27 per cent., or more than a fourth, of the wealth of the country. On the other hand, three-fifths of the wage earners have but one-sixteenth of the wealth.

A FORECAST OF THE FUTURE

In the preceding pages our nation's progress has been traced for a century, in territory, population, and industries; in the development of its resources, and of its wealth. At the beginning the United States was one of the feeblest and poorest of civilized nations. To-day, in numbers and power, in industry and wealth, it leads them all. It is the exponent to the world of all that makes civilization. Its history, that marvelous history which we have tried to picture, will forever serve humanity as an object-lesson of the beneficent results of perfect freedom in thought and action.

The spectacle afforded by this wonderful development under the freest of governments, has already borne abundant fruit among the monarchies of Europe. Its influence has been exerted quietly, but with the greatest effect. The absence of classes in this country has tended to break down the barriers of caste in the older ones. Universality of citizenship on this side of the water has aided in its extension upon the other side, and the high standard of living among the masses here has helped to elevate the condition of the serfs of Europe.

The Government.—What will be our future? Is our form of government destined to endure? With ignorance born of selfishness and prejudice, the older nations of Europe a century ago, and for many years thereafter, condemned as weak and vacillating a government in which the people were allowed to rule themselves. Our civil war undeceived them. For four years, the United States prosecuted a war of self-preservation, upon a scale unknown to history, with uniform singleness of purpose, pouring out blood and treasure without stint, and fought it to a successful finish.

Neither adversity nor prosperity has developed any material

weakness in the fundamental idea of our government. It is not to be supposed for a moment, that a government by all the people possesses less strength or tenacity of purpose than a government by one person; the former is infinitely the stronger, just as the power of many men is greater that that of one man; and a government in which all participate, and whose officers are simply the agents of the people, is necessarily stronger than one which is above and over them, and in which they take no part and can have but little interest.

There appears to be no reasonable question as to the permanence of our institutions and form of government. There is every probability that they will increase in strength as the nation increases in numbers and in wealth.

No government ever stands still; least of all, the government of an active, progressive nation. We cannot expect ours, excellent as it is, and well suited to our needs, to remain the same. Even under existing conditions it is susceptible of great improvement; and as these conditions change, as change they will, it must in turn be modified to meet the new demands upon it.

The government will develop, not on socialistic lines, which tend to make the people dependent upon it; but under the opposite policy of making them individually independent and responsible. Thus and thus only can the highest development of man be reached. The aim of the public school system is to fit the American youth for freedom and citizenship, and the training commenced in the schools is carried forward in the town meeting, where he takes his part in the affairs of government. The township system of local government will be extended to all parts of our jurisdiction. A man's feeling of responsibility, and his usefulness as a citizen, are increased by the ownership of land and a home; and the private ownership of land will be encouraged by the government of the future, as it has been encouraged in the past.

The government will undertake for the people only those matters which it can do better than they can do in their individual capacity. In other words, it will supplement the work of the people. It will continue to carry out great projects of improvement, which, while necessary for the general welfare, do not offer sufficient pecuniary reward to tempt private capital. It will continue to make surveys, and to prosecute scientific researches, which redound to the benefit of all, and to collect and disseminate information in aid of the industries.

The utter savagery and folly of the spoils system will be thoroughly realized long before the second century has passed, and the reforms recently introduced into the civil service will have been perfected and extended, to a point where the governmental machinery will remain unaltered while administrations come and go. A change of administration will, in the future, involve a change in those offices only which are concerned with the policy of the government, and not with its routine.

When that day arrives, the political party as it now exists—a party well-nigh without an issue, an utterly illogical grouping of men, held together by a name and a thirst for office—will cease to exist. In its place will be found men grouping themselves about a preëxisting issue for the purpose of maintaining and carrying it out under the government. The party will have a reason for its existence, and its members will be able to account for their allegiance.

The People.—Our vast preponderance over the other nations of the North American continent will, ere long, draw them into our body politic; our descendants will be citizens of a republic whose dominion shall extend from Greenland to Panama, and whose sixty-three millions of to-day will have swollen in a century to half a billion.

But it must be remembered that the enumeration of population conveys little idea of the industrial strength of the country. We have grown in numbers from four to sixty-three millions; but this proportion of nearly sixteen to one is utterly inadequate to characterize the growth of our industrial capacity. Within the century, we have invented and perfected machines for making almost everything, and our productive capacity per man has become thereby at least ten times as great as it was a century ago.

The substitution of machinery for human labor will go on indefinitely. Our children will see man fully emancipated from manual toil, and his productive capacity vastly increased beyond even its present proportions.

This increase will be attended by a corresponding improvement in man's physical condition, and necessarily in his mental and moral condition as well. Wages for all classes of service, which have been advanced so rapidly in recent times, will continue to increase with the increased efficiency of labor; at the same time the cost of the necessaries and luxuries of life will go on diminishing. The masses will be better fed, clothed, and housed. As civilization advances, their sanitary condition will improve, the death rate will diminish, and man will live longer. Indeed, it is possible that in the dim future our descendants may live to greater ages than the patriarchs of Mosaic times.

The time is near at hand when immigration will be closely restricted, and only the intelligent and industrious of Europe will be allowed to make their homes with us. This restriction of immigration will greatly check the additions to our numbers from abroad; but their places will be filled by our own flesh and blood, since natural increase, which has been depressed by the flood of immigration, will quickly recover its normal rate. With this restriction, also, illiteracy will rapidly disappear, and before the close of our second century, the illiterate will be reduced to as small a percentage of the population as they now form among the native born of New England. The restriction of immigration will have a like salutary effect upon crime. Our courts and jails, now full to overflowing with the criminals unloaded upon us from Europe, will be found almost unoccupied.

Indiscriminate charity breeds pauperism. With the general increase of intelligence, the community will consider the subject of charity more thoughtfully and philosophically than hitherto, and will better realize the extent of the mischief to be wrought by taking counsel only of its sympathies. It will rightly conclude that the only safe way of helping a needy person is to assist him in helping himself, and that he who will not help himself should, in mercy to his fellow-men, be permitted to suffer the penalty. The coming century will see our provisions for charity greatly reduced, and greatly changed in character. It will aim to reduce pauperism, not to increase it. Instead of offering money to the unfortunate, they will be given an opportunity to better themselves, and the incorrigible will be allowed to go to the wall.

With the restriction of immigration and the exclusion of its worst elements, the trades unions, whose members are almost entirely of foreign birth or parentage, will disappear from our midst.

The colored race, upon which the south depends for its agricultural service, will continue to increase in numbers, but less rapidly than the whites, as has been the case heretofore. There will be little mixture of races. Having no predilection for manufacturing pursuits, the colored people will remain wedded to the soil. As manufactures extend and increase at the south, and the whites leave the farms for the city, their places will be taken by the colored people, who will thus become the farmers of that section. The colored people will also become the landholders of the south and will produce the cotton of the world.

Woman.—The position of woman in the future, already dimly foreshadowed, will be realized. She will no longer be secondary to man, but his equal, or rather his supplement. All arts, all professions, all occupations, will be open to her. It does not follow from this, however, that she will enter them all; for the distinctions of sex, her mental peculiarities and physical limitations, will still enforce certain restrictions. As she acquires greater ability to reason logically, to control her impulses and sympathies; as she familiarizes herself with business methods, she will take a more active part in business affairs. Among other things, she will naturally assume her share in the control of those great corporations known as municipal, state, and national governments, as soon as her assistance in that work becomes of service.

Language.—Prominent among the other improvements we are destined to make, will be the simplification of our language. It is estimated that two years of the life of every American child is to-day wasted in learning the intricacies and inconsistencies of the orthography of the language. Add to this the time devoted, in later years, to searching dictionaries for the accepted spelling of words, and to the mere writing of unnecessary letters, and one can appreciate the enormous expense entailed by the defects of our language—defects originally introduced mainly by the whims of the first makers of dictionaries.

Language is merely a means for the expression of thought. As such, it should be as simple and as efficient a tool as possible; and matters concerning the origin of words and the development of language should be held as trifles, compared with its efficiency as a means of communication.

This view is sure to prevail sooner or later; and phonetic spelling and a simple, consistent grammar, are only a question of time.

Cities.—Among the reforms of the future which will contribute toward long life, improvement in health, and reduction in the death rate, is the extension and spreading out of cities, referred to in connection with the subject of street railways. By the aid of electric roads, carrying passengers swiftly to and fro between the heart of the city and the suburbs, the crowding and congesting of our great centers of population will cease. Tenement houses will be depleted of their teeming and suffering thousands, and in place thereof square leagues will be dotted with detached cottages and villas surrounded by green grass and waving trees. The densely settled states of the future will become continuous cities, and the city, as a crowded, congested congregation of human beings, will cease to exist. The only closely built areas will be those devoted to the needs of commerce.

Corporations.—Corporations will continue to increase in wealth and power, consolidating with one another until they become of enormous magnitude. But as their wealth and power increase, and as they grow more independent of competition except from the community they serve, more and more will the government assume control over them, acting upon the theory that they are agencies for the service of the people, and to be controlled, so far as may be necessary, by the people. The business of transportation, grown to such dimensions as to dwarf our present enormous traffic, may pass into very few hands and yet be as easily controlled and serve the public needs quite as well, as the telegraph business of to-day.

Agriculture.—Before the lapse of many years we shall

have reached the conviction that our manufacturing industries are no longer in their infancy, but have grown to the stature of manhood, and are able to maintain themselves. When that time arrives we will make haste to pull down the barriers of protection which we have erected, and thereby enlarge our markets so as to include the nations of the world. Then will our foreign trade become of relative importance. Then will we supply not only food, but clothing, and all other kinds of manufactured articles as well, to the rest of the civilized world.

Let us run over the list and see what we are likely to be able to do for the support of mankind in the coming century. In the matter of agriculture we have subdued and devoted to the service of man only about one-sixth of our area, excluding Alaska. This is less than one-third of the territory which we can reasonably hope to bring under cultivation. Our rugged mountains and waterless deserts, which comprise possibly two-fifths of our territory, we can hardly expect to devote to agriculture; but by utilizing all our arable land we may hope in the future to produce three times as much from our territory as at present. Furthermore, all experience goes to prove that as the country becomes more closely settled, cultivation becomes more thorough, and the soil is made to yield a richer return per acre. Thus by extending the area of cultivated land, and by more thorough cultivation of the soil, our agricultural industries will yield year by year a greater surplus over the needs of our population; and year by year, a constantly increasing proportion of the products of our soil will be sent abroad, to aid in the support of the overcrowded millions of Europe.

Another score of years will see all the lands within the arid region, which are susceptible of irrigation, taken up and placed under cultivation, and a reflex wave of migration will occupy the abandoned farms and plantations of the east, and restore them to the service of man.

Migration to Canada, Mexico, and the Central American states, which has never prospered under their present forms of government, will receive a great stimulus when these countries become integral parts of the Republic. The American farmer will spread across the border and occupy the fertile fields of the

Saskatchewan and the mountain valleys of the Columbia and Fraser, pushing his outposts northward as far as the cereals will grow. Southward he will occupy the rich lands of the *tierra caliente* and the *tierra templada* of Mexico and the valleys and plains of Central America, where he will introduce to the people of those regions enlightened methods of farming, and will energize the whole community.

Manufactures.—Meantime, while the farmers, the vanguard of civilization, are extending our frontier of settlement, the frontier of manufacturing industry will continue its steady advance. From Mason and Dixon's line, the Ohio river and the Mississippi, which now define its line of march in general terms, it will spread both southward and westward. In the southern Appalachians, in the mountains of the Virginias, Kentucky, Tennessee, the Carolinas, Georgia, and Alabama, will soon be developed a second Pennsylvania, greater and richer than that of the north.

It seems a curious waste of energy to transport the raw material of manufactures thousands of miles, there to undergo a change of form and to be returned to the starting place, perhaps, in the shape of the finished product. In this way two-thirds of the cotton crop of the United States is annually transported to Europe, where it is manufactured into cloth. A considerable proportion of the resulting cloth is transported back to this country, some of it to the very states in which the cotton was grown. This is a maladjustment of things, which in the future will be remedied. The manufacture of cotton will be carried on mainly at the south where the material is raised, and the cost of transportation and handling will thereby be greatly reduced. Indeed, the cotton states will become the center of the cotton manufacture of the world, and it is safe to conclude that when this time arrives the cotton factories of New England and Great Britain will have seen their best days, and that manufactured cotton will be exported from New Orleans, Mobile, Charleston, and Newport News, as it is now from Liverpool and London.

Coal.—The coal supply of this country is simply incalculable. Hundreds of thousands of square miles are underlaid by coal beds. Their extent is so vast and the quantity of coal so immense, that although thousands of millions of tons have already been taken from the bosom of the earth, the comparative loss is utterly inappreciable. For many centuries to come the United States can supply the whole world with fuel without materially depleting her resources of coal. On the little island, which is our mother country, a different state of things prevails. Its coal supply is limited, and at the present rate of mining a few score years will exhaust it, and the mother may be obliged to turn to her child for fuel, which is the source of power. But this is not all. The failure of England's coal supply may cause the failure of her iron industry; and in this event America will be called upon to furnish the world with its iron and steel as well.

Electricity.—The transmission of power in the form of electricity is destined to work great economies in industry, transportation, and social life. There is no longer a doubt that in this form power may be developed on an immense scale; transported to great distances from the point of its generation; retained on draught, as it were, for long periods of time; subdivided at will, and changed in volume or intensity. Therefore, who can question that force, in the form of electricity, will become as completely subject to the needs and uses of civilized man, as matter itself?

The time is not far distant when our railway passenger trains will be run by it, thus obviating the use of heavy locomotives and tenders, with their cargoes of coal and water. This will permit of attaining greater speed, and greater comfort to passengers. By electric trains, running on improved alignments, grades, and roadbeds, we may reasonably expect our descendants to cross the continent in twenty-four hours, with less discomfort than now attends a journey from New York to Chicago.

Horses, deposed by the storage battery, will disappear from our roads and streets; and all work, from rocking the cradle to drawing the hearse, from running a sewing-machine to the operation of a railway system, will be done by electricity. The next will, indeed, be the electric age.

FINIS

LITTLE did the great admiral imagine, when, on the early morning of October 21, 1492, from the lookout of the *Santa Maria*, he first descried the shores of America, what tremendous results were to follow his discovery, what world-wide changes it was destined to produce. He little foresaw that upon the land which he, an Italian, in the service of Spain, unfolded to the world, would develop a nation of English blood, greater and stronger, and with a higher civilization, than any of the powers of Europe.

Like many another of the world's heroes, he builded better than he knew. The long list of those to whom this country is chiefly indebted must forever open with his name.

INDEX

	PAGE
Accessions of Territory	46
Agriculture	163
" Department of	21-23
" general statistics of	164
" importance of, relative to manufactures	164
" of the future	236
Agricultural capital	164, 165
" products, value of	164, 165
Alabama	25
Alaska	4, 25
" purchase of	46
Algonquin Indians	99
Aliens	126
Allegheny plateau	7
Altitude, distribution of population according to	84
American Federation of Labor	143
Annexations of territory	46
Apache Indians	100
Appalachian mountains	6
" valley	6
Areas of states and territories	30
Area of United States	5
Arizona	25
Arkansas	25
Army	41
Artesian wells	175
Assessed valuation in 1890	227
Athabascan Indians	100
Atlantic coast	5
" plain	7
Attendance at schools	131
" " colleges and professional schools	132
Austrians in the United States, distribution of	111
Baptists	148

INDEX

	PAGE
Bighorn mountains, Wyoming	9
Black mountains, North Carolina	7
Blue Ridge	6
Bohemians in the United States, history of	110
Books, publication of	183
Brazil, commerce with	214
British in the United States, distribution of	111
Budget	40
Building associations	221
Bureau of Statistics of Treasury	21
Cabinet	18
Cable railways	216
Caddo Indians	99
California	26
Canada, commerce with	214
Canadians in the United States, distribution of	111
" " " " history of	110
Carolinas, settlement of	52
Cascade range	11
Cash sales of public lands	49
Catholics	147
Cattle, distribution of	172
Causes of prosperity	2
Census Office	23
Center of population	71
" " movements of	71
Cessions of lands, by states	46
Charity, future reforms in	234
Cherokee Indians	100
Chickasaw Indians	100
Chinese in the United States, statistical history and distribution of	98
" number of, in the United States	90
" Exclusion Act	98
Choctaw Indians	100
Christians	148
Church members, proportion to population	150
" property, value of	146
Circuit courts	19
Circulating media	219
Cities, constituents of the population of	121
" of the future	236
Civil divisions of counties	31, 32
Civil Service Commission	24
Coal	187
" supply for the future	238
Coast and Geodetic Survey	22

INDEX

	PAGE
Coast ranges	11
" traffic	208
Coinage	220
Colleges	132
Colonies, population of	52
Colorado	26
Colored, number at each census	91
" race, future of	235
" " relative diminution of	92
" rates of increase of	92
" southward movement of	97
Commerce	209
Comptroller of the Currency	21
Congregationalists	149
Congress, committees of	19
Conjugal condition	159
" " of colored	160
" " " foreign born	160
" " " native whites	160
Connecticut	26
Constituents of population, summary of	123
Constitution of United States	1
Copper	191
Cordilleran plateau	8
Cordilleras of North America	8
Corporations of the future	236
Cotton	169
" manufactures	182
Counties	31, 32
County debt	33, 37
Creek Indians	100
Crime	156
" restriction of, in future	234
Cuba, commerce with	214
Cumberland plateau	7
Death, causes of	153
" rate, general	152
" " of future	234
" rates in foreign countries	155
Debts of government	33
Delaware	26
Density of population	62
" " " by groups	67
" " " " states	68
" " " in foreign countries	64
Departments of Government	18, 20

INDEX

	PAGE
Desert Land Act	49
Disposal of Public Lands	48
District courts	19
District of Columbia	25
Divorce	161
Early settlements	51
Education	130
" Bureau of	23
" expenditures for	131
Electors for President	17
Electric railways	216
Electricity, future development of	239
Elements of population, summary of	123
Elk mountains, Colorado	9
Engineering works	204
Engraving and Printing, Bureau of	21
Enrollment in schools	130
Episcopalians	149
Ethnology, Bureau of	24
Executive departments	20
Expenditure on public schools	131
Expenditures of government	40
Exports	211
Extent of settlement	63, 64
Families, size of	86
Farming tools and machinery, value of	164, 165
Farms, average size of	164, 165
" number of	164, 165
" value of	164, 165
Finance and wealth	219
Finis	240
Fish Commission	23
Florida	26
" purchase	46
Foreign blood, amount of, in country	119
" born, birthplace of	108
" " by states	105
" " distribution of	105
" " history of different nationalities constituting it	109
" " illiteracy of	115
" " in cities	113
" " nationalities of	108
" " occupations of	114
" " population	102
" " proportion of, by states	106
" commerce	219

INDEX 245

	PAGE
Foreign commerce, history of	213
" parentage	118
" " distribution of population of	119
" " population of, in cities	121
Forests	15
France, commerce with	213
Front range, Colorado	9
Future, forecast of	231
Gadsden purchase	46
Geographic distribution of population	82
Geological Survey	23
Georgia	26
" settlement of	52
Germans in the United States, distribution of	111
" " " " history of	110
Germany, commerce with	213
Geysers	12
Geyser basins	12
Gold	190
" in circulation	219
Government	16
" debts	32
" general	17
" of states	24
" future development of	231
Great Basin	10
Great Britain, commerce with	213
Great cities	80
" plains	8
Hay	171
Hogs, distribution of	173
Homestead Act	49
Horses, distribution of	172
Hot Springs	12
Hungarians in the United States, history of	111
Hydrographic Office	22
Idaho	26
Illinois	26
Illiteracy	127
" census statistics of	128
" distribution of	128
" reduction of, in future	234
Immigration	103
" character of	104
" constituents of	104
" effect of, upon natural increase	115

INDEX

	PAGE
Immigration, effect of, on native element	118
" future of	234
Imports	211
Improved land	164, 165
" " distribution of	166
Increase of population, considerations affecting	58
Indian corn	168
Indian Territory	26
Indiana	26
Indians	99
" citizen, in the United States	90
" cost of maintaining	101
" number of	100
" progress in civilization	101
" treatment of	100
Industrial republic, an	1
Interior Department	21, 23
Interstate Commerce Commission	23
Invention	144
Iowa	26
Irish in the United States, distribution of	111
" " " " history of	110
Iron and steel manufactures	180
Iron ore	189
Iroquois Indians	99
Irrigated area	174
Irrigation	173
Italians in the United States, history of	116
Jamestown, Va., settlement of	51
Japanese, number in the United States	90
Judiciary	19
Justice, Department of	20, 22
Kansas	27
Kentucky	27
Kiowa Indians	100
Labor, Department of	24
Land bounties	49
" grants to railways	49
Language, development of	235
Latter Day Saints	149
Lead	192
Life Saving Service	22
Light-house establishment	22
Live stock	171
" " distribution of	172
Louisiana	27

INDEX 247

	PAGE
Louisiana purchase	46
Lutherans	148
Mail service	217
Maine	27
Maize, production of	168
Malt liquors, production of	184
Manufactures	176
" general statistics of	176
" of great cities	179
" " the future	238
Manufacturing capital	178
Maryland	27
" settlement of	52
Massachusetts Bay colony	51
Merchant fleet of the United States	206
Method of survey of public lands	47
Methodists	147
Mexican cession	46
Michigan	27
Middle Park, Colorado	9
Military forces	41
Militia	41
" potential	42
Mineral resources	186
Minnesota	27
Mint Bureau	21
Mississippi	27
" valley	7
Missouri	28
Moki Indians	99
Money in circulation	219
Montana	28
Mortality	151
" census statistics of	151
" in registration cities	154
Mormons	149
Mulattoes, number in the United States	90
Mules, distribution of	172
Municipal debt	33, 37
Muskogee Indians	99
National banks	220
" debt	33
" domain	4
" Museum	24
Native born population	102
" " white population	102

	PAGE
Nativity of population	102
Natural gas	194
Nautical Almanac Office	23
Naval Observatory	23
Navy	44
" Department	20, 22
Nebraska	28
Negroes, number of, in the United States	90
Nevada	28
New Hampshire	28
New Jersey	28
New Mexico	28
New York	28
" " the greater	81
" " when colonized	52
Newspapers	183
North Carolina	28
North Dakota	28
North Park, Colorado	9
Oats	169
Occupations	133
" changes in	141
" criticism of census schedule of	133
" distribution of classes of	135
" nativity with relation to	138
" of immigrants	140
Octoroons, number in the United States	90
Ohio	29
Oklahoma	29
Oregon	29
Ozark hills	7
Pacific coast	5
Park range, Colorado	9
Pauperism in the United States	158
" classification of, by race and nativity	159
Pennsylvania	29
" when colonized	52
Pensions	45
People, future progress of	233
Periodicals	183
Petroleum	193
Pima Indians	100
Plateau region	9
Plymouth colony	51
Poles in the United States, history of	110
Population	51

INDEX 249

	PAGE
Population by states in 1890	55
" density of, in the United States	62
" geographic distribution of	82
" increase of	53
" of colonies	52
" " countries of the globe in 1890	54
" " states, rate of increase of	56
" " " recent changes in	60
" " the United States at each census	53
Post Office Department	20, 22
" " statistics of	218
Potatoes	171
Powers, distribution of	20
Preëmption	48
Presbyterians	148
Presidency, succession to	18
President	17
" salary of	18
Prisoners in the United States	156
" classification of, by race and nativity	157
Professional schools	132
Prosperity, causes of	2
Public lands	45
" " amount alienated	49
" " method of disposal	48
" " method of survey	47
" schools	130
Puget Sound	11
Quadroons, number in the United States	90
Quicksilver	193
Races	90
Races, distribution by states	94
" " at each census	96
" proportions of, at each census	91
" statistical history of, in the United States	91
Railway accidents	203
" companies, consolidation of	201
" land grants	49
" mileage compared with population in countries in 1890	199
" mileage of all countries in 1890	198
" transportation, cost of	202
Railways	196
" growth of system, 1830 to 1890	197
" mileage of, in 1891	196
" objects of construction	203
" of United States, general statistics	200

	PAGE
Railways, organization of	201
Rainfall, distribution of population according to	83
" of United States	13
" " eastern United States	13
" " western United States	14
Rainier, Mount	11
Receipts of government	40
Register of the Treasury	21
Regular army	41
Relative standing of states in population	62
Relief of the country	5
Religion	146
Religious communicants, distribution of	149
" denominations, membership of	146
Representatives, House of	18
Rhode Island	29
River traffic	208
Rocky mountains	9
Rolling stock of railways	203
Rural population	75
" " increase of	77
Russians in the United States, history of	110
Salt	194
Salt Lake basin	11
Sangre de Cristo range, Colorado	9
San Juan mountains, Colorado	9
San Luis Park	9
Savings banks	221
Sawatch range, Colorado	9
Scandinavians in the United States, distribution of	111
" " " " history of	110
School district debt	35, 38
Seminole Indians	100
Senate	18
Settled area	66
" " and population, rates of increase compared	67
" " classification of	67
Settlement, extent of	63
" in 1890	65
Sex	88
" proportions of, in foreign countries	88
" " " " states	89
Shasta, Mount	11
Sheep, distribution of	172
Ship building	214
Shoshone Indians	99

INDEX   251

	PAGE
Sierra Nevada	11
Silk manufactures	183
Silver	191
" in circulation	219
Sioux Indians	99
Size of families	86
Smithsonian Institution	24
South Carolina	29
South Dakota	29
South Park, Colorado	9
Spirits, production of	184
State debts	33, 36
State, Department of	20, 21
States, organization of	24
Statistics, Bureau of	21
Steel	190
Street railways	216
Summary of constituents of population	123
Subdivisions of states and counties	31
Supreme Court	19
Swamp lands given to states	49
Telegraphs	215
Telephones	215
Temperature, distribution of population according to	82
Temperature of the United States	12
Tennessee	29
Texas	29
" annexation of	46
Timber Culture Act	49
Tobacco	166
Trades unions	143
" " future of	235
Traffic statistics of railways	200
Transportation	195
Treasurer of United States	21
Treasury Department	20, 21
Urban population	74
" " by states	79
" " distribution of	77
" " increase of	77
Utah	29
Vermont	29
Vessels in foreign trade	207
Vice-President	17
" salary of	18
Virginia	30

	PAGE
Volcanic action	12
Voters, potential	124
Wages	142
" in manufactures	178
Wagon roads	195
War Department	20, 22
Water transportation	206
Wealth	221
" distribution of	228
" historical résumé of	224
" in 1890	223
" methods of estimating	221
" sources of increase in	227
Weather Bureau	23
West Virginia	30
Wheat	167
Whites, number of, at each census	91
" rates of increase of	92
Wind River Range, Wyoming	9
Wines, production of	184
Wisconsin	30
Woman in the future	235
Wool manufactures	182
Wyoming	30
Yellowstone Park	12
Yuma Indians	100
Zinc	193
Zoölogical Park	24

www.ingramcontent.com/pod-product-compliance
Lightning Source LLC
Chambersburg PA
CBHW020248240426
43672CB00006B/664